Determining the Requirements for the Design of Learner-Based Instruction

Fred L. Gale

*University of North Carolina
at Chapel Hill*

Charles E. Merrill Publishing Company
A Bell & Howell Company
Columbus, Ohio

Published by
Charles E. Merrill Publishing Co.
A Bell & Howell Co.
Columbus, Ohio 43216

This book was set in Caledonia and Eurostile.
The production editor was Deborah Worley.
The cover was designed by Will Chenoweth.

International Standard Book Number: 0-675-08709-0

Library of Congress Catalog Card Number: 74-28563

1 2 3 4 5 6 7 8 9 10—78 77 76 75

Printed in the United States of America

*To Rick, Dave, Judy,
Billy, and Ellen*

Preface

This book is an attempt to look at the educational process as an instructional system. Each chapter is a major part of the system and is discussed from the standpoint of its unique characteristics as well as its relationship to other parts of the system; consequently, no one area assumes greater importance than another area. What is important in this design is that all of the major factors work together toward satisfying the requirements associated with learning.

The theoretical concerns presented have been discussed by many authors. In this respect the reader will find nothing new because this is not a text that describes instructional theory, nor is it a description of instructional materials and educational media. Rather, it is an effort to conceptualize the educational process as a system of logical interrelationships, showing how these factors contribute to the ultimate goal of accommodating the learner.

It is my feeling that educating students is a difficult process and that we need an approach that is equal to the task. You will recognize this bias in efforts to change the present emphasis regarding the functions of certain roles. The teacher is depicted as a decision maker who concentrates his energies on the orchestration of learning experiences. He designs instruction for learning needs instead of just presenting ideas. Media assumes the role of an enabler; as a management tool, it allows us to extend beyond our limitations and accommodate the variance among learners. This book presents an array of strategies that will help teachers cope with the growing complexity of education.

The danger one faces when looking at the practical side of theory is that verbal expressions of the practical often become nothing more than further extensions of theory. To prevent this outcome, a deliberate effort was made to force practical considerations by treating a topic within the context of a teaching situation. Thus, in one chapter we may discuss an idea as it relates to the task of teaching a science lesson, and in another chapter we may consider the topic as it relates to teaching an English lesson. From this vantage point, we are able to scrutinize more carefully the worth of the theory presented.

Further effort was expended to serve this practical cause in the form of students' projects that represent, in different ways, an application of the system discussed in this book. This has been a fruitful experience for both the students and the professor, for it appears that only when students are given an opportunity to test ideas are these ideas understood and, more importantly, considered for acceptance.

Whatever value this book may have will be due to the efforts of those who have helped me. Credit for the illustrations goes to Mr. Jack Weaver whose talent so ably complemented the ideas presented. I extend my thanks to Dr. Alan Schueler for the photographs he provided.

I wish to extend special thanks to my wife Ann who gave me encouragement and honest criticism when it was needed. Her support and efforts were significant contributions. Assistance with the typing offered by Mrs. June Haas and Mrs. Lynn Ray is gratefully appreciated. I particularly want to thank Ms. Deborah Worley, production editor of Charles E. Merrill, for her efforts. Her keen perceptions were significant to the final composition. I also extend thanks to Mr. Fred Kinne who, although he inherited this project, has assisted me greatly in his role as administrative editor. Finally, to my colleagues, Dr. Ralph Wileman and Mrs. Betty Cleaver, I extend my thanks for their valuable criticisms.

Contents

INSTRUCTIONAL SYSTEM

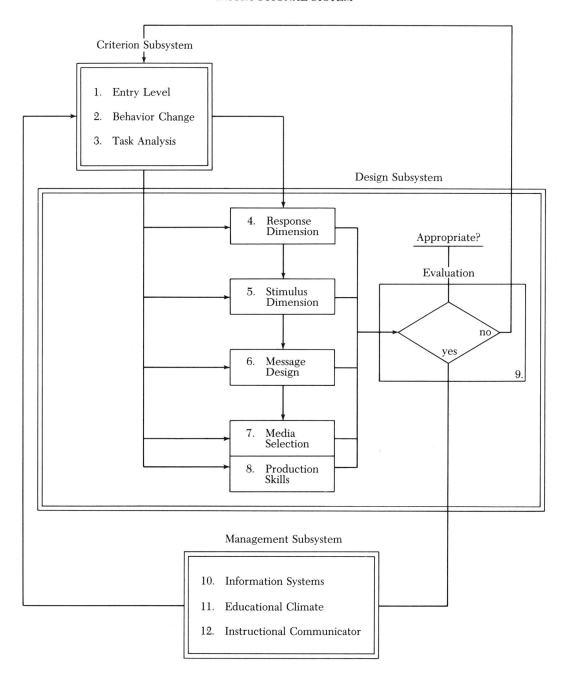

Introduction

Purpose of This Book

The cutting edge of change is far less damaging if it approaches its victim from the situation which presently exists. Acknowledging one's position may substantially improve the palatability of innovative measures. The vantage point in approaching the topic expressed in this book is to look closely at the status quo as answers are sought to certain issues. Some of the issues are presented in the following questions:

    I. Can an instructional approach provide for individual learner characteristics?

   II. Is it feasible to consider attending to individual differences within the context of a traditional educational setting?

 III. Can teachers become classroom managers of the instructional-learning process?

The responses to these questions are plentiful and are vented with considerable emotion from all channels of communication. The consensus seems to point in one direction—schools appear to be riding the crest of past successes. This success, however, has reached a state of obsolescence. The emergence of students questioning the precepts on which they were weaned testifies to the obsolescence of traditional methods. The educational system must now respond with answers to these questions.

Education today is a mixture of old and new concepts. The unification of old concepts with new ones is a difficult task and, in the minds of many, an impossible dream. Yet, the impetuousness of change and the tenaciousness of tradition must hold hands if a better methodology is to be found.

Many schools are flirting with change by attempting innovative techniques, and it is evident that a movement does exist to separate instructional methods from the security of the past. Yet, this is primarily a note of indulgence with what appears to be a trend of fashion. A variety of experiments with media, individualized instruction, and modular scheduling denotes serious attempts by educators to respond to the demands for accountability. Unfortunately, the record shows little promise of permanent change. A contributing factor to this dilemma is the role that institutions which train teachers have played in preparing teachers to maintain the status quo in schools. Prospective teachers are prepared with skills and knowledge suitable for content-teacher-oriented instruction. This would suggest that the attempts to change do not demand new competencies from teachers. Yet, teachers represent the principal participants who will be charged with the responsibility of making new programs work. New demands require skills and knowledge that were not a part of the previous training experiences. Change that consists of more than a modest alteration to a past condition often brings with it the need to consider the respecification of roles.

The respecification of the teaching role is one of the targets of this book. Emphasis is placed on the competencies which changing views on the role of the teacher seem to demand. This book is predicated on the assumption (not untested) that there presently exists little if any relationship between teaching behaviors and learner achievement. This text suggests that certain teaching competencies are necessary to provide instruction that is appropriate to learner characteristics. Without such skills and knowledge, it is doubtful that teachers will ever succeed in adapting instructional methods to students' individual differences.

The demands of society are far less forgiving than in the past, and the unrest will not be subdued, although it may be sedated, by false attempts to reform. New programs must follow certain antecedent conditions; namely, the training and retraining of teacher personnel. The teacher as a communicator has enormous limitations that can interfere with the students' reception of intended meanings. For this reason, a variety of media options are presented throughout the book rather than confining the issue to one chapter. The knowledge of media usage is necessary to the management of a learner-based instructional program mainly because such an approach involves the communication of a considerable amount of information.

In essence, the purpose of this book is to offer a response to the often repeated question: Are there better ways to teach prospective teachers? The design of this text goes beyond an affirmation of the question by penetrating the more fundamental question of how it is to be done.

Design of the Text

The interrelationship between chapters is described visually on the Instructional System Chart which appears at the beginning of each part division of the text. At the beginning of each part, the reader can see where in the overview a particular chapter fits. This organization will serve as a reminder that the relationship between chapters as well as the unique identity of each chapter is important. Although each chapter makes a unique contribution, it does so partly because of its relationship to the other chapters. Keeping this individuality and interrelationship factor in mind will help make the reading of this text a less arduous task and the occasional reference to other chapters reasonable.

As a text, this book is in part a brief excursion through a consideration of certain competencies. The knowledge and skills which seem to be most relevant to the teaching and learning process are stressed. Throughout the book an emphasis is placed on the use of media options to facilitate teaching and learning. How the teacher can use a particular technique under numerous constraints is an ever-present issue in each chapter. The treatment accorded each competency, therefore, is in terms of what it is, why it is important, and, most critical, how it can be used.

The contents of this text are divided into three sections; namely, Criterion Subsystem, Design Subsystem, and Management Subsystem. The categories (Criterion, Design, and Management) are presented as major parts of an instructional system and as such they are referred to as subsystems. Each category will attempt to describe a cluster of factors which appear to have a strong bond of relationship. Interwoven throughout each subsystem is an expressed concern for the learning process. That is to suggest that when the reader confronts a teaching-learning situation, a bias for accommodating the learner will be apparent. The murkiness of learning theory is somewhat alleviated by establishing as targets the achievement of certain behavioral tasks. This approach will, if nothing else, focus attention on particulars rather than vague generalities. Student accomplishments in the teaching-learning situation as viewed from a behavioral vantage point will be in terms of observing behavior change. As a means of assess-

ment, observing resultant behavior change is an indirect measure of learning performance.

The first step to establishing an instructional system is to collect relevant information. The entry level of the students, the expected terminal behavior, and an analysis of this behavior (i.e., task analysis) are the major milestones of data collection. The summation of this information is crucial to the design of instruction which follows. It is from such a foundation that the design of learner-based instruction emerges. Success with the elements of Part One provides a base that is essential to the desired systematic approach. The control function of this category as it serves to alter the design of instruction when learning performance is below minimum standards is of equal importance to this approach. Learner characteristics, terminal behavior, and response demand (task analysis) represent a yardstick against which decisions are made for altering the design of instruction. In this respect Part One serves a criterion function which recommends the particular instructional treatment needed.

The adaptation of instruction depends on several design considerations. The second major subsystem, the design of instruction, considers those competencies that enter into the selection of the appropriate instructional conditions. After the responses of the learner have been identified, the stimuli needed are expressed in the most appropriate design and conveyed by the most suitable medium or media. In other words, the instructor determines what the learning needs are and then considers the media conditions required. Approaching media options in this fashion prevents the tendency to adapt instruction to media rather than to the learner. Consequently, the evaluation will consider more than just the learner's performance; it will include in equal measure the instructional conditions used. The learner benefits from this approach because of the optimal linkage established between learning conditions and instructional strategies. Teaching and learning, in this context, assume a posture worthy of the challenge posed by demands for accountability.

The demand for accountability has influenced the respecification of the teacher's role to a managerial status. It is now imperative that teachers view their role as a part of a rather complex system with many priorities to satisfy. In this capacity, teachers need to confront problems systematically with appropriate decision-making tools. The accessibility and utilization of human and nonhuman resources is one of several concerns demanding a good decision. The present era in education is becoming far less forgiving of content oriented instruction and it is apparent that the interface between man, machines, and information will compose the teacher's arena. The teacher as a manager of the teaching-learning process is in the business of designing learning environments. Success with this design responsibility depends greatly on the selection of alternatives to overcome the persistence of unwanted constraints. If instruction cannot be individualized, what options are available? What alternatives are evident when a facility is not suitable for an innovative program? Many problems such

as these need to be viewed as constraints for which there are suitable alternatives. Without certain management competencies, the prospective teacher will find transplanting many academic experiences into real-life situations exceedingly difficult.

Using the Text

The text describes a systematic approach to learner-based instruction. Each chapter is a component of the instructional system and describes areas for which competencies need to be developed. For the purpose of this book, competency is defined as the ability to do a particular job which includes the skills and knowledge involved. The reader is assisted in the development of these competencies by a different exemplary classroom lesson presented at the beginning of each of the first six chapters and chapter nine. In order to clarify the competencies discussed, information will be given by using the exemplary situations. Although media is presented in chapter seven in considerable depth, it pervades each chapter when appropriate. Consequently, the reader is able to see a media mixture for specified learning outcomes.

A wide range of teaching-learning situations and media options is presented to the reader along with a systematic approach to learner-based instruction. In this respect, the prospective teacher may find this book a convenient reference when assuming a real-life teaching position.

INSTRUCTIONAL SYSTEM

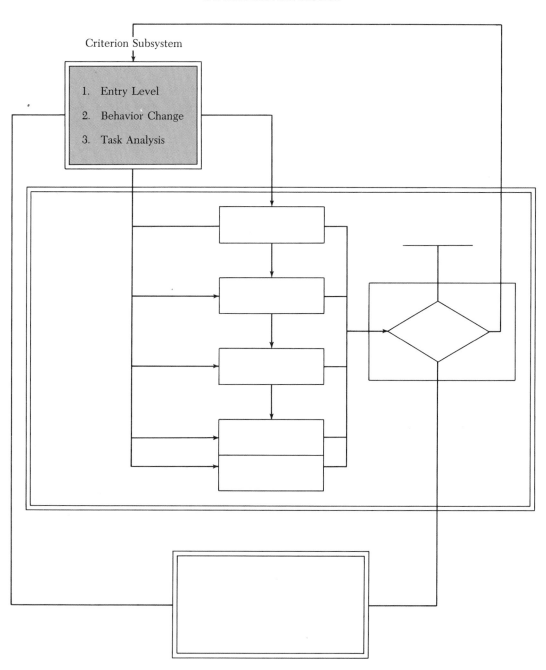

Criterion Subsystem

1. Entry Level

2. Behavior Change

3. Task Analysis

Part 1

Criterion Subsystem

Criterion is defined as a rule for making a judgment (Bloom et al., pp. 185–192). On a continuum ranging from low to high achievement levels, the expectations of students' performance dictate the course of instruction and learning. Subjected to a myriad of instructional strategies, the student emerges from the heat of such confrontation with his achievement a product of chance. The alarming feature of this approach is its guarantee that some students must fail. Since there is no defense for deciding which students should fail, the educational system should strive for the presently unpopular goal that none shall fail.

With this course so defined, the criterion goals of the subsystem become clear. There are decisions to be made, and these decisions influence other areas (design subsystems). As indicated in Figure 1–0 A (p. 10), this relationship is established, and the consequences of these decisions are evaluated. Decisions made about the learner influence the decisions made about instruction. The margin of error is measured (Figure 1–0 B), and inappropriate decisions initiate a reassessment. Various areas may be responsible for inappropriate decisions: a learning objective may be inappropriate; the medium selected may be too abstract, or a host of other possibilities could intervene. Whatever the cause, a mismatching of learning and instructional conditions (Figure 1–0 C) dictates that new assessments be made. Expressing the learner's needs, the criterion function serves as a guide for the selection of the appropriate instructional conditions (Figure 1–0 D).

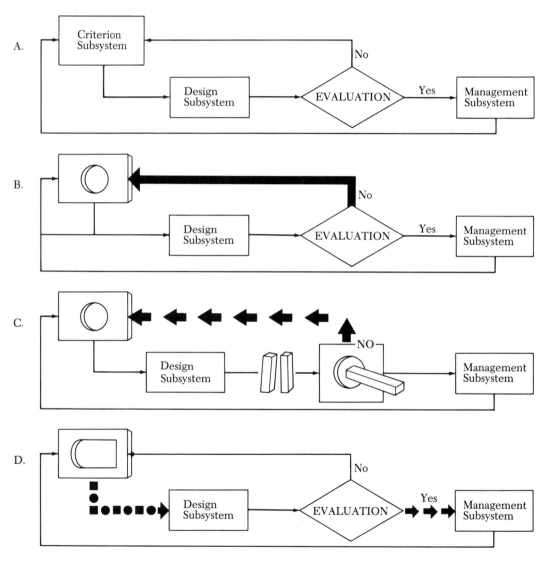

FIGURE 1–0

Chapter 1

Entry Level Assessment

Introduction

John Holt describes the following incident in his book, *How Children Fail* (Holt, p. 3):

> Several times she would make a real effort to follow my words, and did follow them, through a number of steps. Then, just as it seemed she was at the point of getting the idea, she would shake her head and say, "I don't get it."

If the language in the above situation had been foreign to the girl, there would have been little hesitation to choose another form of gesture. However, when the language is not foreign to the learner, the tendency is to peruse different levels of abstraction but often within the same mode (verbal in this case); and the idea remains unknown. It is strange that little consideration is given to the possibility that the instructional conditions and learning styles are mismatched, and yet there exists a wide range of instructional options that await the discretion of the instructor.

It would be unpardonable of a doctor to prescribe self-administered insulin shots for a patient when the patient had not demonstrated the competence this task requires. Likewise, the tendency of educators to make assumptions should be equalized with the tendency to test these assumptions. With this thought in mind, the reader is encouraged to seek out from this chapter a process for testing the assumption that students, with respect to the lesson, are where they ought to be. The goal of this chapter is to present an approach to entry level assessment that prospective teachers will be able to implement in the real-life teaching situation.

The following objectives represent the skills and knowledge that one must possess in order to achieve the competency necessary for conducting entry level assessments:

I. Identify the skills and knowledge needed for assessing entry level behavior.

II. Provide reasons for making an entry level assessment.

III. Discuss the use of media as a means for facilitating the attainment of entry level information.

IV. Adjust content to the entry level assessed.

V. Express an approach for determining the entry level of students as well as the adjustments to the lesson that subsequently will follow this assessment.

VI. Explain how the entry level of students can be assessed in a manageable way within the context of the present educational system.

VII. Design an entry level approach that is not intimidating to students.

Exemplary Situation

Chapters one through six and nine consider competencies that are important to the development of an effective instructional system. In each of these chapters the competency is discussed with frequent references to an exemplary situation. It is hopeful that the reader will find some of the exemplary situations used related to his subject area of interest or that generalizations can be made from the exemplary situation to his area of interest.

Chapter one refers to a biology lesson whenever examples are needed to explain some facet of entry level. It is expected that as a result of associating subject matter with a teaching situation, the exemplary situation will be more meaningful. The intent is that you will consider the lesson only in terms of entry level, thus avoiding any need to comprehend the content of the lesson.

The situation is a biology class which consists of an average group of boys and girls. The average figure denotes that the performances of the class generally describe a normal or bell-shaped curve. As such, when the students are tested, a certain percentage of them are destined to fail; a large percentage will fall in the seventy and eighty range, and a small percentage will fall into the coveted range of ninety and above.

The lesson to be presented is concerned with relationships between oxygen and blood in the circulatory system. The class is in the process of learning the various physiological systems of the body. Up to this point, they have studied the nervous and respiratory systems and have been taught the important parts of the circulatory system.

Answers to the following questions are to be explored in the lesson: How does oxygen get into the bloodstream? What happens to oxygen within the bloodstream? Where does oxygen go from the bloodstream?

Pretend that you are the teacher of this class. You not only know what you intend to present, but you also know how the class has done on previous tests that have been concerned with other physiological systems. Although the students' performance on the previous lesson was not a true bell-shaped curve, it was not enough of a departure to demand the reteaching of the lesson. Yet, more students fell in the lower and middle range than you had anticipated. Because you wish to help the poorer students achieve better results than were displayed on previous lessons, you have decided to approach this lesson differently.

In the past, you have included models, diagrams, films, and other audio-visual aids in your presentations. In other words, you have attempted to positively motivate your students toward the topics being discussed. Therefore, by using audio-visual aids for this lesson, students will not only receive a description of how the red blood cells pick up oxygen from the air sacks of the lungs, but real-life cues will be provided in terms of actually seeing the process portrayed on film.

It is not, however, the intent of this chapter to present a biology lesson but to acquaint the reader with the significance of entry level assessment. So, with this consideration in mind, the teacher should reflect on those problems which might interfere with students' learning the intended lesson.

It is already known that certain students had difficulty with previous lessons which have some bearing on the topic being discussed. It is important to know to what extent these students are restricted by this deficit and, of course, to what extent they can be helped. Is it possible to reveal information about those things that can interfere with a student's performance without getting into great detail about the dynamics of the lesson? Just by asking what can interfere with learning a lesson, important direction can be provided that will help the assessment process. The following questions about relevant factors should be considered by the instructor prior to the lesson:

I.   Of those students who failed related test questions based on previous lessons, to what extent are they unprepared for this lesson?

II. Of those students who passed the previous tests, to what extent are they prepared for this lesson?

III. Is it clear to each student what is expected of him from the forthcoming lesson?

IV. Are there any students who have problems that will require special handling of the content information?

V.   Has an attempt been made to attach importance to the lesson?

VI. Is it possible that some students already know the lesson?

A good place to start the discussion of entry level assessment is to consider answers to these questions, and in the course of seeking answers, perhaps a framework of entry level assessment will emerge.

Question One: Of those students who failed related test questions concerned with previous lessons, to what extent are they unprepared for this lesson?

Assume that in a previous lesson the students received instruction as to how oxygen is transformed in the lungs from air and then transferred to the bloodstream. Students who missed test questions pertaining to this process might experience difficulty with the following lesson which considers the nature of oxygen in the bloodstream. Knowing, for example, that small air sacks in the lungs serve as areas through which oxygen is transported into the bloodstream will contribute to establishing an important point of reference.

One of the first things that you might consider is to make a simple analysis of the previous test results to determine which students missed those critical items. A problem may exist with this approach, however, for the time that it would take to check each student's previous test results would make implementing this approach prohibitive.

An alternative worthy of consideration is to present all students with questions that consider prerequisite information. Although a few moments of time would be taken from the class period for this experience, it would prove more profitable to the student than time frequently donated to quizzes and other evaluative exercises. If the student is not ready for the following lesson, it is important that the instructor be aware of the deficit before presenting the next lesson.

Question Two: Of those students who passed the previous tests, to what extent are they prepared for this lesson?

If the information presented in the previous lesson was designed to help students resist forgetting, this is not a problem. Long-term memory does not just happen; it happens by design. If the meaning of the content is not clearly displayed, the chances are good that the knowledge will not be retained. Evidence indicates that the human brain has a limited storage capacity and in this respect old information is displaced by information that is new (Kumar). However, given the proper incentive and the appropriate instructional conditions, the human brain can be taught to store information indefinitely.

It is possible that the test questions did not test all of the important information. It may seem unreasonable to suggest this possibility; yet, in the interest of expediency, a mere sampling of information often must suffice. One often wonders what mysterious insight allows the instructor to select those questions that pass those who should pass and fail those who should fail.

The solution to the problem appears to be similar to that which was suggested for the first question. Prior to presenting a new lesson, the instructor should review those questions that represent the prerequisite information.

Question Three: Is it clear to each student what is expected of him from the forthcoming lesson?

Students frequently know the topic which is to be considered when asked to read an assignment from the text or related reference material. However, communicating in concise terms what is actually expected of them is more the exception than the rule.

Displaying the intricate relationships between the respiratory and the circulatory systems when oxygen is exchanged may be the main intent of one lesson. Discussing the unique characteristics of the circulatory system is another possibility. Studying the various parts of the systems and their particular functions is also a possible consideration. Each of these approaches is a reasonable means of presenting the lesson; however, each approach places different demands on the learner and on the instructor. If the instructional intent is not clarified beforehand, it is possible that the learner and the instructor will approach the lesson from a different and conflicting point of view.

Question Four: Do some students have problems that will require special handling of the content information?

This consideration ranges from extreme learning difficulties to particular styles of learning. The inability to manage the left-to-right format used with verbal displays can pose a severe problem to students with this handicap who are constantly facing this type of instruction. Color blindness can interfere if, in the case of the biology lesson, the blood with oxygen is depicted as red and the blood without oxygen is depicted as blue.

Students have unique learning styles. Some students have a low tolerance for ambiguity; others lose interest if an element of difficulty is not present. Certain students work well under authority, while others are relatively self-directed. It may be that individualizing instruction is the only solution to this problem. If a learning style is unique to the individual, these idiosyncrasies need to be accommodated. This means that the teaching and learning processes encompass a multi-sensory approach designed to adapt to specific learner characteristics. The learner who displays some rigidity toward facts will have difficulty with conceptual approaches. For example, some learners will experience difficulty if the following concept is presented: The heart as a muscle is susceptible to the strains of excessive abuse but loses its vigor with prolonged inactivity. Developing this concept throughout the process of identifying the unique characteristics of a muscle and then associating them with the heart as a muscle may make the concept more meaningful. On the other hand, the learner who is stimulated by self-discovery will find the tediousness of this step-by-step approach frustrating and boring. The method of instruction alluded to by these cognitive styles depends upon those conditions dictated by the learner's needs.

In some respects Question Four can be handled like the previous questions; it differs, however, in design. Presenting a lesson that adapts to the individual learner is to a large extent a decision-making process. Performing this role effectively depends largely on the teacher knowing something about the learner. A teacher, in this capacity, not only gathers information but also controls it to some extent. How this information is collected and controlled is a concern of this book and specifically a solution to Question Four.

The first solution sought information about the learner's knowledge of the lesson. The second solution sought information about the student's style of learning. Each category is equally important but quite different, and each category provides data about the learner which the teacher needs to know before presenting the lesson.

Question Five: Has an attempt been made to attach importance to the lesson?

The importance of the learner's acceptance rests on the premise that a veto power may be exercised by the learner at any time. A student can reject information presented by the instructor for other information being received at that time. Research describes the human information processing system as being limited. Consequently, certain information received is perceived in a vague, crude manner, whereas other information is perceived clearly. It is much like the peripheral vision of the eyes which views the outer ranges of a person's sight as less definite than the central areas of vision. This might be described as figure versus ground perception (Fleming, pp. 124–26). As processors of information, human beings tend to separate information into dichotomies: important, unimportant; clear, unclear; interesting, uninteresting; or more generally, figure, ground.

Information is labeled by the receiver (learner) in a process often referred to as coding. Information which is being sent or transmitted is encoded; information which is received is decoded (Figure 1–1). It is possible, therefore, to look at teaching

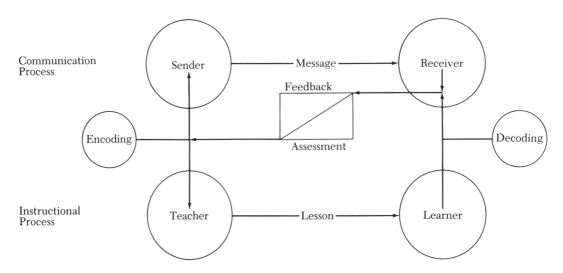

FIGURE 1-1   Education is a communication process.

and learning as a communication process during which information is encoded (teaching) and information is decoded (learning).

If this approach is used, it would seem that two conditions may influence the learner's choice to select or reject the information being presented in a lesson. Is it meaningful? Is it of interest? Ignoring these two questions may make subsequent teaching efforts futile. The particular label a student places on a lesson may very well dictate its destiny.

A counterpart of equal importance to learning is the clarity of the information being presented. Without a clear expression of the message, interest and/or meaning may be compromised. In either case, the presentation of a lesson must attract the attention of the learner away from interference. Interruptions may range from obvious distractions to the presence of meaningful but irrelevant stimuli which attract the learner's attention. Perception is selective and people tend to categorize information on the basis of their expecta-

tions (Bruner, p. 38). Information that is similar but not relevant to ideas that are being processed can filter into the mainstream of learning. Accommodating information that is not a part of the message transmitted is, in some respects, a manifestation of the learner's processing style. Shannon and Weaver describe the impact of noise on the communication process in their model (Figure 1-2). Noise to the communicator is like tooth decay to the dentist, crime to the lawyer, and disease to the physician. Every profession has a culprit, the demise of which serves as the prime target for creative energies.

When the encoding and decoding processes agree, communication has occurred. Before the lesson is presented, some consideration should be given to assisting this process. Presenting the learner with questions about the lesson will alert him to the topic and, more importantly, express what he is expected to do with the lesson. This introduction, if handled correctly, may suffice to capture the attention desired. A possible approach at the entry

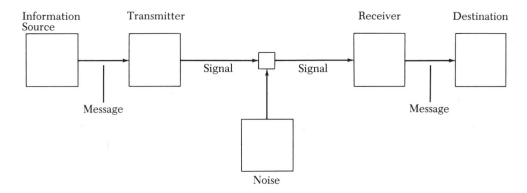

FIGURE 1–2   The Shannon and Weaver model describes the impact of noise on the communication process.

level stage might be to give the learner a clear statement of what value the topic will be to him. If this question cannot be answered, perhaps the lesson should not be taught. In the case of the exemplary lesson, a question pertaining to student health could be presented. Such a presentation might reveal the biological conditions of emphysema and heart disease, their relationship to smoking and, in a more positive light, the importance of breathing properly for the maintenance of good health. Hopefully, the consequence of this approach will convince the learner that, of all of the information impinging on him at that time, this lesson is the most important.

Question Six: Is it possible that some students already understand the lesson?

It is possible that the learner is repeating the subject, and although he did not meet the minimum standards of this particular course in biology, he, nevertheless, might have done well in certain areas of it. The student who has failed demonstrates a deviation from the expected learning behavior, and to treat him like an achiever would be to ignore his particular problem. This is not to suggest that the learner who

has failed previously should be made conspicuous but that the instructional design should be appropriate for him specifically. Part of individualizing instruction is to give the learner who has demonstrated a mastery of the appropriate skills and knowledge a chance to move on to those problem areas where he has experienced difficulty. Allowing him to bypass knowledge he understands may also bolster a damaged self-concept.

In this same category are students who for one reason or another already understand the subject and meet the minimum standards. This could be a student who because of personal interests has acquired some knowledge of the topic. A strong interest in medicine at an early age, for example, may have stimulated the student at a level that accomplished learning; much of the information may have already been comprehended.

Another situation where the learner may have successfully mastered the lesson is revealed when a teacher of a different subject has included similar content. A general science teacher at a previous grade level may have had a particular affection for a biology unit and, consequently, may have covered in great detail the topic planned.

Regardless of the reasons, a student in this category should be given an opportunity to move on to new areas. Assessing this condition prior to the lesson may save some students from boredom and teachers from the inevitable consequence of spending time managing disruptive social behavior. The need for discipline may arise from problems which are the result of inappropriate instructional designs.

Entry Level

It is unrealistic to assume that all students enter a lesson at the same learning level. Yet, the guilt of neglecting this common understanding has not been sufficient to alter the practice of starting all students at the same level. If the learning needs of students are to be accommodated, an assessment of entry levels should be high on the list of teaching priorities.

From the variety of responses accorded questions raised in the previous section, four critical areas can be identified. In the following statements these areas are expressed as important checkpoints for entry level assessment.

I.   Identify the skills and knowledge that the learner should possess in order to succeed with the lesson.

II. Determine whether or not the learner has the skills and knowledge to be presented in the lesson.

III. Identify the learning styles which may influence the student's effectiveness with the lesson.

IV. Identify the learner's attitude toward the intended lesson.

The **first checkpoint** refers to a student's background in relation to prerequisite information. In the case of the exemplary situation, some knowledge of cells and tissues is essential to understanding the function of the circulatory system. Prerequisite knowledge establishes the foundations on which the structure of the lesson is to be built. Without this assessment, the lesson rests precariously on the factor of chance.

The **second checkpoint** suggests that the learner may already possess the skills and knowledge of the lesson. An assessment should be made to determine how much the learner knows about the subject matter. What does the student know about the circulatory system (in the case of the exemplary lesson)? Posing this question will not only give the learner an idea of what is expected of him but it will also give those students who can meet the minimum standards of the lesson the opportunity to move on to something else.

The **third checkpoint** is directed toward assessing learning styles which may have a significant influence on the student's ability to handle the lesson. The three questions of the example lesson (How does oxygen get into the bloodstream? What happens to oxygen within the bloodstream? Where does oxygen go from the bloodstream?) are at a level of learning that demands an ability to see relationships as well as to identify certain parts of the circulatory system. Some students may be able to handle this with little difficulty; for others, it will be a problem. Unlike the two previous checkpoints, this one considers *how* students learn rather than *what* they learn. Therefore, questions asked will be designed to demand responses at predetermined learning levels. How a student processes information (verbal/visual) may be determined in part by exposing students to both modes of communication and maintaining the content at the same level of difficulty. Colored visuals (e.g., a film) of the blood passing through the thin one-celled walls of the capillaries in the circulatory system can be presented, or a written passage can describe the event. The objective for each presentation can be the same. Then, before the assessment period ends, the learner will be asked to recall the information. A record of those students who had difficulty with a particular mode can be made and if in subsequent assessment experiences a pattern is observed, the reason for suspecting a verbal or visual style is justified. Of course, by exposing the learner to verbal and visual stimuli while keeping other learning conditions constant, the teacher can make a valid analysis sooner.

It may appear to the reader that teaching rather than gathering information about the learner is being discussed. In some respects, there is only a fine line of difference between the two situations. In both instances a concern is expressed for communicating information; in the case of teaching, the primary concern is the transfer of experiences from academic to real life, whereas assessment is mainly concerned with finding out where a person is with respect to certain experiences. Although, in the preceding example, we have presented specific stimulus conditions (i.e., film or written passage) and demanded a response from the student it is unlikely that the student will hold on to the information for any period of time if nothing more is done.

The **fourth checkpoint** refers to the attitude of the learner toward the lesson. In the case of the exemplary lesson, if the student is not interested in the content or if he does not see it as important, the chances are very good that other sources of information will succeed in attracting his attention. Constructing a prelesson question which offers the learner a choice may indicate a preference for a particular mode of instruction. The questions should express different degrees of involvement with the content of the lesson. For example: If you had an opportunity to dissect an animal to observe its circulatory system directly or if you had an opportunity to see a film on dissection, which of the two experiences would you prefer? Granted, one question will not serve to establish a particular attitude for determining a particular response. Several questions describing different situations of choice must be asked before a clear assessment of the learner's attitude can be made.

Learning Styles

A student's learning style is more theoretical than other entry level considerations. However, it is a critical factor in the selection of an appropriate instructional system. Considering the possible styles which we suspect exist is of little value to our particular goals. Instead of being snarled by a process of abstracting several different learning styles, two differences have been delineated. These are low cognitive complexity or high cognitive complexity and low verbal reception or high verbal reception. Encompassed within these four categories can be found other differences such as impulsiveness and reflectiveness in responding, figure and ground fixation, and other styles that enter into the learning process.

It is important to realize that assessment and not the diagnostic measures associated with the normative testing of learning disabilities is being discussed. The latter demands some commitment to statistical methods and validity which is beyond the scope of this chapter. The concern of this chapter is to provide information of a general nature that will be manageable and relevant to learning behavior. Because of this emphasis, these two learning styles (low cognitive complexity or high cognitive complexity and low verbal reception or high verbal reception) were selected as being relevant and implementary within the context of classroom teaching-learning situations.

If one is expected to master the assessment of students for their learning styles it is important to go beyond the *why* and answer the questions of *what* and *how*. The first step towards providing the answer is to become acquainted with Bloom's taxonomy of the hierarchy of cognitive levels. This document represents the work of several people and has a variety of uses. The taxonomy attempts to classify cognitive instructional objectives according to levels of complexity in thinking. The following six levels represent the hierarchy (Bloom et al., pp. 201–7):

    I.   Knowledge

   II.   Comprehension

  III.   Application

  IV.   Analysis

   V.   Synthesis

  VI.   Evaluation

Presenting questions at any one of these levels challenges the learner's ability to cope with the different demands of a particular level. An analysis of the students' answers to questions will provide information about his style of learning. If the learner correctly answers a low level cognitive question but misses the higher level question and if the content is the same in both questions, then it would appear that the learner has trouble with the level of the question. In this case, perhaps the student is more factually than conceptually oriented. On the other hand, if the learner misses both questions, it would indicate that his lack of knowledge about the content is the major problem.

Using the exemplary lesson on the respiratory system, the following statements might have appeared on the test:

    I.   *Low Cognitive*

        A.   Describe how oxygen passes from the lungs into the bloodstream. (Comprehension)

   II.   *High Cognitive*

        A.   Describe how a reduction of air supply to the lungs influences the passage of oxygen into the bloodstream. (Application)

Missing either question may occur for reasons other than a student's learning style. A poorly presented test question is one possibility. Therefore, more than one attempt to assess a particular style should be made. Recognizing and providing for a learning style or attempting to alter an undesirable style may make a substantial difference in a student's learning behavior.

The second learning style (low verbal reception or high verbal reception) refers primarily to visual versus verbal stimulus conditions. Whether ideas are presented visually or verbally may make a difference in the learner's ability to respond correctly. If the use of a nonverbal means as well as a verbal means for testing is a standard procedure, the instructor should not have to do any additional work. Two questions with the same content which are presented in different modes (verbal and visual) will suffice to express the desired information.

The following statements may serve as examples of low and high verbal questions:

I. *Low Verbal*

   A. A colored slide of the respiratory system is available for you to project on a motion picture screen. As you will note several areas are numbered. Write on your answer paper the numbers which you feel represent those areas which are associated with the transportation of oxygen into the bloodstream.

II. *High Verbal*

   A. The following statements describe parts of the respiratory system. Identify the parts which are referred to.

      1. Oxygen passes through these one-celled tissues into the bloodstream.

      2. These small structures located in the lungs transport oxygen into the bloodstream.

      3. It is the upward and downward movement of this structure which influences the passage of air into the lungs.

It should be noted that in the examples of the two learning styles, a previous lesson was referred to when students were tested. It is necessary to use knowledge that a learner has comprehended in order to determine how he is learning instead of what he is learning. If a student has demonstrated that his knowledge is lacking in a particular area, test questions covering that area should not be used in an attempt to determine his learning style.

For the high and low verbal reception styles, it is important that the level of learning remain constant while the stimulus conditions change. The more closely this guideline is followed, the more relevant the assessment will be to learning style.

Each learner approaches a question in a unique way; for some learners, a visual approach presents problems, and for others, a verbal approach is more difficult. An understanding of where the learner is with respect to this problem will be helpful in the accommodation or modification of his learning behavior.

The learner may be placed in a situation of varying risk. That is, the level of learner involvement may incur an element of risk to the student. As the student pits his ideas against possible questions or conflicting opinions of others, a psychological risk may be created. The following questions will serve as examples:

I. Check the word that agrees with your attitude toward the following statement: When the stomach is forced out, the diaphragm is pulled up and air rushes in. When the stomach is forced in, the diaphragm is pushed down and air is forced out.

Wrong   I don't know   Right

_____   _____   _____

(Note: The learner is given a possible way out; it is not necessary for him to commit himself.)

II. During the process of inhaling, the diaphragm is forced down into the abdomen. During exhalation the diaphragm is forced up into the chest cavity. Are these statements correct? Defend your answer.
(Note: The learner is required to defend his answer; thus, he experiences a risk.)

III. Describe the process of how you breathe, and include the movements your stomach makes when air is inhaled and exhaled. Is this the correct way to breathe?
(Note: A higher risk is involved here because if the learner reflects on what was learned in the previous lesson and relates this to what he actually does, he may reveal an error in his breathing process.)

The knowledge demanded in each question is essentially the same. The questions differ, primarily, because of the degree of risk the respondent will experience. If the instructor notes the responses to this type of questioning, he will gain some insight into the willingness of the learners to perform at different levels of risk.

Attitudes

Attitude assessment can be performed easily if one becomes familiar with Krathwohl's taxonomy of the affective domain. This work represents the efforts of several persons, and it provides an instructional tool which will assist the teacher who desires to influence the attitudes of students. The taxonomy's behaviors are listed in hierarchical form. The behaviors represent a continuum of an internalization process. Students' responses, as indicated by the following description, can range from lack of choice to greater choice (Krathwohl, pp. 176–85).

I. Receiving
II. Responding
III. Valuing
IV. Organization
V. Characterization

This taxonomy is valuable because it describes a range of possible responses that a learner might express. The nature of a learner's response is partly a question of choice which is influenced by the degree of threat an individual expects to experience; e.g., a student may be dissatisfied but appears to respond attentively. Such compliance is proportional to the level of imagined threat. How a learner approaches a learning task emotionally is critical to his performance.

A student's attitude can be assessed by requesting him to indicate a preference between different content areas. The following question is an example:

Three 8mm film cartridges are available on an independent basis for your viewing. So that they can be available when needed, indicate in the blank provided which topic you would prefer to see.

   I.   Human Circulatory System ___
   II. Human Respiratory System ___
  III. Human Nervous System ___
  IV. None of these ___

At this stage, the student is under no pressure to respond; that is, the information appears to be concerned with managing the distribution of 8mm cartridges (see chapter 8).

A response to one of the first three items might indicate a preference; and if the item is related to the intended lesson, this should be noted. A response to the last item allows the student to avoid a commitment; this may be an expression of reluctance or a revelation of other priorities.

These responses are indicators only, and more than one situation should be provided. Whatever approach is used, remember that choices made on the basis of expected consequences are the instrumental factor. It is unlikely that anyone will deliberately choose a direction that will bring adverse consequences.

One method of implementing this approach is to pose a question at the end of the previous lesson. From the standpoint of management, this will save time and provide information early in the game.

Media Options

Chapters seven and eight present a description of various media options. However, because of the assistance media provides in classroom instruction, a brief discussion of this topic will be of value to the reader. The task of gathering information about the learner is a communication process. Which medium is best suited to convey the lesson? Which medium is best suited for gathering information about learners in the least amount of time? These and other questions suggest that media should be considered at the outset of preparing a lesson plan.

The student's level of learning is assessed at entry level; the teacher instructs the student; then the learner's exiting performance can be assessed. In all three stages, different media may be used. Often the problem in each of these areas is a question of management; e.g., expense, time, and other constraints.

Media may be used at the entry level stage to seek information about a student's level of learning for which written stimuli are not appropriate. The expectations of a learner do not necessarily require a response to a written question. It is reasonable to expect a performance response from the learner. A student could be asked to diagram the relationship between certain parts of the circulatory system. Another possibility is to require a written response from an auditory stimulus. In this instance, the learner could be asked to distinguish between the sounds made by the heart when it is forcing blood into arteries and the sounds made when it is recovering oxygenated blood from the lungs. Both of these conditions will require a different means of assessment than is normally

used. For example, to achieve a performance response (i.e., diagraming), stimulus conditions appropriate to this response should be selected. A visual might be preferable to words in this instance. The visual could be an incomplete diagram, or it could be slides or a film.

Media as it appears in the context of this chapter provides a means for obtaining information about the learner. Media allows the teacher to accommodate a wide range of learner behaviors. Without such options, it is doubtful if assessment can be covered on a scale that will make it a meaningful experience.

Media plays a supportive role throughout the text; therefore, media options are discussed in terms of a variety of classroom management decisions. It is not chance that caused this redundancy to occur but rather the acknowledgement of media as a vital link in the teacher-lesson-learner communication process.

Entry Level Profile

The results of procedures give some evidence of their worth. What does all that has been said about entry level assessment lead up to? The answer to this question depends on the ability to focus on both the content of the lesson and the learner for whom the lesson is intended. Most of the discussion so far has centered on the learner because it is he who must process the content of the lesson. However, in the majority of school systems the teacher is given a fixed curriculum to cover in a limited period of time. There are, of course, exceptions to this rule depending on the age of the students and whether the school is public or private.

Assume that the teaching circumstance is a public school system, and as a teacher, you have a fixed amount of information to cover. If you assess the entry level of your students for the checkpoints that were previously identified, you will generate information about the students' learning abilities; specifically, the learners' ability to succeed with the lesson, the students' knowledge of the lesson, their individual differences, and their attitude toward the lesson. If the experience is to be worth the effort and time required of you, the effectiveness of this approach toward improving the teaching and learning process must be shown. The question is not what can be done with the entry level assessment but *how* the instructor's job can be done more effectively when given the constraints of classroom teaching.

The assumption that the teacher can be a facilitator of learning is accepted in this text and, therefore, influences the answer to the above question. The learner is expected to do something with the content presented in the lesson, and it is expected that the competencies achieved will be transferred. As Mager so aptly puts it, "If the learning experience cannot be transferred beyond the initial learning setting, perhaps it should not have been taught in the first place" (Mager, pp. 9–10). Collecting data about the learner before the lesson is taught should help the desire to provide meaningful experiences.

Entry level assessment will provide four different kinds (i.e., four checkpoints) of information about each student from which will emerge certain requirements for instructional design. A profile can be established for each student that will show his position with respect to the categories expressed by each checkpoint.

A basic format expressing each of the four checkpoints for entry level and exit level is described on the graph in Figure

1–3B. The numbers on the graph represent the prerequisite and learning objectives offered to each student. The diagonal line connecting each corner of the graph represents a common linkage between entry and exit level performance. It is expected that between the entry level and exit level points, all of the prerequisites of the lesson will be accomplished and all of the prelesson objectives will be accomplished. The other two categories (learning style and attitude information) will vary considerably between individuals because their purpose is to identify learner characteristics rather than information about content. The graph expresses the linkage between content and the learner as well as the pre- and postlesson learning experience.

This graph should be passed out to students with clear acetate, colored flow pens, and a ruler. They should also be given a copy of their entry level performance results. Students should proceed to draw connecting lines in the entry level section of the graph using the color which the instructor designates for each category. Each line will connect the objective to the corresponding point on the diagonal line. Lines are drawn only when the entry level information indicates that the objectives have been performed correctly.

Although exit level will be discussed in chapter nine, the graph reveals a record of the student's performance for this section. Students should fill this section out in the same manner as described for entry level.

EXPLANATION OF THE STUDENT LEARNING PROFILE

The four checkpoints of entry level assessment (A, B, C, D in Figure 1–3A) will furnish information relevant to the instructional design. A student's performance (entry level and exit level) is pictured in Figure 1–3B. In the case of the exemplary lesson, there are four prerequisite objectives that are necessary to succeed with the lesson. The profile graph (Figure 1–3B) shows that of the four possibilities, the student has mastered two of them (e.g., P-Obj. One and P-Obj. Two). The other two objectives (P-Obj. Three and P-Obj. Four) will present a problem to the student if they are not learned prior to the lesson. A glance at the exit level of the graph indicates that success was achieved.

Throughout the graph wherever a line is extended, the characteristics exist. For the entry level of this student, look at the left side of the graph and see that P-Obj. One and Two and L-Obj. Four and L-Obj. Nine of the lesson were acquired in some previous learning experiences.

Checkpoints C and D express four learning styles and two attitude possibilities. The graph shows that the student has a high verbal style (i.e., LSHV—he does well with printed materials) and a high cognitive style (i.e., LSHC—he can organize ideas). Also, the student expresses a negative attitude toward the lesson (NA).

The exit level side of the graph indicates that the student has mastered all of the prerequisites. Two of the lesson objectives (Eight and Ten) have not been mastered. The student shows no change of attitude toward the lesson.

At the end of the lesson, the teacher should have two sheets of acetate for each student. When these two sheets are combined the basic graph will reflect the entry level and exit level performance of the student. This student profile will show the student's performance level prior to the lesson as well as the student's performance level following the lesson. Also, a compari-

	Entry Assessment	Exit Assessment
A. Prerequisite Information: P-Obj. One P-Obj. Two P-Obj. Three P-Obj. Four B. Lesson Information: L-Obj. One L-Obj. Two L-Obj. Three L-Obj. Four L-Obj. Five L-Obj. Six L-Obj. Seven L-Obj. Eight L-Obj. Nine L-Obj. Ten C. Learning Style: LSHV LSLV LSHC LSLC D. Attitude Information PA NA		

Legend: P-Obj. (Prerequisite Objective)
L-Obj. (Learning Objective)
LSHV (Learning Style High Visual)
LSLV (Learning Style Low Visual)
LSHC (Learning Style High Cognitive)
LSLC (Learning Style Low Cognitive)
PA (Positive Attitude)
NA (Negative Attitude)

FIGURE 1-3A Student learning profile.

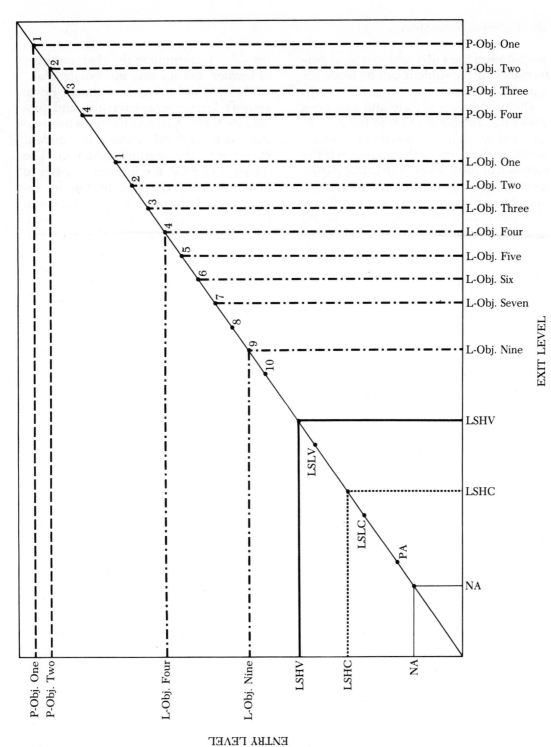

EXIT LEVEL

FIGURE 1-3B

27

son between the entry and exit level performance of the student can be made for a particular lesson.

The use of clear acetate and flow pens allows the instructor to reuse the acetate for subsequent instructional experiences. Another advantage of this approach is the inclusion of the learner as an active participant in the assessment. Assessment of both the entry and the exit levels will provide information that is important to the design of instruction.

Management

Given the constraint of a 25:1 student-teacher ratio, nonteaching duties, and a time schedule that makes deviating from traditional presentations risky, a teacher may find entry level assessment as presented in this chapter unrealistic. In essence, the question deals with management which, unfortunately, is a concern frequently ignored.

To resolve this problem we should establish what it is that the educational process hopes to accomplish and consider this a criterion. The direction of this text is to move toward the provision of adaptive instruction, that is, education which adapts to learner characteristics. Such a position places us in a confrontation with individual differences, and this enhances the possibility of providing fulfillment for individual learner needs.

This goal places different demands on instruction than are evident with a group oriented approach. Whether process or content oriented, teaching to a group dictates that instruction cater to the average student. If, on the other hand, students are considered as individuals, some method of collecting relevant data about them is im-

perative. Determining the characteristics of learners becomes an immediate goal.

The mission of teachers should be to identify learner characteristics and provide for them. A step in this direction is to start with the level at which the student enters into the learning situation. The question of what the instructor hopes to find out about the student can be responded to in terms of four critical areas; namely, prerequisite skills and knowledge, lesson skills and knowledge, cognitive styles, and attitudes. These areas have been labeled checkpoints. It is important for the instructor to know how to gather this entry level assessment information. It would appear that one of the constraints to entry level assessment is time. Prerequisite assessment (checkpoint one) can rely on questions from previous lessons. Therefore, if the teacher is willing to use previous test questions for this assessment purpose, the factor of time posing a constraint is reduced. It is possible to use posttest questions for the task of assessing students' knowledge of the lesson. Although the presentation may be different, the level of learning will have been identified. This is a good reason for designing the post or exit level test before presenting the lesson.

The difficulty with the learning style area of assessment lies with approaching questions from the unusual standpoint of detecting how a student learns rather than what the student has learned. Yet, shying away from this task because it appears overwhelming is to overlook the critical relationship between learning styles and expected learning outcomes. Once it is realized that students describe a behavior pattern when making choices, the difficulty of assessing learning styles is reduced. Referring back to the exemplary lesson the instructor could show a cartridge (8 mm) film to show oxygen passing from the air sacks into the thin-celled capillaries. Although this may have been used during the instructional situation, there is nothing preventing the use of it a second time to assess whether students are verbally or visually oriented.

It is not necessary to make an assessment of students' learning styles each time a new lesson is presented. Once it has been conducted enough times to reveal a pattern, the objective has been reached. The teacher's decision to accommodate it or attempt to change it will dictate the direction of future strategies.

In a similar fashion, the assessment of attitudes may be made by using materials which will also serve the instructional situation. Media such as films are suitable for eliciting value responses from students. This assessment requires few questions. The attitude of the learners could be ascertained by asking them whether or not they want to attend the lesson.

The management of time required to make an entry level assessment is related to the instructor's willingness to change procedures and his ability to reallocate and reuse resource materials. Perhaps it is time for teachers to include efficiency on their list of priorities.

IS ENTRY LEVEL A THREAT?

Many educators believe that pretesting may interfere with learning. This attitude stems from a feeling that frustration will result if students are exposed to several questions which they cannot answer. Entering into the learning experience with such frustration will possibly interfere with students' receptiveness to the lesson.

Because of this belief, educators range in their approaches from excluding entry level testing to alerting students that they are not expected to correctly answer all of the pretest questions. With the former approach, an opportunity to determine appropriate instructional conditions may be compromised because valuable learner information is missing. With the latter approach, student anxiety may prevail because the sincerity of this standard is not believed.

The testing feature is a big problem of entry level assessment. Students frequently generalize from past testing experiences that questions are meant to be answered correctly; or stated differently, questions answered incorrectly or questions not answered leave the learner in an undesirable state. However, it is possible to assess the entry level of students without the usual trappings of testing which may reduce the amount of generalization, thus removing the fear of failure.

Even if disguising entry level assessment to appear differently from testing is a viable means of reconciling the problem, the question of how to do it might be asked. The testing format is often used because it is relatively inexpensive to use; it is not difficult to give; and it is expeditious. The task then becomes one of finding an approach to entry level assessment that is different from the posttest (exit) experience and which retains three priorities; namely, lack of expense, freedom from difficulty of administration, and expediency.

Once again, the use of technology comes into the picture. It is important to realize that any media selection will not suffice; there are three priorities which need to be accommodated. For example, films, television, and slides may be too ex-

1. Small veins
2. Arteries
3. Veins
4. Arterioles
5. Capillaries
6. Heart
7. Ventricles
8. Aveoli
9. Pulmonary

FIGURE 1–4A

pensive, too difficult to prepare, or too time-consuming.

The selection of appropriate media is a competency which will be developed in subsequent chapters (i.e., chapters seven and eight). These chapters will discuss the importance and versatility of transparencies as a medium for displaying information. If you are not familiar with this particular medium, a look at the portion of chapter seven which describes the production of transparencies will prove helpful.

The materials required to make transparencies are simple, easy to acquire, and inexpensive. A simple design developed in color can be produced quickly. If the exemplary lesson (the conduction of oxygen within the bloodstream) is considered, a prerequisite knowledge of the parts of the circulatory system is required. A transparency, perhaps one that was used for teaching a previous lesson, could be presented to the class. The use of a transparency rather than a diagram of a written test is

less like the usual testing approach. This is the objective, and if the transparency is produced in color, the difference is even greater.

Now that stimulus conditions have been altered from those of the usual testing format, the same attention should be given to the other half of a testing situation; that is, the response demand of the learner. In the usual testing format, the student would be required to write a label on a diagram. It would be ideal if the response could be an auditory expression on tape because this would be quite a departure from the usual demand. However, all three priorities, especially expense, would be challenged by this choice.

In a previous section of the chapter, it was recommended that students participate in the development of their entry level profiles. It was suggested that each student be given clear acetate and colored flow pens. In the assessment situation, perhaps these materials can be used by the students to provide responses to the trans-

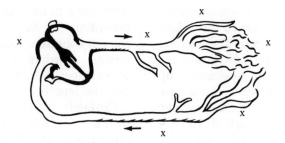

FIGURE 1–4B

parency. The diagram might appear as displayed in Figure 1–4A. If the master for the transparency is copied for a student handout, it would serve as a base over which the clear acetate can be placed as indicated in Figure 1–4B. In Figure 1–4A a small x identifies the areas of the diagram which should be labeled. The handout has, in addition to the diagram of the circulatory system, a list of possible labels. In addition to the appropriate labels, the list contains labels that are not appropriate selections. Students are expected to write on the clear acetate the number which precedes the label chosen. This can be done with the colored flow pens. Because it is relatively easy to write a number in lieu of the correct label, the learner will be tempted to do so and may not have the frustrating experience of leaving blank spaces where responses are expected. In other words, students will undoubtedly render a response whether correct or incorrect when the effort required is minimal. The end result will be a piece of clear acetate on which is placed the student's name and a pattern of numbers.

The acetate with the pattern of numbers can be put aside until the entry level assessment is completed for each of the four checkpoints. If the answers are not corrected or handed in to the instructor, the procedure will not appear like a testing situation. When the time comes to refer to the acetate, it will be for the purpose of transferring information onto the second sheet of acetate which will describe the prerequisite portion of the entry level profile. Involving the learner in this fashion minimizes the evaluative nature of assessing student behavior and, hopefully, the anxiety that accompanies such evaluation.

With this approach there is a definite attempt to make the experience less demanding for the student. Even though requiring a written response from recall might reveal more about a student's entry level, it carries with it an aura of urgency and the trappings of testing procedures that may contribute to frustration. This compromise is not unreasonable when a little thought will reveal that some students who score highly on entry level assessment pretests do so because of good guessing.

Another suggestion for this particular prerequisite assessment task is that a colored transparency be revealed on an overhead projector to the whole class; each student responds with a colored flow pen on a piece of clear acetate which overlays a handout of the diagram.

The conditions of the entry level assessment should be different from the exit level assessment of a student. This needs to be emphasized for it is the generalization from the one situation to the other which should be prevented. The recommendation that pre- and posttesting be the same for an accurate assessment of learning that occurs between these two extremes is interpreted to mean that the level of learning on both tests should be the same. In other words, it is possible to keep the entry level and exit level assessment the same as far as the level of learning is concerned by altering the stimulus and response conditions between the two assessment situations. If application is the desired learning level planned for students, it may be accomplished with a variety of verbal and nonverbal materials. Although the stimuli may change between entry and exit level assessment, the demands on the learner should remain the same.

The example that has been given to explain this section is for one of the four checkpoints (i.e., knowledge of prerequisite information) and for a particular subject area (i.e., biology). The medium described will not necessarily be appropriate for other situations. It is the procedure that should be noted; the procedure can be generalized to other lessons.

Summary

Four areas of information have been identified that contribute to students' learning behavior. These are prerequisite skills and knowledge, skills and knowledge to be presented in the lesson, learning styles, and learner attitudes.

The task of assessing these areas is essentially a management function with media playing a significant role. Avoiding this process of entry level assessment causes instruction to fall into that dubious role of providing for the average student. Although considerations may enter into decisions regarding the design of learning experiences, without entry level information the targets of design are too obscure.

Certainly without pretesting and posttesting one cannot, with any conviction, infer from grades the effect of teaching influence. For all the instructor knows, the success of the student may be due to experiences that occurred prior to the presentation of the lesson.

REFERENCES

Bloom, B. S.; Entlehart, M. D.; Furst, E. G.; Hill, W. H.; Krathwol, D. R. *A Taxonomy of Educational Objectives: Handbook I, The Cognitive Domain.* New York: David McKay Co., 1956.

Bruner, J. *Beyond the Information Given: Studies in the Psychology of Knowing.* Edited by J. M. Anglin. New York: W. W. Norton & Co., 1973.

English, H., and English, A. *A Comprehensive Dictionary of Psychological and Psychoanalytical Terms.* New York: David McKay Co., 1972.

Fleming, M. "Perceptual Principles for the Design of Instructional Materials." *Viewpoints* (Indiana University) 46 (1970): 124–26.

Holt, J. *How Children Fail.* New York: Pitman Publishing Corp., 1964.

Krathwohl, D. *A Taxonomy of Educational Objectives: Handbook II, The Affective Domain.* New York: David McKay Co., 1974.

Kumar, V. K. "The Structure of a Human Memory System and Some Educational

Implications." *American Educational Research Journal* 41: 379–411.

Mager, R. F. *Developing Attitude toward. Learning.* Palo Alto, Calif: Fearon Publishers, 1968.

Ofiesh, G. "University without Doors." Lecture presented March 1972 at University of North Carolina.

Shannon, C. E., and Weaver, W. *The Mathematical Theory of Communication.* Urbana, Ill.: University of Illinois Press, 1964.

Skinner, B. F. *Beyond Freedom and Dignity.* New York: Alfred A. Knopf, 1971.

Smith, O. *Research in Teacher Education.* Englewood Cliffs, N.J.: Prentice-Hall, 1971.

Chapter 2

Behavior Change

Introduction

Learning is a term which educators banter about with ease. Learning is a deceptive term which appears to convey much meaning but, like a surrealistic painting, its meaning is within the eye of the beholder. To many teachers, learning is expressed only when signs of pleasure emanate from the child. To others, it is expressed when the firmness of a problem gives way to the tenaciousness of a probing mind. The very nature of the term's ambiguity and the persistent efforts of educators to keep it so gives them the license to be condescending.

It is assumed that educators, being managers of the learning process, know something about this enigma. If educators are interested in guiding young minds, then they need to alter the nondescript nature of the term, learning. The Dictionary of Psychological Terms (English & English, pp. 290–292), for example, identifies fifteen variations of learning which have unique stimulus and response characteristics.

Teachers who have experienced a formal introduction to learning theory often exit with a theory that defies their efforts to use it. If teachers are to fulfill their mission, then they must relegate this phenomenon to a useful level.

With each learning situation, antecedent and contextual conditions are changed, and these conditions regulate the type of learning behavior manifested. The teacher's task will be to influence such conditions in the direction of desired learning behavior. Behavior change, whether it be internal or external to the learner, is evident in all cases. The learner is expected to do something with the instruction. Learning as a process of changing behavior can be observed and treated; and more importantly, it can be managed.

There are many circumstances where the instructor expects nothing more of a student than to think about an idea. However, sooner or later, the instructor desires some evidence from the learner that ideas have been assimilated. If teaching and learning is viewed as a communication process, the teacher's intent to persuade or influence the student is obvious. Ultimately, the intrinsic (internal) behavior of the student is manifested in some form of outward expression. Behavior change in this context serves as an expression of knowledge and skill acquisition; such behavior is the focal point for observing the learning process. The instructor should direct his objectives and strategies toward some form of behavior change. In other words, the content of the lesson should be treated in a special way based on expected changes in the learner's behavior. Objectives should not only be written in behavioral terms but they should also be shared with the student. Robert Mager states that for the instructor and the learner to reach the same destination, information stating where the learner is expected to go with the lesson and what the learner is expected to do with the lesson should be shared (Mager, p. 10).

This chapter attempts to communicate how expected learning is expressed at various levels of behavior. In essence, this chapter is a response to the question raised in chapter one; i.e., Is it clear to each student what is expected of him from the forthcoming lesson?

The goal of this chapter is to present a format for expressing desired behavior change which will lead to the development of an instructional plan. The following objectives represent the skills and knowledge that one must possess in order to achieve the competence necessary for expressing instructional goals in behavioral terms.

I.   Translate instructional goals into behavioral expressions.

II. Construct an objective that will express learning in terms of expected behavior change.

III. Express the desired behavior change at all levels of cognition.

IV. Translate affective concerns into indicator behaviors.

V.   Select media that can be used to communicate the learner's expected behavior change.

VI. Reveal a method for accomplishing the writing of behavioral objectives within the context of classroom teaching and learning.

Exemplary Situation

Imagine that you are a fifth-grade teacher who is going to present an English grammar lesson. Your desire is that students will comprehend verb tenses.

The class is fairly large with a wide range of individual differences. You suspect the prevailing attitude to be a lack of interest. This factor is supported by the entry level assessment. Some students do not comprehend the parts-of-speech concept and, therefore, are not prepared to pursue the lesson.

Because of the size of the class and the age level of the students, you have decided to focus on their lack of interest with sufficient concern given to those students who lack certain prerequisites. Using the method suggested in chapter one, you have determined the entry level of each student and have decided on the best instructional approach for these learners.

Among the factors which will determine the particular instructional strategy to be used are the characteristics of the class. A very large class or a wide range of individual differences may force you to consider certain objectives before other objectives which seem more important. Keying in on factors which appear to cause interference to the learning process is one way of determining what objectives to compromise. If interest appears to be a necessary prerequisite condition to learning and if the entry level assessment of a class indicates a large negative factor in this category, designing the instruction toward emphasizing this end is a reasonable approach.

The particular approach used in the learning process is related to the instructional objectives. If no objectives are specified for a particular lesson, the adaptability of instruction to learning becomes a factor of chance. On the other hand, expressing objectives that defy interpretation are little better than none. If the teacher and the learner see different targets, it is almost certain that they will not meet. The first step in planning the lesson, therefore, is a clear statement of objectives.

Characteristics of Behavioral Objectives

An objective is defined by Webster as "an aim of action or a point to hit" (Webster, p. 579). Although action and specificity are intricate parts of an objective, most educational objectives do not contain such priorities. This is especially true of administrative goals and curriculum policy. A potpourri of attempts to accommodate this need is evident in classroom teaching and learning. The range consists of extreme specifications that border on triteness to some deliberate attempts at perpetuating general goals which are often ambiguous. Agreement rests on a belief that some indication of direction is necessary. However, confusion and disagreement hinge on the degree of specificity that is associated with this direction.

Will concentrating on behavior change stifle creativity? Will specificity dilute the learning experience, relegating it to a simplistic level? These are two questions frequently raised by critics of a behavioral approach to instruction. These are reasonable concerns. Few will deny the need for spontaneity and unique expressions; few will deny the importance of the instructor in cultivating the necessary learning climate. Most educators desire to explore the intricate and sometimes mysterious relationships of ideas. Perhaps it is from such a position that we should launch our inquiry into the nature of behaviorism via behavioral objectives.

There is a proliferation of written materials on behavioral objectives that consider the common characteristics and the writing of objectives for different levels of learning. Most authors seem to agree that objectives are clear when they include the following three characteristics:

I. Terminal Performance—the expected behavior change at the end of the learning experience.
II. Conditions—stimuli necessary to the expected behavior change.
III. Criterion—means for evaluating the learner's performance.

As a teacher faced with the problem of presenting a lesson on verb tense (exemplary lesson), investigate the behavioral objective approach from the standpoint of the challenge posed by the lesson. The goal is for students to understand verb tenses to the extent that they will be able to apply the principles of this topic when it is necessary to do so. The range of difficulty will extend from comprehending verb tenses that follow a regular pattern to comprehending those that are exceptions to this pattern. A general objective could be: The student will be able to indicate the correct verb tense of several sentences with 80 percent accuracy.

If this objective is analyzed in terms of the above pattern, the *terminal performance* is the ability to *indicate the correct verb tense,* the *conditions* is the use of *several sentences,* and the *criterion* is the completion of the task *with 80 percent accuracy.*

Compare the preceding objectives to an alternative way of presenting the same lesson. The students could be told, "Today we are going to take a look at verb tenses." All that the students know is that verb tenses will be presented in the lesson. Which objective will help grade the students' performance? Which objective will help focus student attention on the intended meaning of the lesson?

The second alternative fails to let the student know what is expected from him. The student is aware of the topic to be covered in the lesson, but no reference is made of what he is supposed to do with this knowledge. Whenever the instructor and the student have different objectives, a problem may arise. Often the consequence is a realization by the student that success rests more with discerning the behavior patterns of the teacher than with understanding the content of the lesson.

In contrast, the first objective specifies not only what the student is expected to do but also the conditions under which he is expected to do it. There is little chance that the student will misinterpret the teacher's intentions. There is little chance that error will occur if test questions correspond to the objectives of the lesson. Frequently carelessness is exercised at this point, and inappropriate test questions nullify any benefit objectives may provide. *The conditions of the test questions should match the conditions of the objective.*

Specificity is a major characteristic of behavioral objectives. Whether or not it leads to simplicity is certainly questionable and appears to be an issue of management. The teacher could reduce learning to a rote level and maintain this level by always specifying objectives which demand little more than recall. This condition can be avoided if a teacher possesses the skills to write behavioral objectives at all levels of learning behavior. Perhaps within this competency also rests the solution to the criticism that attitudes may be compromised along the way. If viewed as a legitimate form of learning behavior, the expression of attitudes in behavioral terms will provoke a desire to attend to affective concerns.

Writing Behavioral Objectives

Although it is customary to express behavioral objectives with the three major components (i.e., terminal behavior, conditions, and criterion), it is important that this format be subjected to a test of appropriateness. The test will consist of comparing the behavioral approach with educational goals. Variance in instructional techniques is enormous. However, most instructional goals attempt to leave students with information which is meaningful or competencies that can be applied after the initial learning experience.

The first of these intended outcomes is typical of what is found in classrooms today. An example is expressed when students are given a final exam which tests their recall of information. Success with this experience may indicate nothing more than the attainment of certain understandings.

If you will refer to the taxonomy of cognitive behavior (p. 20), it will become apparent to you that there are several levels of learning. One should challenge the justification for failing to attain certain levels of difficulty with particular students. This is especially true if the students are teacher candidates. If the prospective teacher does not attain at least the level of application, he will find little need for the application of abilities in real-life teaching roles.

It is reasonable to expect that teachers will have some abilities which are more developed than others. An opportunity for demonstrating these abilities should be provided during the learning experience. Comprehension of subject matter is obviously important; however, somewhere during the course of instruction the student's teacher's ability to use knowledge should be determined. The alternative to this approach is to assume that ability is cultivated by simply exposing students to knowledge. It is known from experience that there is a vast difference between understanding and applying knowledge.

The aim of this text is to apply an instructional approach that will enable the teacher to adapt instruction to individual learning differences and to manage this system within the traditional school struc-ture. A fundamental goal of this text is that this instructional system will be appropriate in a real-life teaching situation. Therefore, opportunities must be provided that will enable the prospective teacher to demonstrate an ability to apply the skills and knowledge learned.

The appropriateness of a detailed approach to expressing instructional objectives can be questioned. Such an approach consists of the terminal performance, the conditions, and the criterion.

An analysis of the condition portion of this approach raises the important question of whether or not all students can handle the conditions. In the case of the exemplary lesson, it is possible that some students will not comprehend the meaning of sentences. Is it possible that one mode of presenting the lesson may be satisfactory for some learners and not for others? It is evident that we cannot acknowledge individual learner differences on one hand and provide an objective that is universal for all learners.

Objectives which specify what the learner is expected to do with the lesson are basically content oriented even though terminal behavior is an important component. Objectives which are content oriented tend to lead to instruction which is designed for students as a group, ignoring individual differences. A troublesome outcome of committing instruction to a group rather than to individuals is the tendency to overwork one format. It is not unusual to find syllabi expressed in behavioral terms with little or no attention given to individual learning styles. Teaching methods may continue as before with the exception that students have some advance warning of the instructional intent. If, however, there are students who have difficulty with the condition because of their individual learning characteristics, this advance notification is of little help.

It is questionable whether appropriate conditions can be selected at an early stage of instructional development. Information which is not available at this stage of planning is necessary to make such decisions. To cite an example, the assessment of where students are prior to the lesson is relevant information. An analysis of the expected terminal behavior may engender certain requirements that will establish the appropriate conditions. Posttest questions generate information upon which instructional conditions can be established.

In consideration of the preceding reasons, an alternative method of phrasing the suggested objective is proposed.

   I. *Old Form:*
      A. The student will be able to indicate the correct verb tense of several sentences with 80 percent accuracy.

  II. *New Form:*
      B. The student will be able to indicate verb tense with 80 percent accuracy.

The instructional objective has been reduced to the terminal behavior expectations and a criterion statement. Other sources of information (mentioned above) will establish the necessary conditions.

Previously, support has been expressed for identifying the expected behavior change; now the worth of the criterion portion of behavioral objectives should be assessed. If the entry level assessment includes each objective of the lesson, then the student will be exposed to the criterion at the outset. This presumes that the pretest questions will correspond to the behavior change expected in each objective. In the exemplary lesson, the learner should be tested on verb tenses and not on defining verb tense.

In the previous chapter we stated that although the stimulus and response conditions of the pre- and posttest may be different, the level of learning should remain the same. It would seem redundant to include the criterion in the objective if the student has already been exposed to it in the pretesting situation. If the learner recognizes a need to relate the criterion questions to the behavior expected in the objective, it is unlikely that the criterion will need to be restated for him.

Since there does not appear to be any interference between expressing the criterion factor in the objective and instructional development, the inclusion of this portion would appear optional. Either of the following forms are appropriate for stating the lesson objective:

   I. The student will be able to indicate verb tense with 80 percent accuracy.
  II. The student will be able to indicate verb tense.

Exposing the desired terminal performance is of primary importance at this stage of instructional development.

WRITING BEHAVIORAL OBJECTIVES FOR ALL LEVELS OF LEARNING

The methods for writing a behavioral objective has been a favorite topic of authors ever since Mager upset the educators' pedestal of ambiguity by pointing out the value of stating educational objectives in clear terms. Educators often use a variety of verb expressions as a means of writing behavioral objectives for certain types of learning. Each author has a scheme for organizing verbs so that they can be used when needed. When this approach is applied, a variance often occurs between the verb and learning level it attempts to satisfy; and the task becomes not only confusing but exhausting.

In *Writing Worthwhile Behavioral Objectives,* the taxonomy of cognitive behavior is considered as a focal point for writing behavioral objectives for learning difficulties (Vargus, pp. 105–110). An understanding of the differences and interrelationships between these levels eliminates the need for a prolonged study of verb expressions. From this point of view, the level of learning to be conveyed by the behavioral objectives is more a question of meaning than of using a particular verb.

In the exemplary lesson, the student who cannot express the correct verb tense for different points in time has a problem. We need to know the nature of this problem; that is, we need to know where the learning process broke down. If objectives are specified at different levels of difficulty, the teacher will be provided with diagnostic information of importance to the instructional design. Remediation as well as preventive measures rely on the teacher's selection of appropriate instructional strategies. For example, the student who cannot comprehend the meaning of verb tense will not be able to apply the correct verb tenses.

Because the levels of the taxonomy of the cognitive domain are arranged on a hierarchy, it is necessary to acknowledge what level the lesson is on and to determine the preceding levels that the student needs to know. Such information is important to the design of an instructional system.

Look at our grammar lesson in terms of specific objectives. You may want students to be able to recognize certain information. The following objectives express this expectation:

I. Identify the six verb tenses.
    (Consideration: The tenses may have been given in class, and they could have been memorized by the student.)

II. Recognize the auxiliaries that indicate tense.
    (Consideration: It is possible for the student to memorize the auxiliaries.)

III. Express the tenses for the verb "to be."
    (Consideration: It is evident that more information needs to be processed but it is nevertheless a memory task.)

Level One (knowledge) of the taxonomy encompasses both recognition and recall functions, which are important to the acquisition and use of knowledge. This level should not be considered unimportant to instruction. Criticisms that have been directed at writing objectives for recall purposes express concern for the preoccupation of those who concentrate almost exclusively on this stage.

Some educators doubt that a concept is understood by learners when all that is required by them is a recall response. Real understanding is expressed when students can relate ideas that have not been experienced in a teaching sequence (Markle, p. 57). Evidence of learning beyond memory should be apparent in the student.

The following objectives are examples of Level Two, comprehension:

I. Write original examples that convey the six verb tenses.
(Consideration: The request that examples be original eliminates the possibility of memorization.)

II. Select the "to be" verb form out of sample sentences.
(Consideration: An understanding of the "to be" concept is necessary to accomplish the task of sorting out conflicting possibilities.)

III. Indicate the correct tenses for an array of verbs.
(Consideration: Associating the appropriate tense for a verb requires that the student understand the tenses.)

Once a property has been isolated, it is necessary to recognize that it may be ascribed to other circumstances. The verb "to be" is associated with various tenses thereby giving the concept of tense a broader meaning. When the meaning is finally understood, the concept assumes a new posture. Tense is viewed differently when regular verbs rather than irregular verbs or the verb "to be" are considered.

If a student understands a concept, then he is ready to apply it. This consideration leads to the next level of the taxonomy: application. In some respects it is unfortunate that application was chosen as the label for this level. Note that application is exercised at the comprehension level. At level two, a concept is applied whereas at level three, a variation is apparent because a concept is applied to different circumstances. Therefore, some logical arrangement or sequence is inherent at this level.

The following objectives are examples for Level Three, application:

I. Apply the principle of writing the emphatic forms of verbs to past and present tense expressions.
(Consideration: The learner must go beyond the concept by coping with how to handle emphatic verb forms with a different tense.)

II. When the learner is directed to go beyond simple anticipation or expectation (e.g., the use of shall in the first person), the correct procedure for expressing determination, threat, or promise will be demonstrated.
(Consideration: Altering expressions to change meaning involves an understanding of the principles.)

III. Use the rule for mixing tenses by correctly altering verb expressions which contain a mixture of past and present tenses.
(Consideration: Using a rule in various situations requires an understanding of the concept and the procedure for it.)

For many learners the terminal behavior will stop at level three. Many educators of prospective teachers believe that the learner who can apply principles to different situations has achieved the expected level of learning. Isn't that what the teaching role demands? This level can be practiced so that the concept is entrenched in the student's mind. We would like to believe this occurs; however it is at this point that we begin to waver in our convictions. This is especially true if students are expected to retain their acquired knowledge or skills to be used at some future date. If transfer is an intended goal, then objectives ought to reflect a concern for long range retention.

An instructor can help students retain knowledge by exposing them to experiences which will develop associative linkages. Each of the three remaining levels requires that the learner *associate* information in a meaningful fashion, and each level accomplishes this in a unique way.

Certain subjects like geometry require analytical behavior. The process of problem solving is helpful to students in and out of the classroom. The following objectives are examples of behavioral objectives for Level Four: analysis.

I. Identify the verb tenses in a written passage.
(Consideration: The accomplishment of this terminal behavior requires that students understand the integral relationships associated with verb tense.)

II. Analyze sentences and identify which verb tense is being expressed.
(Consideration: Success with this task demands that the learner be able to see the differences and relationships between each of the six verb tenses.)

III. Label the parts of speech in a sentence.
(Consideration: It will be necessary for the student to apply and interrelate a variety of rules.)

In the next two levels, synthesis and evaluation, the expected terminal behavior depends on the learner's willingness to participate. Synthesis is the conveyance of an idea in a unique way. Synthesis may range from a simple verbal interpretation to a visual expression of the idea. This level is not reserved for the creative person. Any individual who wishes to express a unique idea is functioning at this level regardless of how the idea is displayed. The following objectives are examples of behavioral objectives for Level Five: synthesis.

I. Create a sentence that correctly expresses mixed tenses.
(Consideration: This task requires that the student understand the relationship between the parts of speech.)

II. Show by a unique diagram the interrelationship between the parts of speech in a sentence.
(Consideration: An understanding of the relationship between the parts of a sentence is necessary to complete this task.)

III. Design a system for expressing the six verb tenses.
(Consideration: Success depends on knowing the six tenses, the rules for expressing these tenses, and the relationship between them.)

The final level is the most demanding because at this level the learner must defend his position or be willing to defend it. At this level it is necessary for the learner to explain the *how* and *why* of a situation. Some readiness is expected at this point, and the absence of willingness may suggest inadequacies at previous behavior levels. Some behavior change occurs at each level of learning, and the instructor should consider the consequences of skipping a level if the terminal behavior of the student is to be at the highest level of difficulty.

Each time that a student approaches a concept from a different level of learning, his chances of remembering it are greater. When the student can associate the concepts that he has learned to different situations, then he is ready for the next level of difficulty: evaluation. The following objectives are examples of behavioral objectives for Level Six: evaluation.

I. Criticize the usage of verb tense in a sample passage.
(Consideration: Criticism depends on the student's ability to generate examples of good and poor usages of verb tense).

II. Defend a method for teaching the concept of verb tense.
(Consideration: An analysis of other methods and the expression of new methods are prerequisites.)

III. Debate the issue of why the verb is the most important word in a sentence.
(Consideration: One's own interpretation of the function of a verb and an analysis of this function are necessary prerequisites.)

Issue of Attitudes

The idea that motivation leads to learning and vice versa contributes to the perceptual emphasis often placed on instructional treatments of attitudes. The issue is often approached as a factor of novelty. Varying presentation modes are often used to provide the learner with an air of novelty that will attract him. Although this may be a worthwhile strategy, there are other important ones to be considered.

The attainment of the various levels of cognition may depend on the learner's attitude. Attitude change is not necessarily an effect of cognitive pursuits; it has its own identity and deserves special attention. The teacher must learn how to express this abstract facet of human behavior in succinct terms.

WRITING BEHAVIORAL OBJECTIVES FOR ATTITUDES

A form of communication needs to be established to express behavioral objectives for attitudes. In the context of behavioral or operational expressions, such a means already exists. The essential factor in writing objectives for attitudes is the ability to associate the desired attitude with its behavioral component.

This task poses great difficulty. For example, consider the word "appreciate." It is not unusual to find an educational goal which states that students should appreciate. What does appreciate mean? The more we try to clarify the meaning, the closer we get to behavioral descriptions.

Can we tell how a student feels about a certain artist? We can ask him but that would only give us a sampling of his feelings, and perhaps only a small percentage of these would be accurate. Most of us are adept at playing roles and if our answers are intended to evoke reinforcing responses, little can be learned about one's true feelings. However, we can observe behavior patterns and gain insight into a student's attitude. The student who chooses to gain more information than was expected from resources about a particular artist might be expressing a degree of interest. On the other hand, the student may be seeking approval from the teacher. Observing one behavior is not enough; several behaviors should be listed that express the desired attitude.

Using the exemplary lesson, look at the task of expressing affective concerns in clear terms. It is desired that the students will not only understand the tenses but also have an interest in writing them. Specifying affective objectives in clear terms will enable one to provide conditions necessary to the attainment of these objectives.

It is a challenge to clearly express an objective for attitudes. An ambiguous objective might read as follows: Students will display a positive attitude toward learning how to express the correct verb tense. The term "positive" becomes less ambiguous if more than one behavior that expresses this objective is identified. Our approach might be to ask the question: What kinds of behaviors does one exhibit when he is interested in learning how to write verb tenses? If a student's class participation increases as the lesson is taught, he may be showing interest. If when given the opportunity to report on some facet of grammar, the student chooses verb tense, a positive attitude toward the lesson can be assumed. Pursuing higher levels of involvement than the lesson requires might be another indication of an interest in verb tense. The selection of behavior is arbitrary.

Once the behaviors are identified, a criterion for assessing attitudes can be established. Our concern is to establish whether an attitude change is desired and what specifically needs to be accomplished. Specifying behaviors beforehand will not only highlight the importance of attitudes to the lesson but will also alert the instructor to those attitudes which may interfere with learning.

If students are aware that the teacher is looking for behaviors, is it possible that the student will comply just to gain the instructor's approval? The question is reasonable if behavioral objectives which include affective concerns are given to the student. Ulterior motives which may influ-

ence the student's behavior patterns can prevent the instructor from assessing behavior for a particular attitude. Therefore, affective objectives should not be shared with students. It is important, however, that opportunities be provided to students for the expression of such behaviors.

The following steps will enable an instructor to express affective concerns as observable behaviors and assess attitude change:

I. Specify the desired attitude.

II. Consider those behaviors that express the desired attitude.

III. Provide opportunities for these behaviors to be expressed.

IV. Do not share this information with students.

V. Identify and provide for more than one behavior.

Media Options

It is important that students comprehend the intended meaning of an objective. It is also important that students recognize the terms used to specify the desired terminal behavior because specifying terminal behavior can be a communication problem. It is our intent, as instructors, to offer objectives that are meaningful. Objectives should stress the expected outcome and the expected activity necessary for achieving a desired end. It is the instructor's task to determine what can interfere with this transaction and prevent it from occurring.

An objective may be ambiguous to a student. The teacher may wish to get immediate feedback from students so that he can determine whether or not they under-

"time of the state of condition"
(*past* or future
reference)

"time of the state of action"
(*now* reference)

FIGURE 2–1 A visual display may help convey the intended
message.

stand the objective. The teacher may wish to provide some cues which will help the learner decode the objective. One way to accomplish this task is to express the objective in several forms.

The media possibilities will depend on the age and learning level of the students. Some modes of presentation (i.e., verbal) will be inappropriate for very young children who usually have a high visual literacy. For them, a visual approach may be necessary to provide additional meaning. In the case of the exemplary lesson, an overhead transparency could be designed that shows verb expressions as they relate to tenses. This can serve to set the stage for the lesson. The medium chosen to communicate the objectives should be selected on the basis of how well it reduces ambiguity.

When the instructor writes behavioral objectives, he should attempt to express them clearly. Some instructors who do write objectives behaviorally tend to believe that their commitment to the learner ends with the terminal behavior expression. However, other portions of the objective may confuse the student. The following statement, although stated in behavioral terms, is ambiguous: Be able to express the part of speech that indicates time of action or the time of the state of condition.

The phrase "time of the state of condition" is vague. In the case of this particular objective, many students will require more cues if they are to understand it. Whenever it appears that the code selected (in this case verbal) is not communicating, perhaps another one should be tried. A visual code (transparency) showing an athlete competing in a foot race using two different captions as depicted in Figure 2–1 illustrates the difficult parts of the objective.

Management

It makes little sense for an instructor to expend the effort to write objectives behaviorally if the meaning goes undetected by the student. Visualizing the objective, vocalizing the objective, and verbalizing objectives all contribute to developing in students the desired state for learning.

It is important for the learner to know what level of learning and type of behavior (i.e., affective, cognitive, psychomotor) is expected from him; therefore, he will not be reluctant to study the lesson because he is confused about the intent of it. Presenting the learner with a preview of the lesson and providing for some means of assessment are other major reasons for writing objectives in behavioral terms. The instructor's ability to choose the appropriate option to communicate the objective will determine the student's success with it.

Because there are several options to choose from when presenting an objective to a class, the instructor should choose the one which requires the least amount of time and is effective. If we view this issue from the standpoint of what the teacher has accepted to be reasonable tasks, perhaps some clue will be given. Most administrators require that teachers prepare a lesson plan. This usually consists of a brief sketch which describes in outline form the content to be covered. If the time that is used to write lesson plans could be used to express what the student is expected to do with the content, lesson plans would be of greater value. The specification of objectives behaviorally will help the teacher make decisions for teaching the lesson and for testing the students' performance. Both of these subsequent tasks are necessary responsibilities of teaching to which a certain amount of time should be allocated. It is possible that time will be saved in both of these areas, thus providing additional time for specifying objectives behaviorally.

Some schools have hired teachers during the summer months to rewrite curricula in behavioral terms. When this is done, objectives which are content oriented may appear to the participants as learner oriented. Basically, all that has happened to the curriculum is that it is organized in terms of what to expect from the learner. The objectives, although behaviorally written, are content oriented and learning depends on effective communication. The level of learning that is expected to occur is in part a question of knowing the learner's entry level as well as the content of the lesson. Writing objectives behaviorally for a unique group of learners may be more effective than writing objectives for an average group of students.

Summary

A student's receptiveness to a lesson may be influenced by the statement of a goal. Once this statement is made, steps which the learner must take to achieve this goal should be identified. A need for direction is one of the principle reasons why objectives should be expressed clearly.

Although there are several characteristics of an objective, the expected behavior change of students is the most important. The desired terminal behavior indicates the demands that are placed upon the student by the instruction. A completed objective should include not only the desired terminal behavior of the student but also his reasons for doing it.

Three factors are basic to the expression of instructional objectives. First, it is important that one can identify the unique characteristics of an instructional objective. Secondly, one should be able to apply these characteristics when writing the objective. Thirdly, it is important to know how to write instructional objectives clearly for all levels of learning.

The expression of instructional objectives for attitudes is challenging. Evidence suggests that the avoidance of attitudes as a target of instruction is often detrimental to the learning process. Although attitudes lend themselves to multi-interpretations, they nevertheless must be expressed behaviorally. Affective goals can be expressed as succinct behaviors which indicate the attitude. The teacher should provide the opportunity for the behavior to be exhibited willingly and observe what happens.

Media can be used to communicate the meaning of instructional objectives to students. The choice of appropriate media is important; expressing objectives which fail to communicate meaning may be reflected in the learner's responses.

The management of time required for writing behavioral objectives is often depicted by teachers as a deterrent factor. The problem lies in the fact that some teachers are reluctant to retrain. However, like so many duties which are performed in education, a reallocation of time and priorities is sometimes all that is needed.

REFERENCES

English, H., and English, A. *A Comprehensive Dictionary of Psychological and Psychoanalytical Terms.* New York: David McKay Co., 1972.

Mager, R. F. *Preparing Instructional Objectives.* Palo Alto, Calif.: Fearon Publishers, 1962.

Markle, S. M. *Good Frames and Bad—A Grammar of Frame Writing.* New York: Wiley & Sons, 1969.

Vargus, J. S. *Writing Worthwhile Behavioral Objectives.* New York: Harper and Row, Publishers, 1972.

Webster's New Collegiate Dictionary. Springfield, Mass.: G. & C. Merriam Co., 1960.

Chapter 3

Task Analysis

Introduction

It would appear that if we have managed to express the objectives for a lesson as clearly as possible, we are ready to teach the lesson. However, this is not the case. Objectives are expressions of content, and if written as prescribed, they are clear expressions of content which should also state what the student is expected to do with this content. Yet, neither of these necessary steps sufficiently bridges the gap between the lesson and the learner.

Other information is needed before we have a complete picture of what instruction is supposed to do. We don't know, for instance, whether a particular terminal behavior depends on a mastery of certain related behaviors. Also, it is not apparent at what level of learning a student is expected to perform. Both of these conditions can remain embedded within a behavioral objective unless some effort is made to release them.

In this chapter an effort will be made to show how one can analyze a behavioral objective and unravel certain requirements for the design of instruction. The following objectives will help us achieve this goal:

I. Be able to analyze the terminal behavior expected.

II. Be able to arrange learning tasks along a hierarchy of difficulty.

III. Be able to compare the desired learning behaviors with learning behaviors which are evident.

IV. Be able to express those specific behaviors that are targets of instruction.

V. Be able to analyze the content of a lesson for learning behaviors.

VI. Be able to express tasks as units of learning behavior.

VII. Be able to show how media can facilitate the management of a task analysis.

Exemplary Situation

Imagine that you are a fifth grade mathematics teacher. The lesson you will present is concerned with the English and metric systems of measurement. The following goal and objectives represent your approach. Goal: Students should be able to convert units of measure from the English system of measurement to the metric system of measurement. Objectives:

I. Be able to identify the units of measurement in the English system.

II. Be able to identify the units of measurement in the metric system.

III. Be able to identify a measurement problem and apply each system as a solution.

IV. Be able to translate units of measurement from the English to the metric system.

Units of Behavior

In the exemplary lesson, it is apparent that an attempt has been made to specify not only what the teacher wishes to accomplish in the lesson but also what the students must do to achieve this goal. Such a commitment makes it necessary for the teacher to provide conditions so that success will be achieved. Has enough information been provided for the teacher to foster these conditions? For example, consider the first objective of the lesson. The terminal behavior expected in this objective is that the student will be able to identify the units of measurement in the English system. What is it that the learner must be able to do in order to achieve this terminal objective? As a math teacher, you might respond with the following list:

I. The student must recognize the symbols which distinguish one unit of measurement from another.

II. The student must be able to comprehend the labels which represent the units of measurement in the English system.

III. The student must be able to apply the base ten numerical approach which is used in the English system.

IV. The student must be able to apply the rules of decimal point placement to the English system of measurement.

It appears that the terminal behavior of an objective is contingent on other behaviors. If these behaviors are satisfied, the expected terminal behavior will be accomplished. Because of this dependency, we will refer to these subobjectives as contingent behaviors.

At this point it would be helpful if you applied this procedure to the second objective. Try it on a piece of scrap paper, and compare your results with the attempt presented below. The terminal behavior expected in this objective is that the student be able to identify the units of measurement in the metric system. In order to accomplish this goal, the student must be able to

I. recognize the measurement symbols of the metric system;

II. comprehend the measurement labels of the metric system;

III. apply the base two numerical system;

IV. apply the rules of decimal point placement to the metric system.

Inventory of Tasks

If you continue with an analysis of each behavioral objective, an inventory of tasks will emerge. It is this inventory of contingent behaviors that will serve as a framework upon which the instructional system can be designed. Applying this scheme to each of the objectives for the exemplary lesson will generate the following inventory.

Objective One: The student will be able to identify the units of measurement that are represented in the English system.

Contingent Tasks:

I. recognition of the measurement symbols in the English system

II. comprehension of measurement labels in the English system

III. application of base ten numerical system

IV. application of decimal point placement rules to the English system

Objective Two: The student will be able to identify the units of measurement in the metric system.

Contingent Tasks:

I. recognition of the measurement symbols in the metric system

II. comprehension of measurement labels in the metric system

III. application of base two numerical system

IV. application of decimal point placement rules to the metric system

Objective Three: The student will be able to identify a measurement problem and apply each system as a solution.

Contingent Tasks:

I. identification of the solution to a problem to be one of applying a system of measurement

II. application of either system of measurement to solving the problem

Objective Four: The student will be able to translate units of measurement from the English to the metric system.

Contingent Tasks:

I. substitution of one factor for another without altering the original relationship

II. application of the rule for expressing ratios

III. application of the rule for solving for unknowns when given a ratio between two systems of measurement

We have described thirteen behaviors upon which the four objectives depend. If any of these behaviors are excluded, the achievement of one of the objectives may be prevented. As you survey this list, you may assume that the learner possesses the skills. This assumption is correct in many cases; yet, a surprising number of student failures can be attributed to making the wrong assumption. Certain requirements for the design of instruction may remain undetected when the instructor bases his instructional plans on too many untested assumptions. If a student is surveyed for prerequisite skills, the teacher may become aware of some critical contingencies that would otherwise have gone unnoticed.

There is a close relationship between the task analysis and the entry level assessment. Both attempt to unfold requirements for the purpose of designing instruction. The entry level assessment measures the learner's ability prior to the lesson; task analysis identifies those behaviors which are essential to success with the lesson. The former is oriented to the learner whereas the latter is primarily concerned with the demands of the lesson. If a teacher relates these two concerns, he will have a basis upon which to build his instructional plan.

If an entry level assessment and inventory of the tasks have been made, the teacher can compose learning experiences appropriate to the difference between these two inventories. Using the exemplary lesson, assume that the entry level assessment of a fifth grade student indicates that he is deficient in the following contingent behaviors:

I.   Objective One: Task 4

II. Objective Two: Tasks 2, 4

III. Objective Three: Task 2

IV. Objective Four: Tasks 1, 2, 3

SUBOBJECTIVES

The results of this comparison between the entry level and contingent behaviors will be called an inventory of target behaviors. They, in fact, represent the targets on which the instruction should focus. Target behaviors can assume the form of subobjectives. For the seven target behaviors represented in the student profile, we have the following subobjectives:

I.   Be able to apply the rules of decimal point placement as it applies to the English System.

II.   Be able to comprehend the measurement units of the metric system.

III. Apply the rules of decimal point placement as they apply to the metric system.

IV.   Apply either system to solve a measurement problem.

V.   Be able to substitute one factor for another without altering the original relationship.

VI.   Apply the rule of expressing ratios.

VII. Apply the rule of solving for unknowns when given a ratio between the two systems of measurement.

Why are subobjectives important to the instructional design? If this question is considered from the standpoint of communication, then your commitment should be to minimize the forces of interference. Controlling forces of interference is the expected outcome of systematically designed instruction.

One of the first steps toward facilitating

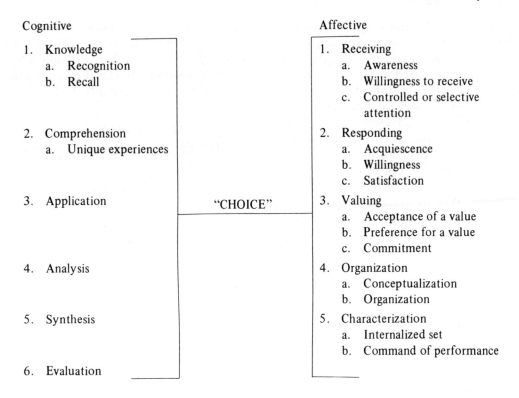

Cognitive

1. Knowledge
   a. Recognition
   b. Recall

2. Comprehension
   a. Unique experiences

3. Application

4. Analysis

5. Synthesis

6. Evaluation

"CHOICE"

Affective

1. Receiving
   a. Awareness
   b. Willingness to receive
   c. Controlled or selective attention

2. Responding
   a. Acquiescence
   b. Willingness
   c. Satisfaction

3. Valuing
   a. Acceptance of a value
   b. Preference for a value
   c. Commitment

4. Organization
   a. Conceptualization
   b. Organization

5. Characterization
   a. Internalized set
   b. Command of performance

FIGURE 3-1   Relationship between cognitive and affective taxonomies.

the learner's success with a lesson is to clearly express subobjectives in behavioral terms. When reference is made to behavior domains, we are usually concerned with one in particular (i.e., cognitive, affective, or psychomotor). However, it is seldom the case that a desired target behavior lies in one domain. For example, a mastery of the knowledge that is necessary to apply the rules of decimal point placement (cognitive) depends heavily on a desire to master this knowledge (affective). The affective concern is almost always a component of behavior that must be reckoned with in the learning process.

Overlooking the behaviors that are perhaps secondary to the emphasized behavior (e.g., primary: cognitive; secondary: psychomotor) may prevent success with the learning task. Before we continue this discussion, make sure that you can distinguish between the two behavior domains that are illustrated in Figure 3-1. Cognitive behavior is the expression of awareness or the attainment of knowledge. Affective behavior is the expression of feeling or emotion.

Psychomotor behavior is the expression of the motor effects of the thinking processes (English & English, p. 427). Distinguishing between certain cognitive and psychomotor behaviors may pose a problem. For instance, if you write the conversion of the density of water from the English system to the metric system, are you exhibiting cognitive or psychomotor behavior? On one hand, you express an awareness of knowledge (i.e., the conversion of the density of water from one system of measurement to another); on the other hand, it would seem that you are expressing the motor effects of thought processes (i.e., writing). However, a closer look at the definition of psychomotor behavior and the act of writing reveals a discrepancy. Writing for the expression of knowledge is the act of expressing a particular knowledge (cognition) whereas writing with the intent of formulating knowledge is an expression of the motor effects of physically manipulating a writing instrument to form the desired symbol (psychomotor).

Any motor behavior that expresses knowledge or meaning that is not associated with the how of performing the motor act is considered to be an expression of cognitive behavior. Therefore, writing, drawing, and using numerical symbols are all cognitive behaviors when they serve as a vehicle for expressing meaning.

Setting up a ratio is a necessary skill that the student must know in order to master the exemplary lesson; as such, it is an expression of psychomotor behavior. When a ratio is used to express a relationship between the two systems of measurement, it is an expression of cognitive behaviors. Obviously both behaviors are necessary; if the student cannot master the skill of formulating a ratio, the cognitive portion of the subobjectives will not be accomplished.

Behavior Chains

Although attention has been focused on behavior domains and behavior expecta-

tions for a particular lesson, these factors have not been associated with possible *types of learning*. Robert Gagne's assessment of learning is classified into eight types; they are (Gagne, pp. 33–57):

   I. Signal Learning
  II. Stimulus-Response Learning
 III. Chaining
  IV. Verbal Association
   V. Multiple Discrimination
  VI. Concept Learning
 VII. Principle Learning
VIII. Problem Solving

An instructional system which is adaptive to learner characteristics would be only partially effective if this hierarchy of learning were ignored. Although the taxonomy of cognitive behavior contains some elements of this hierarchy (i.e., types V through VIII), there are others which are also relevant.

Gagne's reference to chaining is of particular interest. The learning experience can be described as a chain of tasks with each task assuming an important link in the chain. When instruction is designed to accommodate chaining as a learning function, the ordering of events is of the utmost importance—skipping a link can cause a serious breakdown.

In the exemplary lesson, the procedure for reading a meter stick could be taught using the chaining principle as follows:

   I. <u>Hold</u> the meter stick so that you can <u>read</u> the numbers from left to right.
  II. <u>Look</u> at the small and large numbers which are arranged in equal intervals.

INSTRUCTIONAL NEED	PERFORMANCE REQUIREMENTS	STUDENT BEHAVIOR
1. Read numbers on the meter stick.	1. Number must be legible.	1. Hold meter stick.
2. Read numbers in the proper sequence.	2. Read from left to right.	2. Read numbers.
3. Identify the units of measurement in the smallest intervals.	3. Stop when number one is reached.	3. Count the number of lines.
4. Recognize the total number of lines in the smallest interval.	4. Record without error.	4. Record the number of lines in the smallest interval.
5. Establish the existence of a pattern of measurement units.	5. Use a different section of the meter stick.	5. Repeat step 4.
6. Determine the nature of the pattern for larger areas.	6. Refer to larger areas only.	6. Count units in the larger areas.
7. Identify the total pattern of units for a meter stick.	7. Add only intervals of equal multiples.	7. Add intervals to obtain the total.
8. Be able to communicate this information.	8. Areas must have some unique quality.	8. Label each different area.
9. Determine student readiness to pursue the next step of applying the knowledge.	9. Include all three units discussed.	9. Draw an outline of a meter stick and fill in the units of measurement.

FIGURE 3–2   **The task analysis of reading a meter stick describes a chain of tasks.**

III. Focus to the far left of the meter stick and count the number of lines which represent the smallest intervals.

IV. Stop counting when you reach the first number. An accurate count will register ten units.

V. Focus your attention to any point on the meter stick and locate the interval between two of the small numbers.

VI. Count the number of small units

again. Each time you repeat this exercise you will find the outcome to be ten.

VII. Focus to the left of the meter stick and locate the larger numbers.

VIII. Scan the meter stick and count the number of small intervals of ten which are represented by the smaller numbers. Again the answer should be ten.

IX. Step back and look at the meter

stick in total perspective and determine the number of intervals that have been marked off in units of ten. You will find that three intervals have been marked with this pattern.

X.   Locate each length measured, progressing from the smallest to the largest distance. The pattern you will find is that each succeeding length is expressed in multiples of ten. Therefore, the total length of the meter stick contains one hundred units of the large numbers and one thousand units of the smaller numbers.

XI.   Before the meter stick is used, it will be necessary to name each of the three lengths. The total length of the measuring device is called a meter (meter stick). The next size lengths (large numbers) are labelled centimeters. The small units (line markings) are labelled millimeters.

XII.   Identify the relationship between each of these units. That is, one meter is equal to one hundred centimeters (1 m = 100 cm); one centimeter is equal to ten millimeters (1 cm = 10 mm), and one meter is equal to one thousand millimeters (1 m = 1,000 mm).

XIII.   When a meter stick is used to measure length, the answer may be expressed in three units: meters, centimeters, or millimeters. Now that the units for measuring length with a meter stick have been identified, you are ready to apply this knowledge to an ob-

ject which has an unknown length. However, before testing your knowledge, draw an outline of a meter stick and fill in the information you have been given.

An analysis of the preceding lesson reveals that in order to read a meter stick, the student must be able to perform several functions (underlined words). Each of these tasks is performed at a special place in the total sequence of events. Figure 3–2 describes the importance of this factor to instructional design.

Each of the steps identified in Figure 3–2 as an *instructional need* is satisfied by an expression of *student behavior* in accordance with certain specified *performance requirements*. The attainment of each area depends upon the success of the previous area. One benefit of analyzing a passage in the psychomotor domain is the emergence of a sequence that has a definite order (i.e., chaining).

The arrows connecting the "need" steps suggest that each need is a necessary precursor to the succeeding need. Figure 3–3 illustrates the nature of this linkage. The success of each need is influenced by its performance requirements. For example, if the numbers on the meter stick are to be read, how must the meter stick be held? It must be held so that the numbers are legible. Unless the "how" is considered, no provision is made for correcting a possible error.

Specifying the performance requirement enables the instructor to maximize his assistance to the learner. As the diagram in Figure 3–3 indicates, a consideration of the next step occurs only when the performance requirement has been met. If the requirement is not met, the instruc-

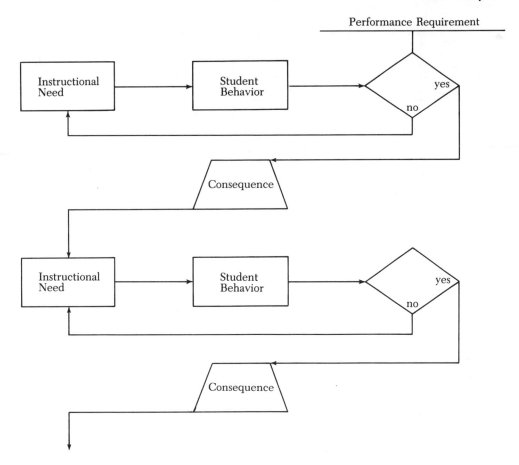

FIGURE 3–3 This flow chart of performance chains illustrates that each need is a necessary precursor to the succeeding need.

tor can help the student so that he will be able to move on to the next step.

Media Options

A glance at the objectives for this chapter (p. 49) will reveal a strong emphasis on the analysis, organization, and expression of information; in fact, a task analysis invariably centers around some aspect of information management. Information

management in this sense refers to the process of making decisions about the proper organization of information.

Is there a medium that is associated with this problem? Computer technology has certain attributes that make it ideal for assisting with the management of information. The ability to store, process, and retrieve information are the characteristics that make computers attractive. For our purposes the computer can facilitate the processing of entry level information

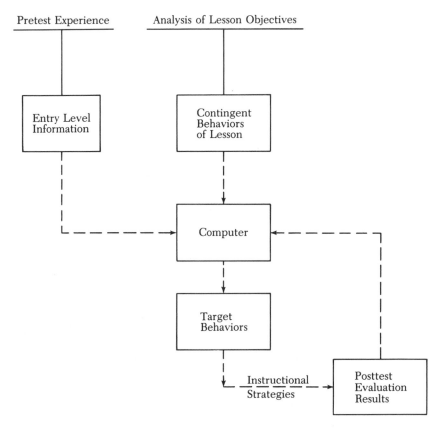

FIGURE 3–4

by comparing the outcomes with the contingent behaviors of the lesson and establishing a student profile of target behaviors; Figure 3–4 illustrates this process. The computer's ability to accomplish this function and retrieve the resulting target behaviors almost instantly makes it possible to establish learning profiles for each student within a school. Since the knowledge of target behaviors is a critical point in the development of instruction, the accuracy of the computer is of considerable value. That is not to imply, however, that task analysis cannot be performed without the assistance of a computer but rather that the computer is definitely an asset to this function.

The use of a computer in school systems is not unusual. Many schools are using this technology for the purpose of scheduling, reporting grades, and other logistical functions. It would not be impossible to extend the service of a computer to the classroom teaching and learning situation. Note that in Figure 3–4 the evaluation of the learner's performance and the instructional approach is fed back into the computer. This feedback provides a measure of control because the instructor can alter the instructional strategies on the basis of assessing what happened. A large percentage of the work done in the classroom is not successful because of untested assumptions.

The computer's ability to simulate experiences enables the instructor to determine beforehand the effect of instructional assumptions on a student population with certain known characteristics. This technique is used in medical education as a means for teaching diagnostic and prescriptive strategies. Testing assumptions without the consequence of producing victims has considerable merit.

Programmed instruction is another medium that can be used for teaching skills. Since a sequence of skills is critical to the achievement of the end product, it is important that the student be exposed to the proper order of steps to be performed and that he have knowledge of this performance. This need is shown in Figure 3–3 where only a positive consequence of action can lead the student to the next step; a negative consequence directs the student back to the beginning (Instructional Need). Whether it be a programmed book, a teaching machine, or other programmed visual and verbal formats, programmed instruction is designed to guide the learner through a learning experience. This technique is designed to establish the linkage that is important to learning a particular skill. Feedback is provided to the student which indicates his particular readiness to pursue the next step in the sequence. In some instances, remediation is provided to the student whose response is wrong. Thus, programmed instruction clearly expresses the desired sequencing and stimulates the interaction needed for the learning of skills.

Skill learning demands a precise instructional approach. Consequently, the options available to the instructor are restricted to a format that systematically conducts the learner through the learning experience.

Management

In an effort to find the time to accomplish a task analysis, the first concern will be to determine if part of the responsibility can be shared. If you will recall, a task analysis involves information that pertains to students' entry level assessments. Part of the procedure is associated with behavioral objectives. Taking this latter point first, fundamental to a task analysis is the expected terminal behavior of the learner. This first important step has been taken during the course of conducting an entry level assessment. At this time, we are not adding anything to the instructor's list of responsibilities.

It will be necessary, however, to look at these objectives, particularly the expected terminal behavior to determine what the student must know in order to perform this behavior. This does not necessarily mean that there will always be a list of contingent behavior needs. For example, if the exemplary lesson is taught to a class of high school physics students, it probably will not be necessary to teach them how to hold the meter stick. Some behaviors, although necessary to the expression of terminal behavior, are obviously a part of the students' repertoire of relevant experiences. The teacher should decide which contingent behaviors will be treated.

Analyzing objectives to seek out the contingent behaviors is a necessary step if the student is to be provided with the essentials for learning. This is particularly critical when sequencing is a vital part of organizing these behaviors. It is possible to share this responsibility with the student to some extent and thus reduce the time required to prepare a task analysis. A student might be given the directions for performing a skill with a request that he write down each step performed when executing this skill; when reviewed, this will provide information about the target behaviors needed.

Summary

We have been discussing the organization of information gathered about the content of the lesson and the learner. As Figure 3–5 indicates, the expected terminal behavior is analyzed and reduced to smaller units of behavior. These smaller units of behavior represent the contingencies which must be achieved before the expected terminal behavior can be achieved.

There are several advantages to the sequencing approach to learning. One benefit is that the student is forced to become

aware of what he is doing because of the need to record the steps taken. This self-analysis gives more clarity to the information to be processed by the learner.

If one or two students from the high, medium, and low achievement range apply this approach, the validity of the teacher's proposed sequence of tasks will be greater. Students from the high achievement range will undoubtedly process information differently than representatives from the low achievement range. If the instructor notes the differences in learning styles, he will be able to provide a sequence of tasks appropriate to individual students (Designing Effective Instruction, pp. 143–54).

The instructor will find that less revision will be needed with this approach than if

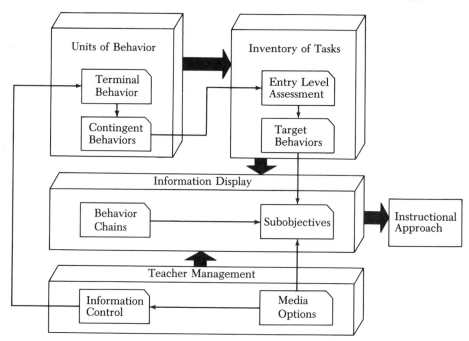

FIGURE 3–5   A task analysis involves information that pertains to students' entry level assessments.

only the teacher's assumptions are represented in the proposed order. Instructional systems based upon teacher's assumptions can be inefficient in the long run. On the other hand, sharing this experience with students not only expands the instructor's sensitivity toward students' needs but may result in a greater degree of efficiency.

A task analysis is a means of manipulating information in a systematic way. Learner deficiencies which are evident when the entry level assessment and the contingent behaviors are compared represent the targets of instruction. The target behaviors can be displayed as subobjectives of instruction, thus providing the necessary direction for the selection of the appropriate means of instruction. An important by-product of such an analysis is the attention given to the arrangement of information to be presented. It is evident that the content of some lessons needs to be sequenced carefully if the student is to master the knowledge. However, it is not enough for an instructor to know what to say; he must also know when information should be presented. Two media options contribute to the desired outcomes of a task analysis. Computers, because of their unique ability to process, store, and retrieve information, can maximize the benefits of task analysis. Programmed instruction can facilitate task analysis because the information is arranged sequentially; thus the learner's attention is focused on the critical aspects of instruction.

REFERENCES

Bloom, B. S. et al. *Taxonomy of Educational Objectives, Handbook I: Cognitive Domain.* New York: David McKay Co., 1956.

"Designing Effective Instruction." *General Programmed Teaching* Unit 15: 143–54.

English H., and English, A. *Comprehensive Dictionary of Psychological and Psychoanalytical Terms.* New York: David McKay Co., 1972.

Gagne, R. M. *The Conditions of Learning.* New York: Holt, Rinehart & Winston, 1965.

Krathwohl, D. K.; Bloom, B. S.; and Masia, B. B. *Taxonomy of Educational Objectives: Handbook II: Affective Domain.* New York: David McKay Co., 1956.

INSTRUCTIONAL SYSTEM

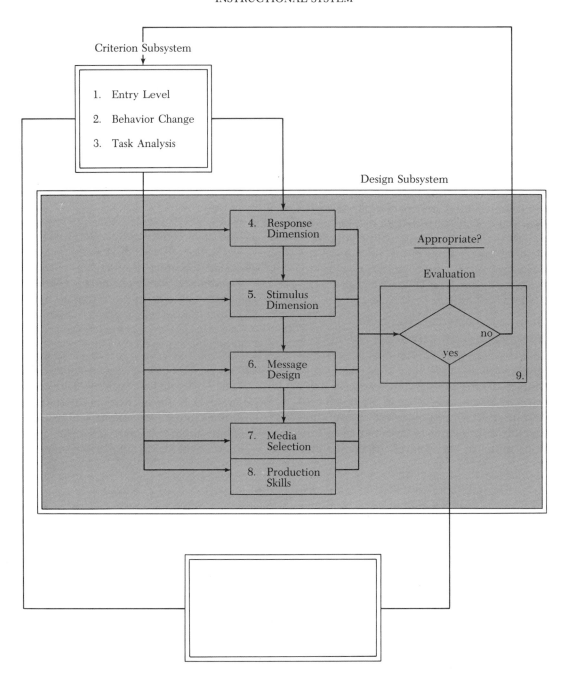

Criterion Subsystem

1. Entry Level
2. Behavior Change
3. Task Analysis

Design Subsystem

4. Response Dimension

5. Stimulus Dimension

6. Message Design

7. Media Selection

8. Production Skills

Appropriate?

Evaluation

no

yes

9.

Part 2

Design Subsystem

The Design Subsystem is unique; yet it has a relationship with the other components of the proposed instructional system. In this area, the educator functions as a designer who conceptualizes the nature of adaptive instruction and designs the appropriate instructional treatment. This heavy emphasis on synthesis prompted the label "Design Subsystem."

As expressed previously, the main concern is the learner. In chapter four the learning experience is viewed in terms of the specific responses which a particular behavior change demands. After this dimension has been established, it becomes easier for the instructor to select the stimulus conditions which will be necessary to accommodate the responses. The success of the match between stimulus conditions and responses depends on the teacher's ability to align the compatible characteristics of the teaching and learning process. The intent of chapters four and five is to state these characteristics in clear terms; therefore, the teacher will

have a model for the selection of instructional materials and strategies that will accommodate the learning process.

Up to this point, we have concentrated on generating information about the learner and instruction. We are now ready to consider instructional procedures. Chapter six is concerned with the various options which an instructor can use to display the instructional message.

If teaching and learning is viewed as a communication process, it is important that the appropriate medium is selected to convey this message. Chapter seven presents the skills most frequently used in the production of instructional media. In chapter eight the strengths and weaknesses of various media options are discussed. A knowledge of these characteristics will enable teachers to select media that are appropriate.

Chapter nine examines how well the selected instructional approach accommodates the demands which have been established for the learner. Have the learner's characteristics been satisfied? Have the terminal behaviors of the lesson been accommodated? Have the learning tasks been treated effectively? On this basis the success of not only the learner but the instructional approach is appraised, and the necessary modifications are recommended.

This closed-loop approach to teaching and learning as depicted in the flow chart which introduces Part Two suggests that the learning process is dynamic. Change appears to be an essential part of the process. In this context the teacher moves from a position of one who imparts knowledge to one who functions as a manager of the learning process.

Chapter 4

Response Dimension

There are two sets of behaviors represented in classroom situations; namely, teaching behaviors and learning behaviors. It is expected that one set will be consonant with the other. Yet, research provides little evidence to suggest a positive relationship between teaching behavior and student achievement (Smith, p. 66).

In this chapter we will discuss student responses and the possible range of responses which will be evident within the desired terminal behavior. We will refer to this range as a dimension, and our goal will be to establish its identity. If we can do this, the uncertainty normally associated with instructional treatment will be reduced. The degree to which we are effective depends to a large extent upon the reduction of unknowns.

To achieve the goal of this chapter, the following objectives need to be accomplished:

I. Identify the target behaviors of instruction.

II. Classify the different strategies apparent when designing learning experiences.

III. Distinguish between the response possibilities evident when designing instruction.

IV. Recognize the importance of attitudes to response types.

V. Show the affect of media selection on the type of response demanded.

VI. Be able to recognize how the methods associated with the development and implementation of a response dimension can be managed.

Exemplary Situation

Imagine that you are teaching a social studies class; the topic of your lesson is air pollution. Your students are high school sophomores who represent an average achievement level. Your goal is to convince your students that air pollution is a serious problem which they can do something about. The learner objectives for this lesson are as follows:

I.   Recognize the hazards of air pollution.
II. Comprehend the causes of air pollution.
III. Be able to recommend a solution to the problem of air pollution and defend your position.

Your affective objective is for pupils to demonstrate an awareness of the seriousness of the air pollution problem. This objective will be indicated by the following behaviors on the student's part:

I.   A greater frequency of nonsolicited involvement with this topic
II. Voluntary expressions of an awareness to the problem
III. Unsolicited requests to pursue the topic beyond the scope of the lesson
IV. Unsolicited suggestions for solving the problem

Behavior Analysis

In this chapter attention will be focused on associating the learner with target behaviors; that is, the expectations demanded of the learner and how they relate to the behavior change designated as the target will be our major emphasis. Let us clarify this point with an analysis of the first objective for the ecology lesson.

Objective One: Recognize the hazards of air pollution.
Terminal Behavior: Recognize the hazards . . .
Contingent Behaviors:

I.   Give an example of a hazard.
II. Identify types of air pollution.

The expected terminal behavior of the objective requires an understanding of the word "hazard" and the ability to identify a type of air pollution. For the first contingency, the learner is expected to be aware of the various attributes of the concept "hazard" whereas for the second contingency the learner needs to recognize examples of air pollution. Presumably the entry level assessment will indicate that the first contingency was mastered by the pupil before he confronts this particular lesson. This being the case, the behavior expectation of the learner is a simple association of information pertaining to a new concept (air pollution) with an old concept (hazard).

The association of information requires that the learner be able to recall knowledge which is given during the lesson. When you provide a student with some example of the hazards of air pollution and he responds verbatim, all that is evident is that he can memorize. No particular understanding of the attributes of air pollution is essential for such a response to occur. Some associations are necessary, however, before this information can be learned.

Recall learning does not involve understanding but simply an ability to identify certain recognized characteristics and an associative code that facilitates retrieval. An example is presented in the following statements: Pollutants interfere with the ecological balance. Waste materials discharged into a stream are an example of a pollutant. At this level of learning, a student may do nothing more than make the association between "waste materials" and "pollutants" and record this association for future purposes. If the learning is not interfered with by competing information, the student may be able to subsequently retrieve this association. The learner's facility with memory tasks will determine the success of rote learning.

Many classroom teaching and learning situations involve this kind of learning. This is not surprising because retention is fundamental to performances at higher levels of difficulty; unfortunately, this fact is often denied. It is critical, at this stage of learning, to convince the learner that the lesson is worthy enough to be retained.

Recall learning demands may be expressed by the following two examples:

I. Air with ____% of pollutants is considered hazardous to human health.

II. Give examples of chemicals which contribute to air pollution.

The recall of information is fundamental to both statements, although the response to each is quite different. The learner can construct a response which can be easily memorized to the first statement. In contrast, the response to the second statement requires that the learner be able to discriminate between those chemicals which are pollutants and those which are not.

In responses such as these, the risk to the learner is less than it is at higher levels of difficulty; therefore, this is a good way to ease the student into a learning situation.

However, if the learner is not provided with experiences beyond the recall point, he may miss out on other meaningful learning experiences. Responses, whether they complete an idea or choose from several possibilities, are necessary to establish conceptual linkages.

When target behaviors are analyzed, the question of whether the learner can provide a response on the basis of memory is indicative of a strategy of thinking that we will call *associative*. Such strategies are primarily concerned with the retrieval of information that the learner has encoded and stored. The recall of this information depends on certain definite attributes that the learner has associated with a particular label. The amount of difficulty that the learner experiences is due to the concreteness or abstractness of the information. The more concrete the information to be memorized, the easier it is to recall (Snowman, p. 4).

It might be helpful at this juncture if we were to look at the second objective of the ecology lesson and extract the contingent behaviors which will be our aim for instruction.

Objective Two: Comprehend the causes and effects of air pollution.

Contingent Behaviors:

I. Recognize the attributes of a cause and effect relationship.

II. Give one example of air pollution which was not presented in class.

III. Give an example of a cause of air pollution which was not provided in class.

The response to the first contingent behavior may be memorized, in which case no understanding is necessary. Therefore, we will refer to this compartmentalyzing process as an expression of association strategies. This appears to be a more difficult function of association because discriminations have to be made between acceptable and unacceptable examples.

The second and third behaviors, however, require that the learner give examples which were not presented during the lesson. The learner will need to go beyond the establishment of certain associations that have been categorized to accomplish this function. It will be necessary that some meaning be attached to these characteristics so that a rule can be applied. Once the rule is established, any example that fits the rule may be given. The following statement may serve as a rule: Pollution is anything that interferes with the principles of ecology. If the student understands this rule, then he can provide examples other than those to which he has been exposed. However, such understanding depends on the establishment of certain associations and discriminations between information which is relevant to the issue. When the learner is functioning at this level of thinking, *conceptual* strategies are activated.

Two major events that are experienced by the learner in the course of translating stimuli into response expressions are presented in Figure 4–1. Information is perceived by the learner in terms of its meaning, and the appropriate strategy is initiated. On the basis of information received, the learner performs certain processing functions which determine the urgency of the response. This over simplification of a rather intricate process will serve to give us a base from which we can delineate a response dimension.

It will be beneficial if attention is focused on the strategies of learning which describe the following hierarchy:

I. Associations—Characteristics are associated with certain identifying labels.
    —Discriminations are made between characteristics

II. Conceptualizations—Consistent patterns (rules) are established with meaningful characteristics.

III. Generalizations—Inferences are made from meaningful characteristics.

When confronted with a learning task, on the basis of the preceding strategies, the learner performs the following steps:

I.   A simple association is made of a label and its referent.

II. The unique characteristics of each identity are recognized and compared.

III. Resting on this ability to make the appropriate discriminations, fixed patterns are established and descriptive rules are fashioned.

IV. A conceptual framework is created that enables one to generalize beyond a given body of knowledge.

It will be easier to understand these strategies if this conceptual model is applied to the following objective: Using the data presented in class, identify the effects of air pollution on the human respiratory system. Assume that the entry level assessment indicates that the following contin-

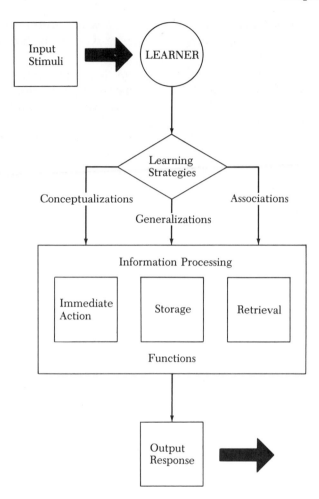

FIGURE 4–1

gent behaviors should be the targets of instruction:

I. Recall data presented in class that is relevant to air pollution.

II. Relate this data to the concept of air pollution.

III. Relate the effects of air pollution to the functioning of the respiratory system.

What strategies need to be activated by the learner to achieve the three behaviors? The first behavior clearly stipulates that the pupil will need to recall information. The second behavior requires that the student associate information (data) with the concept of air pollution. The third target behavior requires the student to go beyond the association process. Even though the learner is asked to establish a relationship, this association is predicated on the need to comprehend the attributes of both air pollution and the respiratory system. The learner is expected to generalize from the known consequences of air pollution to the circumstances peculiar to the functioning of the respiratory system. Building on this conceptual structure, judgments are made about the cause and effects of these attributes. Strategies that are based on the transfer of meaning and the initiation of judgments may be called *generalizations.*

Skipping, as we did, from association strategies to generalization strategies may be confusing to the student. The third target behavior demands a great deal from the learner, and it might be advisable to include another target behavior before it. For instance, the student might be asked to give an example of a solution to air pollution which was not discussed in class. If a student could do this, we would be assured that he possessed an understanding of the concept of air pollution and that he was ready to cope with the third target behavior. The management of this situation depends on the learning characteristics of the students being taught. Obviously, if students reveal a tendency to move better with more guidance, smaller steps should occur between target behaviors.

Each learning strategy can be distinguished by proposing three questions:

I.   Is the strategy involved with associating or discriminating characteristics? (Associations)

II. Does the strategy demand the establishment of meaning? (Conceptualization)

III. Does the strategy involve interconceptual relationships from which inferences can be made? (Generalizations)

The learning strategies which have been described are closely associated with the cognitive taxonomy of learning difficulties. It is possible to relate learning strategies with the taxonomy as follows:

Learning Strategies	Taxonomy Levels
Associations	Level One: Knowledge
Conceptualizations	Level Two: Comprehension
	Level Three: Application
Generalizations	Level Four: Analysis
	Level Five: Synthesis
	Level Six: Evaluation

Note the third response type (Generalization) and the learning difficulties which are referred to. Whether you are considering the attributes of different concepts, generating unique relationships, or judging the effectiveness of these attributes, such involvement is within the context of an interconceptual framework. Several concepts are being considered; the relationship between these attributes is fundamental to the assortment of responses that result. This is the case whether these responses function to analyze data, explicate a process, judge the degree of effectiveness, or extrapolate from the known to the unknown.

Perhaps it would be helpful if the preceding procedure was applied to the

ecology lesson. Look at Objective Three and determine the response strategies.
Objective Three: Recommend a solution to the problem of air pollution and defend your position.

The following is a possible response to the question:

Terminal Behaviors

    I. to recommend a solution

    II. to defend the recommendation

Contingent Behaviors

    I. to recognize that air pollution is a problem

    II. to express the interrelated factors associated with air pollution

    III. to take a position relative to air pollution control

Learning Strategies

    I. Conceptualization

    II. Generalization

Target behaviors were left out because without an entry level assessment, it would be difficult to determine which contingent behaviors should be treated and which should not.

It is apparent that none of the contingent behaviors can be achieved without some element of understanding. Although the first behavior suggests the act of recognizing, it is more than a simple recall of knowledge. Relating the concept of air pollution to a set of standards, which classify the concept as a problem or not, requires that the learner comprehend the knowledge. Thus, the abstractions of this conceptual task must be understood, and

the execution of discrimination strategies must occur.

The addition of support or nonsupport which must be shown in the third contingent behavior is judgmental and requires the activation of other response strategies. When one takes a position on any issue and defends that position, several concepts are interrelated and categorized from which a judgement is made. For example, the solution to the third contingent behavior might preserve a financial gain for employees that support air pollution control and reduce the environmental contamination caused by air pollution. This type of solution involves broader conceptual systems to which the learner employs unique processing strategies. In this particular instance, the social-economic stability of the community and the well-being of the natural environment may be scrutinized carefully for solutions that will not compromise the priorities of either. This inferential process of surveying a sequence of judgements typifies response strategies where generalizations are paramount.

Halting the analysis of the learning situation with the terminal behavior may leave the instructor without some valuable information—valuable in the sense of his role as a facilitator. In the previous example (Objective Three), treating the terminal behavior directly with instruction might entail a considerable amount of guesswork on the part of the instructor. Without an analysis of this behavior, the levels of learning difficulty might not be as apparent. Overlooking any level of difficulty is critical to the learning process.

The association of learning behaviors with the learner's response displaces relevant information from the context of content (i.e., Instructional Objectives, Taxonomy) to the learner's actions. To ignore this process is to invite into the instructional approach an unnecessary amount of unknowns. A large percentage of an instructor's success depends on an ability to focus on the learning conditions posed by a proposed lesson.

Response Dimension

The expression of behavior in terms of response strategies can focus the attention of the instructor on the learner. Once it is clear what the learner is expected to do, it becomes much simpler for the instructor to determine what he needs to do. That, of course, is the intent of an instructional system.

Three types of learning strategies have been identified which refer to how the learner internalizes. The recall of information results from a decision to activate strategies for retrieving knowledge. This type of response may involve the memorization of a mnemonic to assist the recall process. The experience is important yet very superficial; no understanding is necessary with such an association process. The recall of "Roy G. Biv" may enable one to remember the colors of the spectrum in the correct order without knowing the different attributes that distinguish one color from another. And, of course, if the mnemonic is forgotten the knowledge is also forgotten.

Each type of learning strategy demands the activation of a different retrieval process. For example, conceptualization involves the association of many attributes associated with a concept and the detection of a certain pattern which requires that the learner comprehend what he is attempting to retrieve. On the other hand, generalization involves the interrelationship of several concepts. The learner, in some respects, programs himself to initiate these strategies. The decision, however, may be the direct result of instructional factors.

Now that we have considered what the learner is supposed to do in order to fulfill the expectations of the terminal behavior, one final question needs to be answered. How will the learner express a reaction to these expectations?

Consider the possibilities by investigating the demands posed by the objectives stated for the ecology lesson. As you will recall, in the discussion concerning each of the three objectives, the following information was generated:

I. Objective One: Recognize the hazards of air pollution.

II. Terminal Behavior: Recognize.

III. Contingent Behaviors: Give an example of a hazard.
Identify types of air pollution.

IV. Learning Strategy: Association

V. Objective Two: Comprehend the cause and effects of air pollution.

VI. Terminal Behavior: Comprehend the cause and effects.

VII. Contingent Behaviors: Recognize the attributes of a cause and effect relationship by providing at least two examples.
Give one example of air pollution which was not presented in class.
Give an example of a cause of air pollution which was not provided in class.

VIII. Learning Strategy: Conceptualization

IX. Objective Three: Recommend a solution to the problem of air pollution and defend your position.

X. Terminal Behaviors: Recommend a solution.
Defend the recommendation.

XI. Contingent Behaviors: Recognize that air pollution is a problem.
Express the interrelated factors associated with air pollution.
Take a position relative to air pollution control.

XII. Learning Strategies: Conceptualization
Generalization

What type of expression will the learner use to convey the strategy? In the case of objective one, the learner is expected to draw from the knowledge which the instructor attempted to communicate. Notice the inference: from instructional intents, learning strategies may be found.

How does one express factual information? There are many possibilities. Incomplete thoughts may be completed. A complete thought may be offered. One bit of factual information may be associated with another. Labels may be associated with meanings, and meanings may be associated with labels. A series of steps may be physically performed. A picture may be composed from a set of directions. Problems may be solved by a memorized solution. A word may be spoken by recalling a particular manner of vocalizing.

Because of this myriad of response possibilities available to association strategies, recall is a common means of learning. Those students who have good retrieval processes may function a large percentage of their academic life on this basis. Conse-

quently, it is not uncommon to hear a student remark, "I got an A in geometry, and I never understood a thing."

The first two examples of a recall response allude to completing an incomplete thought or offering a completed thought. A phrase which has been used as a common expression among instructional programmers seems fitting here: a *constructed response;* this is a response which the learner provides to a situation where certain information is lacking in total or in part.

In the case of objective one of the ecology lesson, the students need to give an example of a hazard. It might be a situation where the example was requested outright. On the other hand, the learner might be required to complete an incomplete example. The following questions solicit a constructed response:

I. Give one reason why smoking is hazardous to our health.

II. Carbon monoxide fumes originate from _____.

A constructed response may not always be verbal; that is, written. It is possible for the pupil to construct a response aurally. It is also possible to construct a response by completing a drawing or by making a complete drawing. Two factors appear to be working together; i.e., the response type which reflects the learning strategy and the response mode that conveys the response. The following classifications could be expressed for the two preceding questions above with constructed responses.

I. Response Type: Constructed

II. Response Mode: Verbal, Vocal, Visual

When a discriminating strategy is ellicited from the learner, it is expressed as a *selective response.* A selective response type may be conveyed in more than one mode. The learner may be asked to match one group of words with another group; thus the association is expressed in a verbal response mode. In similar fashion, the learner might be asked to express the association in a vocal mode. A student may be asked to physically join objects together; thus the association is expressed in a motor mode.

We typically consider a response as the act of doing something which can be observed. It is not unreasonable to include subjective or covert expressions as responses. These expressions, although not observable, are outputs of our learning system.

As a student, were you ever told to think about an idea? The instructor may have suggested that you think about an idea which would be discussed at a later time. When watching a motion picture film in class, the expectation usually is that students retain the information of the film for future consideration. The response demanded is covert and, of course, its nature dictates that no mode of expression is required. There is, however, an implicit expectation that at a future time the content will be overtly expressed.

Any one of the three learning strategies might demand a covert response. Because it is a response that may be expected of a learner, a covert response is recognized as a legitimate response that differs from other types only in terms of the absence of a particular mode of expression. Once it is translated into an overt response, it may be expressed in any of several response modes.

As indicated in Figure 4–2, responses may be classified according to type or mode. The feature that determines the type of response is the learning strategies applied whereas the response mode is determined by the response to be expressed.

In Figure 4–2 we see that there are four modes of expression for a particular instructional demand. More than one mode may be activated at a given time. The instructional intent may suggest that the student do something physical (motor) and state aurally (vocal) what he is doing. A student might be asked to construct a drawing (visual) and label certain parts (verbal). However, if the request is to label a drawing which has already been constructed, the situation is different; the constructed drawing is part of the instruction and therefore serves as a stimulus rather than response condition. In this latter example, the only response is a verbal demand.

Note that the term "demand" is used frequently to describe the functions that occur in the response dimension. Instruction carries with it implicit or explicit expectations of a student's performance. This is especially true of test questions which state precisely what the student will exhibit as indicative of learning performance.

RESPONSE MODE

The mode which conveys the response has important implications for instructional procedures. Specifying the mode of expression beforehand directs the selection of instructional strategies. For example, if competence is desired in a verbal mode, the learner must be given the necessary experience.

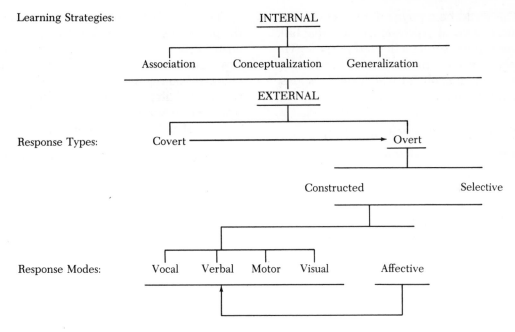

FIGURE 4–2 **Responses appear with the activation of certain response types which are conveyed in a particular mode of expression.**

Several factors influence the selection of a mode for conveying a response. Up to this point, the options have been described. Each of these may serve a given purpose; although, since the verbal mode represents our expected code of expression, it is often the dominant selection. What is important to the appropriate choice is the realization that there are several contingent factors.

High on the list of factors is the entry level accomplishments of the student. Has it been determined that the learner has a particular learning style; e.g., visual? If this is the case, a particular mode may prove to be more beneficial in aiding the learning process. Even if the ultimate goal is proficiency with verbal expressions, preceding the verbal mode with a visual response demand may be helpful to the student.

Some students need a "hands on" experience. Without this physical contact, they appear to be lost. For such a student, a motor response mode may be the key to his success with learning.

Of equal importance to the selection of the appropriate response is the instructional intent. There is the need to determine what a student should do with the expectations of a lesson. Although it is an important part of the teaching role, content decisions should not compromise other considerations.

The difficulty factor is an important consideration. If you want the learner to be able to apply a set of principles, the mode which lends itself to this intent is desired.

This could be a physical interaction, a visual or a vocal expression, or a verbal task; each option serves a desired purpose. The factor that is critical here is the level of learning difficulty at which each response is functioning.

AFFECTIVE RESPONSE MODE

The affective response mode is an area that threatens many instructional strategies and remains one of the factors most critical to the achievement of desired responses. Without an attitude supportive of the instructional intent, the learner will most likely fail to give his full attention to the lesson.

The following are examples of positive affective expressions:

    I. Visual Mode—As an art student you *choose* to construct a cartoon that will convey your attitude toward the issue of environmental control.

    II. Motor Mode—Given several options for expressing your attitude toward air pollution, you *choose* to demonstrate your feelings by walking more frequently than you ride.

    III. Verbal Mode—Provoked by the rate at which environmental control procedures are adopted, you *choose* to proclaim your attitude by writing a senator.

    IV. Vocal Mode—Incensed by the passivity displayed toward environmental control recommendations, you *request* an opportunity to express your views to the class.

The act of choice is expressed in each of the preceding instances. The learner demonstrates a positive attitude, and a mode of expression is chosen that facilitates this effort. If you replace desired outcomes by required outcomes, affective concerns wane into cognitive pursuits.

The instructor is instrumental in the impediment or nourishment of the expression of an attitude. Therefore, the appropriate conditions need to be provided which are peculiar to the affective response. The learner should be encouraged to select the mode for which he has the skills. Given the opportunity to express an attitude, a student might find a picture series more attuned to his particular learning style, even though ultimately you want the student to be able to verbalize the attitude. If we wish to know what students really think rather than how well they comply, the opportunity to choose their mode of expression must be evident.

Media Options

While the response mode expresses one's reaction to an idea, the medium serves as the vehicle for communicating that reaction. A photographer may react with a series of visual expressions which are conveyed via film and equipment to the viewer. Figure 4–2 suggests that a response which is to be expressed verbally may be conveyed in at least four media options. Each of these have certain strengths and weaknesses, and each demands that the learner apply different skills. It is this latter point that is relevant to our immediate concern. Often overlooked, it is this point that contributes to a successful transaction between communicator and audience or a communication breakdown.

Using the ecology lesson, imagine that you wish to have the student respond vocally. This decision should not occur without some consideration for the expected terminal behavior of the learner. What special skills are required to use the appropriate media?

Obviously, you might respond, if one is to use a microphone or a tape recorder, the necessary skills must be evident. Yet, frequently the most eloquent speakers fall short of their intended goal because of a careless use of the medium. It is a common trait for speakers to minimize the importance of the medium. Their preoccupation with the content of a message often relegates the medium to a very low priority level.

This tendency in the classroom may impede the expression of learning to the extent that the efforts expended toward building the learner up to the point of responding may be seriously hampered. If it is important to the terminal behavior that a student vocalize the hazards of air pollution, there is a commitment to expose the learner to the medium chosen for accomplishing this task.

The dynamics of presenting information to an audience deserve the same critical scrutiny that the message deserves. It is probably apparent from the options presented in Figure 4–2 that media is a label which is not reserved for machines. For example, presenting a response to a group is a unique means of vocalizing. It carries with it certain advantages and restrictions that may influence the nature of the response. This position is predicated on the following definition of media: "to be that through which something is accomplished" (English & English, p. 314).

"That" in the above definition may be a person who conveys the message.

The placement of a response on tape for future appraisal and the presentation of a response to a live audience are two different situations. The recording may be critiqued and revised by the learner before the listener is exposed to it; yet the physical constraints of the medium demand a certain level of mastery. For some, the challenge is sufficient to make other options more attractive. Presenting a message to a live audience forces one to compete with many unknowns which may be vying for the receivers' attention.

Some learners will be so uncomfortable when asked to vocalize their responses to a group that the amount learned will be stifled by fear. There is some justification to altering the choice of the medium to learner characteristics. A student's attitude toward the medium is as important as the skills needed to operate the medium. Because more than one medium option exists, it is possible and advisable to let the student choose the means of expression. Of course, if the instructional intent is to cultivate public speakers, that is a different story. Failure to accommodate the learner at this stage of the teaching and learning process may seriously dilute all of the good intentions that have preceded.

Management

There may be some question in your mind as to how much time it will take to implement the processes discussed in this chapter. Although a great deal of information has been presented, actually little new information has been generated. Rather, our concerns need to be organized in the interest of making the proposed system manageable.

It is difficult to manage information which is in such huge chunks that much of what is important is hidden. This is often the case, however, when instruction does not specify clear objectives. The expression of what the learner must do to achieve the specific objectives is often not clear. The teacher who desires to effectively and efficiently manage such learning environments can only do so when the guesswork is kept to a minimum. Of course, that has been the purpose of this chapter; i.e., to pull out information that is important.

The time factor cannot be slighted. Our approach to this problem is to assess the situation and implement as much of what is desired as we possibly can—each successive time creeping closer to the optimum.

If the lesson's content has been analyzed in the fashion described, only the contingent behaviors that are so relevant to a particular learner's needs have to be selected. The learning strategies, the response types, and the response modes need to be established only once. Time which is spent on lesson plans can be organized in this fashion until eventually all that would be necessary are occasional revisions for changes in content. The advantages of knowing what responses to expect from a learner will make the composition of instructional approaches much easier with far less guesswork.

In most schools, there are at least two teachers for each subject. It is desirable, from the standpoint of improving the quality of content analysis and the subsequent transformation of it into learner responses, to have more than one person contribute their particular interpretation. It is also desirable to have teachers working together toward a unified goal.

Ultimately, when confronted with such decisions, the factor of compromise becomes the only reasonable solution. The problem is one of deciding what to compromise. The route to this decision is through the channel of adequate information. A teacher's obligation is to provide students with instruction that will fulfill their learning needs (whether these are cognitive or affective in origin). Therefore, you need to know how the response dimension will help you to perform this function. Hopefully, you will find some assistance in the following chapters.

Summary

Profundities which attempt to describe the intrinsic processes of learning may leave one with a definition which is vague. The best that we can do to focus on a student's learning behavior is generalize from behavior that exhibits the consequences of subjective involvement.

Yet, to focus on a student's learning behavior with uncertainty is to leave the issue virtually unattended. Much of what is observed about a student can be used. We can conjecture from our own experience and that of others that we use certain unique strategies in our efforts to process information. We often take our cue from what appears to be the expectations of instruction. At times we have been misled or we have misinterpreted the signs; yet, we continue to depend on this source for guidance.

If instruction is to be meaningful, the learning behavior of students cannot be ignored. Some semblance of organized thought should be evident. Chapter four describes one way of looking at this problem. Mindful of the need to manage the process of implementing any proposed model, considerable emphasis has been placed on delineating learning behavior as a series of discrete unified steps.

The learner is expected to do something in response to the expectations of instruction. Expressing these expectations clearly communicates with minimum error the desired behavior change. What the learner must do to accomplish this change is another question. The answers, it would seem, rest heavily on the instructor's ability to manage what he has observed.

REFERENCES

English, H., and English, A. *A Comprehensive Dictionary of Psychological and Psychoanalytical Terms.* New York: David McKay Co., 1972.

Smith, O. *Research in Teacher Education.* Englewood Cliffs, N.J.: Prentice-Hall, 1971.

Snowman, J. "The Research on How Adults Learn from Pictures." *Viewpoints* (Indiana University) 49 (1973): 4.

Chapter 5

Stimulus Conditions

Introduction

It is possible, although impractical, to trace learner responses to some source of provocation. When presenting instruction, teachers sometimes, often inadvertently, prompt students to respond in a particular way. By viewing the interaction between these two relevant aspects (stimulus and response) of learning behavior, it would appear that one would gain a better insight into the nature of the instructional plan.

In this chapter responses will be considered to be the representations of learning behavior. We expect a lesson to induce certain changes in the learner's behavior which may, if solicited, be revealed. Stimulus conditions are those factors within instruction that evoke responses; and stimulus control is the management of these factors toward a desired response.

Instruction should begin with an effort to determine the requirements of a partic-

ular learning task, and the focus should be on the learner. With this as the target, the teacher selects stimuli that seem appropriate. Within each learning situation, there exists expectations of a student's learning performance. These expectations are clearer if they are viewed as specific responses to be expressed by a learner. Instructional planning should begin with a delineation of what responses are desired from the learner.

The proposed suggestion is that the circumstances of instruction and learning should be interrelated. If conditions are viewed in this manner, then certain requirements or specifications must be satisfied. Fulfilling these requirements is the challenge that teachers face.

A traditional focus on instruction which emphasizes content negates the existence of certain requirements and the need to provide for them. With such an approach the *what* becomes the dominant force, relegating the *how* to a lesser priority. It is our intent to seek a means for accommodating the student's learning needs; therefore, the approach must bring to a level of awareness the requirements that should be served.

The purpose of this chapter will be to assess the learning requirements by identifying the conditions of instruction (stimuli) that will prove to be satisfactory. Subsequent chapters will attend to the design and composition of the learning experience. Therefore, a large percentage of the following pages will be devoted to describing stimulus possibilities.

To achieve the goal of this chapter, the reader will be able to prescribe stimuli that are appropriate for specified response conditions. In order to satisfy the goal, the reader must meet the following objectives:

   I. Indicate the relevancy of response information to instructional design.
  II. Describe a stimulus dimension.
 III. Prescribe the most appropriate stimuli for certain response conditions.
  IV. Accommodate desired changes in attitude.
   V. Describe the role of media as a vehicle for conveying stimuli.

Exemplary Situation

Assume that you are a high school math teacher who is about to present a lesson on the concept of functions. An assessment of the students' readiness for the lesson indicates that the concept of functions is not clear to them; also, the prerequisite concept of sets is not clear. Because of this assessment, the following objectives are the targets for this particular lesson:

   I. Identify a set.
  II. Identify a function.
 III. Provide an example of a set which has not been presented in the lesson.
  IV. Provide an example of a function which has not been presented in the lesson.
   V. Differentiate between the concept of a set and the concept of a function.
  VI. Apply the function concept to a mathematical expression.

Response Analysis

Achieving the first target behavior involves an ability to recognize attributes associated with the concept of set. Associations are established between the concept (set) and its descriptors (attributes of the elements that characterize the set). The learner's first concern will be to identify an example of a set. Notice that no reference has been made of the need to comprehend the meaning of the concept.

The terminal behavior requires that the learner be familiar with the attributes of the concepts presented, i.e., elements in the set. This discrimination strategy is expanded to include not only an understanding of the attributes of the elements but also an ability to distinguish between the elements.

If the learner is to express his knowledge of a set or function, he may do so by providing an example; thus a response is constructed. The learner may express his knowledge of the concept by selecting the characteristics of a concept from an array of examples; thus a response is selective.

Mathematical expressions may be considered on the same level with verbal expressions. Both expressions represent an abstract form of coding. Because of this similarity we will classify both codes under the same response mode: verbal or vocal.

Through the process of delineating what the learner is supposed to do with the objectives for the math lesson, we will reveal stimulus options that will help him to perform the desired function. Stimulus conditions are the strategies, materials, and media options that compose instruction. Which stimuli are relevant to classroom instruction? How do we select the appropriate stimuli for the desired response? Once identified, how do we relate stimuli to the response they supposedly stimulate? These are only a few of the questions that must be answered before instruction can be adapted to students' learning characteristics.

Stimulus Dimension

As Figure 5–1 indicates, there is an interrelationship between the behavior, response, and stimulus dimensions. Questions we might pose about the learner's behavior will have some relevance to our present concern. You can look at our task as being similar to a physician's assessment of a patient's symptoms. Usually there exists a limited range of possibilities within which one remedy is suitable. Questioning the patient's behavior with scrutiny will often make the difference between a prescription which succeeds and one which does not. Responses, like symptoms, are assessed deductively. Inferences are made on the basis of expected patterns of behavior.

In the exemplary lesson on functions, we realize that outcomes will be verbal/vocal responses. We are simply acknowledging the possible response modes. The instructional objective for the lesson will indicate the desired terminal behavior, but the test question will specify the desired response.

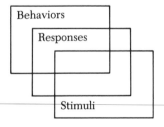

FIGURE 5–1 Each dimension contributes important information to a search for the appropriate stimulus conditions. There is an overlapping between dimensions; therefore, the emergence of one depends on the preceding dimension and the functions of each are interdependent.

The first objective (Identify a set.) makes unique demands on the learner that suggests the type and mode of the response. Because there is no indication that the learner has an opportunity to recall examples, it is assumed that only recognition is desired. Thus, the learner is expected to construct a response (e.g., {2, 4, 6, 8} as an example of a set) that will associate the label "set" with the correct example. It is optional whether the response is to be written (verbal) or spoken (vocal).

Can instruction help the learner to perform this response function? Obviously, the answer lies partly with the conditions expressed in the objective. The expected behavior is for the student to identify the concept "set."

As Figure 5–2 indicates, an analysis of the learning objective and the criterion test question will provide information about the conditions to be satisfied. From the objective, we can determine the conditions which are relevant to the expected terminal behavior; from the test question, we can determine specific conditions of the desired response. Thus, for the first

objective of the exemplary lesson the learner must be able to recognize an example of a set. We could add to this condition (to recognize) additional information from the following test question: From the four numerical patterns identify examples of the concept "set." In order to satisfy the conditions of the test question, the learner must be able to recognize a numerical pattern.

As a result of considering the objective and the test question, information is revealed that will help determine the kind of stimulus conditions that should be provided. This step demands nothing new in the way of information; rather, it uses what has been developed previously. An advantage of considering the conditions prior to the lesson is that the selected stimuli will be consonant with the learner's needs.

In the case of the exemplary lesson, we may identify a set for students or we may ask that they identify the example. Our desire is to clearly present the stimuli. Our concern can be described as a perceptual one. Do the stimuli confuse the issue? Do

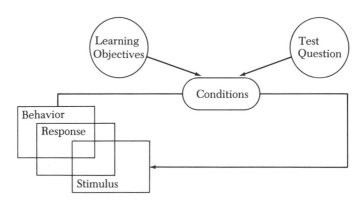

FIGURE 5–2 Stimulus conditions may be determined from an analysis of conditions expressed in learner objectives and test questions.

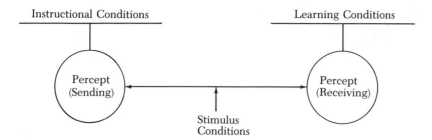

Instructional Conditions

Learning Conditions

Percept (Sending)

Percept (Receiving)

Stimulus Conditions

FIGURE 5–3 How the learner perceives the intended meaning of instruction is influenced by the nature of the stimuli selected.

the stimuli attempt to direct the attention of the learner toward the relevant aspects of the lesson? Perception considers the degree of difficulty one experiences when perceiving or receiving information.

As indicated in Figure 5–3, the stimulus may drastically affect the learning outcome. A percept has an identity that must be preserved from the point of sending to the point of receiving. Inappropriate stimuli can obscure this identity. For example, if we wish to communicate that stimuli can be arranged along a continuum from low to high cues as a set, we might choose to use words, visuals, or some manipulative means. As an example, we could show an apple as the word "apple," a line drawing of an apple, a photograph of an apple, etc. Displaying this set with visuals that can be arranged into a pattern or set provides the learner with perceptual assistance. The visuals will present more clearly than words the elements of this particular set. Being able to manipulate these elements to form a set provides additional exposure. The best guidance that instruction can provide at this point is to present the example so that its elements are clearly expressed.

The elements 1, 3, 5, 7, 9 form a set. Each member conforms to the requirement of a particular rule; namely, sequence of numbers less than ten which consists of odd, positive integers. Successful identification of this set of numbers involves recognizing the attributes expressed by this example and associating these with a verbal label.

The task of composing the set involves a recognition of certain key characteristics that should be associated with the label "set." The following key points are emphasized in Figure 5–4 which illustrates the information graphically.

I. The integers are odd.

II. The integers represent numbers below ten.

III. The integers are positive.

IV. A set is a unity that results from a designated arrangement of elements.

The learner initiates internal strategies when thinking and these strategies are influenced to some extent by the stimulus conditions to which he is exposed. From this standpoint, each learning process is associated with a functional counterpart. Discriminations and associations require that the instruction be presented with *clarity*. Conceptualizations require that

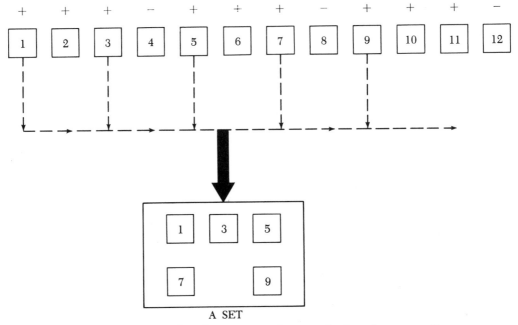

FIGURE 5–4   The above example reveals the elements of a universe of integers that compose this particular set.

the instruction be presented with *meaning*. Generalizations require that the information be presented in a *logical sequence*. Each function (clarity, meaning, and logical sequence) can be construed as a requirement of the instructional presentation if the appropriate learning strategies are to be initiated.

The transactions that occur between the teacher and the student can be described as an interplay between the instructional stimuli and the learner's stimuli. This interplay may or may not be fruitful depending on what is communicated to the learner. A factor which is equally instrumental is *how* information is communicated. As you can see in Figure 5–5 a range of stimulus options exists. Each option provides something unique to the transaction with varied results de-

pending on its consonance with the learning requirements.

The five options in Figure 5–5 are arranged along a hierarchy of cues. Each category can be divided into subcategories which may be arranged along the same hierarchy. An extensive breakdown of stimulus possibilities is described by Jack Edling (Loughery et al., pp. 31–44).

We can see from this diagram (Figure 5–5) that the transactions, which occur with the stimulus options, range along a continuum from high to low cue possibilities. Verbal options offer less cues for helping the student to initiate learning strategies than other options. The amount of information one must process has an inverse relation to the number of cues provided. Thus, stimulus options that offer many cues may produce a negative effect

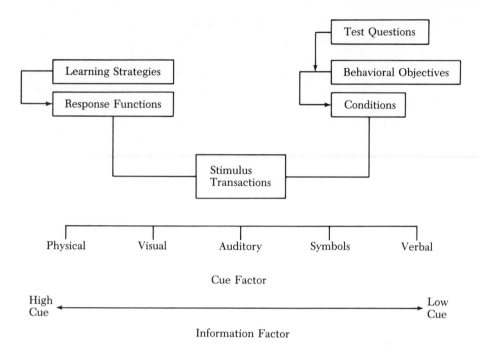

FIGURE 5–5 The stimulus dimension has its origin in the response dimension in terms of how response demands affect the transactions of students with particular stimulus conditions. Stimulus options can be arranged along a continuum of decreasing and increasing cues.

of provoking the need to process more information.

Increasing the amount of involvement (transactions) with stimuli may be beneficial towards students establishing strong associations between information. However, with this benefit, there is a possibility that the student may be exposed to irrelevant information which may interfere with learning—especially if the irrelevant information is more strongly cued. This condition is often a problem with illustrations that accompany a reading text. Because illustrations are not always designed for information processing purposes, they frequently distract the learner more than

they assist. Instruction, if it is to assist the student, needs to provide stimuli that are appropriate.

Stimulus Dimension

PHYSICAL

The actual physical contact which is characterized by direct involvement may be a desirable stimulus option in some cases. If this option is used in our math lesson, what are the possibilities? The elements 1, 2, 3 are more recognizable as a set when associated with the presence of a set of golf clubs. Although it might appear that this option is ideal and the ultimate stimulus choice, it does have a certain weakness. Such a strong prompt might do little to enhance one's understanding of the concept "set." Keep in mind that appropriateness is less of a consideration here than with any of the other possibilities because of the predominance of strong real-life cues.

VISUAL

Another possible stimulus option is to present a visual representation of reality. A motion-picture film may appear to be the most desirable stimulus condition, yet for certain situations it may not be appropriate. You are probably becoming aware of the fact that within the stimulus options a range of different combinations can be found (e.g., Visual: motion/color; motion/B&W; still/color, etc.).

AUDITORY

Of equal importance to learning are auditory experiences. For some learning situations, this is often the only suitable choice; e.g., foreign language instruction. Research has shown that the auditory aptitude is very instrumental in learning to read. The auditory dimension also has certain limitations and is not appropriate for all learning situations.

If, for instance, we consider an example of a set to be a musical chord, the set would consist of a series of notes expressed in a certain pattern. Naturally, an auditory presentation would be a fitting stimulus option to use here.

SYMBOLIC

In the case of the exemplary lesson and certainly in many other learning situations, symbols are a dominant choice of stimulus inputs. Symbols describe a code of expression. Symbols, like other stimulus options, depend on cues for their effectiveness as a means of communication.

Symbols are not necessarily limited to their association with the language of mathematics. Other symbols (e.g., circles, lines, brackets) can be used to enhance meaning. We are using the term "symbol" in its broadest sense; that is, anything that stands for something else (English & English, p. 539).

VERBAL

Probably the most common stimulus option is verbal. However, verbal stimuli are often difficult for the learner to perceive. Some would suggest that visual literacy is a solution to this problem. However, research indicates that verbal stimuli play a vital part in the human storage and retrieval process. As with the other elements of the stimulus dimension, the question of appropriateness is important here.

Here, the option consists of only written communication; thus it is distinctive from the auditory option.

The Relevance of Cues

We have described five levels of stimulus options which may be used in instruction. Either of these options or a combination of them may be appropriate. As indicated in Figure 5–5, each option possesses certain cues. For example, the physical option displays the highest cue level. This condition is not as ideal as you might think for with each cue, there is more information to distract the viewer's attention from the situation. Anyone who has tried to teach a child something outdoors realizes how often it becomes necessary to refocus the learner's attention on the subject matter.

Cue, as used here, means a signal for action (English & English, p. 132). Color may serve to attract one's attention either intentionally or unintentionally and thus initiate a response. In real life many cues (e.g., color, movement, texture, smell) titillate our senses. Consequently, a communicator faces the problem of attracting the viewer's attention from competing stimuli.

In an effort to understand the relevance of cues to stimulus selection, look at Figure 5–5 and compare it with the numerical/verbal expression of this set (1, 3, 5, 7, 9). The critical idea associated with this particular example is the selection of a pattern of elements to form a set. Figure 5–4 graphically expresses this pattern which offers cues that may prove helpful to the learner's processing function. The graphic display is, therefore, at a high cue level.

You will notice that at these higher levels (left of "symbols" on the continuum), more information is provided than occurs with the original expression. As you might suspect, there is a point of diminishing returns if the additional information to be processed does not justify the increased assistance provided by the additional cues.

The nature of the content limits the selection of options. For example, Paris, Rome, and Washington denote a set. These terms identify cities which are capitals of a country. If one were to present this set pictorially, the additional information might interfere with this identification.

The difference between additional cues and additional information is one of degree only. Words are helpful in eliciting desired responses when they are meaningful to the learner. The imagery created by words depends on the learner's experience; therefore, to impose this option on learners who do not have the experience is futile.

Symbols, on the other hand, provide additional information by offering to the learner signals that help him to internalize the information. In some instances, a symbol may aid in the organization of information. For example, the arrow as a symbol generally connotes direction and conveys a sense of movement. As a cue, it directs the viewer to attend in a certain way. Because of this spatial quality, assistance is provided for the task of organizing information.

At a higher cue level of the stimulus dimension, a photograph can be used. Consequently many signals are transmitted to the viewer; i.e., colors, irrelevant information, shapes. At first, this option might appear to be an ideal stimulus display. However, it may be difficult for the viewer to concentrate on the main figure of the photograph because stimuli are competing for his attention. Color, for instance, may cause certain information to seem more important than it really is.

The issue of stimulus cues can be approached from the standpoint of stimulus control. The instructor has less control of the stimulus options which have a higher cue value. For example, unless you alter the content of a photograph, the learner is exposed to everything depicted whereas with a lower stimulus option (symbols), the teacher can compose the display. There is greater stimulus control in the latter example.

If a particular instructional presentation consists of an option that includes stimuli which interfere with learning, the desired response may not be forthcoming. This is one reason why a certain medium choice may impede rather than facilitate the learning behavior.

One solution to this problem that may prove effective is to consider the mode which is to display the information. Information contained in a photograph can be displayed in more than one manner and still maintain the general characteristics of the stimulus option; i.e., visual. For example, a photograph can be presented as a line drawing or cartoon; both of these modes reduce the amount of information originally displayed.

A careless use of stimulus options can cause the interaction between the learner and stimulus conditions to be different from the expected result. It may seem that a motion film is ideal for a particular lesson. However, if you will recall what has been said about the arrangement of stimulus options along a hierarchy of cues, it will be apparent that the potential for a film to transmit a variety of signals to the learner is relatively high. Consequently, the information in the film that is irrelevant may cue the learner away from the intended message. This could easily happen if the film was presented in color—bright colors have a tendency to pull our attention toward them. Such competition is undesirable and unnecessary.

There is another characteristic of films which can create a problem for the learner. This mode of presentation has time built into its design. That is, the learner is expected to get the critical information during the length of the film. In view of the fact that students are seldom told what the critical information is before seeing the film, it is assumed that the learner will process all of it. Teachers would be helpful to learners if they included the following question in their criterion for selecting instructional media: What is demanded of the learner?

The goal of instruction should be to provoke some form of interaction between the learner and the instructional stimuli. This may happen in different ways and to different degrees. For example, an instructional presentation that includes a programmed format may demand periodic overt responses from the student. Somewhere throughout the program the learner is expected to write, draw, vocalize, or present an observable answer. The nature and frequency of the overt response depend on the programming format chosen.

A linear program demands frequent overt responses. The response is usually of the constructed type. Proponents of this style feel that the overt response is an integral part of the learning experience which forces the desired interaction.

An intrinsic program demands a response after the learning experience has occurred. The response is usually of the multiple choice type; and because it occurs after the expected learning, it serves as an evaluative function.

The learner who interacts with the linear program provides an overt response during the learning experience. The learner who interacts with the intrinsic program provides a covert response during the learning experience. Research has not suggested that one type of response is superior to the other. Therefore, the decision of which response to elicit depends on other factors. These are the expected learning behavior, the objective of the lesson, and the student's learning style. Certainly, the strengths and limitations of the stimulus conditions selected for an instructional presentation have implications for learning.

Using the exemplary lesson, consider an instructional strategy for objective three (Provide examples of a set which have not been presented in the lesson.) of the math lesson. The objective of being able to identify a set and the one we are working with now are quite different. Objective three demands more from the learner. Some understanding of the relationship that links together the elements of a set is needed. The suggestion evident in this objective is that understanding will occur when the learner can provide an original example.

What can instruction do to help the learner give an original example of a set? First, we have to determine the nature of the expected response. The terminal behavior suggests that the learner will need to distinguish the attributes that make the concept "set" unique. The learner may search for the attributes that cause elements to compose a set. As an outcome of initiating this discrimination *strategy,* an *inference* is made that allows the student to *generalize* to other possibilities. An *overt response* is expected to display the learning behavior. The *mode* of expression depends on an assessment of the learner—it must be a selection that he can handle.

We commence the process of providing adaptive instruction by assuming the "other role" (Mead, pp. 135–140). We put ourselves into the role of the learner and, providing we know something about learning behavior, we can imagine what he would do. The processing of information to accomplish objective one was primarily perceptual in nature. It is essential that the learner be given an opportunity to clearly recognize the example. In contrast, objective three demands that the learner understand the interrelationships that exist between the elements of a set.

In addition to knowing the nature of the expected response and the strategies that a learner must initiate to provide such a response, it is important to know the stimulus options. It has been emphasized that the response demands that the learner search for the common bond that links elements together as a set. Therefore, an option which displays this linkage effectively will be helpful. The elements of a set should not be obscured by the stimulus display.

The student needs not only to experience a clear perception of the elements which compose a set but he also needs to know the methods for searching out the pattern which makes a set. Teaching behavior can serve as an example for the student.

Our assessment reveals that the learner is to construct an example of a set which was not presented in the lesson. The mode of presentation is dependent on the learner's ability and the conditions associated with the concept. What are the implications for instruction? If the learner is expected to make a contribution, appropriate experience should be provided. That is, one should not go through the learning experience without constructing a response if this is what the lesson demands.

It would be expected that the information in a math lesson would be displayed with a symbolic format, i.e., numbers to a large degree. This is not to say that other possibilities are not reasonable; however, the particular display the learner is expected to be proficient in should be a dominant part of the stimulus offering.

Other stimulus possibilities depend on the student's ability and style of learning. If a student possesses a low spatial aptitude, he might experience difficulty with seeing the interrelationship between the elements of a set. Emphasizing the linkage during the learning experience may compensate for this weak aptitude. A visual display may serve this need.

It may be that the learner needs to be involved with the elements of a concept before he can associate their attributes. Manipulating the elements physically as though they were pieces of a puzzle may be helpful to the learner. A series of pictures mounted on cardboard squares can be arranged into a sequence that represents an example of a set.

The conditions of the learning objective may suggest that the student process verbal stimuli; it is possible that the student may experience difficulty with this option because of his learning style. The instructor may select a visual approach to provide additional cues that will enable the learner to discriminate better.

It would be unfair to provide stimuli to compensate for a deficit during the learning experience and then test the learner's success with a different stimulus option. Ultimately the learning outcome needs to be in agreement with the response that will evaluate the learning experience.

Although we now have made a choice of stimulus options, there is another question to be answered before the instructional presentation is complete. What stimulus mode will be used to convey the information displayed? A consideration of the type of interaction expected will provide an answer. Also, a consideration of the characteristics of each mode will prove helpful. For those students who learn better with a visual stimulus, a motion picture with an animation treatment (see chapter 7) may be helpful. A still picture series might be suitable. Before the learning experience is terminated, an association must be made between this visual approach and symbolic stimuli with which the learner must become proficient.

Each mode of stimulus expression demands a specific type of interaction from the learner. For certain displays of information the interaction is on a covert level and for others it is on an overt level. Some modes force the learner to interact (e.g., programmed instruction) while others await the decision of the learner. To discuss interaction without considering the learner's attitude is to omit the major catalyst which accounts for the learning outcome.

Attitudes and Contingency Management

A student's decision to interact or not to interact with the stimuli in an instructional presentation will depend to a large extent on his attitude. Skinner states that our choices tend to move in the direction of consequences we find reinforcing. This reinforcement may be a direct association with a pleasant consequence, or it may be the result of avoiding an aversive consequence. Whatever the case, these contingencies may be viewed as stimulus conditions that affect a behavior change (Skinner, pp. 50–53, 59–60, 131).

What stimuli can a teacher provide that will induce a positive attitude towards learning? A clear expression of direction is certainly necessary. A clear expression may be revealed as an objective that indicates an attitude. It is within this format that we will attempt to elicit an attitude change.

We want students to comprehend sets and functions as an outcome of the proposed math lesson, and we are also concerned with their attitude towards this experience. Are they interested in the topic? If we wish this to be an attainable objective, we must start by clearly expressing our desire.

There are several ways a student might indicate a willingness to learn the concepts of sets and functions. Let us consider a couple of possibilities:

I.   A student may present an unsolicited example of the concept.

II. A student may volunteer to go beyond the intended lesson with no anticipation of reward.

III. At a later time a student, when given a choice to select from several concepts presented, opts to do an assignment with sets and functions.

A student may display a positive attitude because of ulterior motives. For that reason, more than one indicator should be presented at a time. In this way, you improve the possibility of the indicator behavior expressing the desired attitude. Several indicators will reduce the possibility of ulterior motives interfering.

The third indicator behavior has no chance of being expressed unless the opportunity is provided. The point of importance here is that opportunities must be offered for attitudes to be expressed. Attitude change is contingent on the appearance of these conditions.

The decision making which is necessary to establish these contingent behaviors is called contingency management. It is characterized by decisions that determine when to provide negative and positive reinforcement.

Behavioral research indicates that out of two possible responses, one has a higher probability of occurring; this concept is known as the Premack principle. In contingency management it is important to identify the reason for the behavior expressed (G.P.T.). Knowledge of this reason enables the instructor to elicit the desired behavior from the learner. How can this behavior change occur? How does this factor relate to the achievement of attitudinal objectives? The answers to these questions are fundamental to classroom management. If a student refuses to participate in the math lesson, what can be done to change his attitude? To answer this question, we must assume that we know what the student's high probability behavior is. In this situation we shall imagine that the student has expressed a desire to be involved with music at several levels (e.g., reading music, listening to records, talking about music and musicians). Knowing this information will enable us to establish a contract with the student; for each five minutes of active participation with the math lesson, he accrues three minutes of involvement with music.

The consequences of associating the desired behavior with the high probability behavior reinforcement will, hopefully, reduce the unpleasantness of the math lesson. Hopefully, the contingency may be removed in the future when the math lesson becomes reinforcing.

It is also possible to elicit desired responses from students when negative reinforcement is provided as a contingency whenever undesired behavior is expressed. Perhaps it is evident to you in the situation of our math lesson that the student desires a considerable amount of attention. On a subtle level the learner may be denied the reinforcement of attention when the undesired behavior is expressed.

Notice that there is a difference between negative reinforcement and punishment. Punishment removes behavior from one's repertoire whereas negative reinforcement attempts to generate behavior (Skinner, p. 63). Punishment seems to do more harm than good.

As Figure 5–6 indicates, the attitudes of students are influenced by the learning climate. Therefore, specifying the desired behavior beforehand will enable the teacher to provide the opportunity for the attitude to be expressed, and the instructional approach will do the rest. In this respect the stimulus conditions are evaluative in nature. They let the teacher know whether the desired attitude was achieved. They make it possible for the indicator behavior to be expressed if the desired attitude is to be forthcoming.

On the other hand, the contingency approach shapes the learner's attitude toward the learning task by associating it with a desired task. Involvement with the learning task is thus reinforced by the desired experience. From this continued association or contingency, a positive attitude toward the learning task is conditioned.

Although different in many respects, both of these approaches influence the attitude of the student. Often this is something that teachers hope to do but do little toward achieving. That is not to say that attempts are not made to make a lesson interesting but rather that no deliberate effort is made to manage the interaction between the learner and the lesson.

CONTINGENCY MANAGEMENT PROCESS

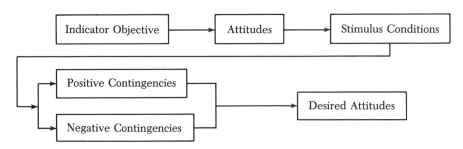

FIGURE 5–6   Desired attitudes may be achieved by providing stimulus conditions that are negative or positive reinforcement. Desired attitudes may occur because stimulus conditions provide the opportunity.

Media Options

Stimuli must be conveyed and, of course, this is the function of media. Whether or not media is supportive to initiating the desired outcomes depends on the characteristics of the media. There are features that distinguish one medium's ability from another to accommodate the stimuli for a particular learning function. Chapter seven is devoted to this issue.

Besides being a means for conveying stimuli, media is also a management tool. Since individual learning differences are a major concern in our approach to teaching and learning, it may be advisable to use more than one stimulus approach for a lesson. If we rely entirely on the teacher to satisfy the different learning styles, he would soon become a wreck. Therefore, several stimuli can convey the same lesson to different students.

The demise of the lecture approach as the only possible means of instruction is not unanimously accepted by educators. Yet, it appears to be necessary to the implementation of learner-based instruction. Without a means for extending the teaching function of the instructor, how can we satisfy the variance we have acknowledged to be evident among learning styles?

Media can do an incredible job of communicating. The potential threat of media is real only to the teacher who displays incompetence, and its value lies in releasing the teacher to perform the management role. The nature of teaching and learning is sufficiently complex to suggest decision making as the essential teaching behavior, with the implementation of these decisions assumed by the versatility of media.

Management

The instructor is expected to perform certain functions which can be viewed as teaching behaviors. Learning results from the inducement provided by teaching. The teacher and learner are partners in a mutual venture; both are seeking a common goal.

In this framework, we can look at media as a means for achieving the desired end. The appropriate teaching behaviors, which include both the stimulus and interactive conditions, are programmed into the lesson. The teacher is a decision maker who determines what stimulus conditions are appropriate. The decisions that need to be made when selecting the appropriate stimulus conditions are predicated on decisions that have been made about prior considerations. Having accomplished the challenge posed by entry level assessment, the specification of clear objectives, the analysis of learning behavior into targets for instruction, and the delineation of response expressions, we are ready to consider their fulfillment. If we have done the job properly up to this point, the choice of stimuli is almost automatic.

This is true only to the extent that we recognize the range of stimulus options. Assuming a possession of such knowledge, the time required to select the appropriate stimuli is practically negligible. In other words, the teacher simply makes a decision to select a particular option on the basis of collected data. It is the collection of data that takes time. But, as we have indicated previously, the solution to this problem depends on the teacher's reallocation of his time.

Summary

Stimulus conditions provoke some type of response. In the context of a teaching and learning situation, these conditions cause the transactions to occur between teacher and pupil.

Inherent in the objectives, the responses, and the level of mastery are certain requirements which must be satisfied. It is the desire to accommodate these requirements which directs the selection of the appropriate stimuli. As indicated in this chapter, the teacher selects from a repertoire of stimulus options. Success with this experience depends, to a large extent, on a thorough understanding of the options which are available.

REFERENCES

English, H., and English., A. *A Comprehensive Dictionary of Psychological and Psychoanalytical Terms.* New York: David McKay Co., 1972.

G. P. T. *A Positive Approach to Motivation,* Filmstrip Series. San Rafael, Calif.: General Programmed Teaching, 1970.

Loughery, J. W. et al. *Man, Machine System in Education.* New York: Harper & Row, Publishers, 1966.

Mead, G. H. *Mind, Self and Society.* Edited by Charles W. Morris. Chicago: University of Chicago Press, 1970.

Skinner, B. F. *About Behaviorism.* New York: Alfred A. Knopf, 1974.

Chapter 6

Message Design

Introduction

Educators frequently emphasize one or two aspects of the total teaching process. The teacher who portrays the expert who imparts knowledge is a good example. Often with this approach, the instructor's responsibility ends when a command of the subject matter is exhibited and questions and answers are well articulated. On the other hand, the teacher may focus on learner disabilities and employ an impressive array of remedial tactics. Both of these strategies may fail if the linkage which joins sender (teacher) and receiver (student) together is missing; both of these approaches may overlook the fact that the learner must process the information.

Every lesson has a message for the learner. Every teacher has an intent when presenting a lesson. A successful transaction has occurred between the student and the instructor when the learner receives the message and indicates through some overt action that the meaning was received. In this chapter we will consider the design of instruction and its implications for learning.

Goal: The reader will be presented with a rationale for selecting information display formats which are appropriate to the content and the expected learning.

Objectives:

I. Identify the role of perception in instruction and learning.

II. Relate message design to stimulus requirements.

III. Select display options which are appropriate for the expected learning.

IV. Use feedback as a means of assessing the effectiveness of a design selection.

V. Relate information display options to media options.

VI. Express the methods and means for incorporating this concern within the teaching and learning schedule.

Exemplary Situation

Imagine that you are a special education teacher. You are working with students who have demonstrated difficulty with the use of phonemes. You have selected as your content six letter combinations (graphemes): *ch* (checked); *ch* (much); *th* (that); *ph* (phone); *wh* (what); *th* (bath). The following statements represent your goal and objectives.

Goal: Students will be presented with six letter combinations (graphemes) which they will be able to use correctly.

Objectives:

    I. Recognize the letter combinations when they appear in a word.

    II. Distinguish examples from nonexamples of words that contain the six graphemes.

    III. Pronounce the six phonemes correctly.

We will consider the goal and objectives of the exemplary lesson in terms of the message design.

Perception

After the stimulus options have been selected, we must consider how these materials will be displayed; the display format of the stimulus options is called the design. A lesson, like a recipe, is the end result of combining ingredients in the correct proportion; and like the recipe, its value lies in testing.

We are constantly extracting information from our environment. This complex process of organizing stimuli is called perception (Fleming, p. 77). Our first encounter with information is on this basis, and at this juncture the stage for learning is set. For this reason, the decisions which are made about the design of instruction are important. Optical illusions like those shown in Figure 6–1 illustrate that things are not always as they seem.

Our experience plays an important role in determining what we see. Shadows fall below a protruding structure in real life. Therefore, any shadow which appears above a physical structure suggests to the viewer that the feature is an indentation. Pock marks on the moon may appear as

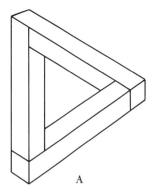

A

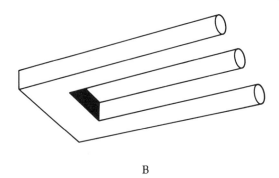

B

FIGURE 6–1   Both A and B have conflicting depth cues which contribute to the difficulty one experiences when trying to accept a particular form (Tibbetts, pp. 140–41).

indentations or craters; when the view is inverted, they appear as mountains. Bright colors attract our attention more than dull colors. Balance in nature is pleasing; so it is with pictorial renderings of nature. Asymmetry causes confusion, and designs which counter the expected may produce tension. How we display information may influence not only the degree to which a student attends to a message but also how the student processes the message.

What does a learner do when confronted with the content of a lesson? The answer depends on the inducement provided. Apart from verbal instructions, the stimulus option and the display format provoke the learner to make certain decisions. In view of this control factor, it is imperative that the instructor be assured of the design's ability to achieve the desired end. The desired end is determined beforehand by expressing the requirements for learning.

Consider objective one of the exemplary lesson: Recognize the letter combinations when they appear in a word. An analysis of this objective suggests that the learner is expected to respond by being able to select the grapheme out of the rest of the word. This perceptual task requires that the student be able to group information. The word "checked" contains the grapheme "ch." The learner must see that "ch" is a part of the word which has a special meaning; it provides the principal sound (phoneme) of the word. For another objective, it will be necessary for the student to put the two letters "ch" together to form the correct sound.

How would you display the letters of this word to provide maximum guidance to the learner? The answer to this question depends on the stimulus option. The range of reasonable possibilities include visual, verbal, and auditory modes. Possibly the most obvious choice would be verbal. The word "checked" may appear in the following verbal display formats:

I.   <u>ch</u>ecked

II. CHecked

III. checked

IV. checked (ch color cued)

V.   CHecked used in a sentence ("He CHecked the figures several times.")

VI. CHecked (accompanied by a picture illustrating the function of the word)

To fulfill the expectation of the objective, the learner should be able to recognize "ch" as the grapheme. We should select the display which will enable the student to separate the grapheme "ch" from the other letters of the word. Options one, two, and four appear to provide the desired assistance. Choice three is not treated in any way, and choices five and six provide additional information which the learner must process that does not necessarily help him separate the grapheme from other letters of the word.

Look at the three possibilities from the standpoint of selecting the one which appears to provide the learner with the maximum assistance. Underlining the grapheme may attract the attention of the learner to the grapheme. The second choice, which capitalizes the grapheme, cues the stimulus, but it conflicts with the rule for capitalizing letters. A solution to a problem which creates another problem has questionable value. Selection four, on the other hand, is not only able to attract the attention of the learner, but color is probably a stronger cue than the others were. Therefore, it would seem that number four is the best selection.

What about the auditory possibility? The "ch" phoneme could be pronounced for the student in concert with seeing the grapheme. If just the grapheme/phoneme is presented, the learner will experience only the sound and letter combination. It will be difficult for him to relate either of these to the world of reality.

Perceptual concerns involve helping the learner to process information. Separating and combining information are the two main functions of perception. The designer of instruction has a resource of means for assisting the learner. Many of these are extracted from a knowledge of how we see reality. From this reservoir of possibilities, appropriate cueing techniques and display strategies can be selected.

Our world consists of an infinite variety of geometrical forms. Shapes appear because of the presence of space which has a definite contour or boundary. We focus on these boundaries. Observe what happens when the boundaries appear to describe two different shapes (See Figure 6–1). If you stare at the drawings in Figure 6–1, it becomes apparent that parts of each drawing spontaneously reverse in depth. There is insufficient information for deciding which part of the figure is near and which part is far. A physical shape is not described in either case because of conflicting depth cues. This type of visual ambiguity appears when we confuse the figure (nearer forms) with the ground (further forms) portions of a design. Depth cues are necessary to our perception, and a good design will accommodate them.

Since perceptual experience has taught us to recognize shapes as space that is sur-

rounded or defined by boundaries, the designer should arrange information so that embedded shapes do not confuse the learner. In most messages, the important information assumes the position of the figure. Therefore, one of the first rules for designing instructional messages is to *display the important information as the figure.* Visually, this means that the important idea is displayed in the dominant fashion. Directing the attention of the learner in this way is sometimes referred to as stimulus control.

Our experience in real life is with much detail. For example, faces consist of eyes, nose, mouth, ears, and other relevant parts of the anatomy. We are able to see faces distinctly at certain points in time regardless of the deficit of detail. This tendency to fill in the blanks is referred to as *closure.* As a matter of fact, we not only are capable of filling in spaces, but we are also willing to do so. Consequently, much of our information processing amounts to skimming material. For some people, closure is a tension relieving experience and may serve as a reasonable target for instruction. If the learner's involvement with instruction is the desired goal, providing just enough information to hold his attention so that he wishes to complete the transaction will provide more interaction.

Flemming discusses perception from the standpoint of an interplay between three groups of factors: complexity vs. simplicity; uncertainty vs. certainty; novelty vs. familiarity (Fleming, pp. 104–10). Understanding that our real-life experiences involve the achievement of some sort of balance between these factors will contribute to our efforts to provide lessons that help rather than hinder learning.

A recent observation of a study on

teaching strategies alluded to the interplay between certainty and uncertainty. How do we react when faced with information which we are certain about and information which we are uncertain about? It appears that we are less attentive to information that we know about. Therefore, providing the student with information which contains a discrepancy between what he expects and what he experiences is an attention-getting strategy. The uncertainty may make him wonder.

There is an alliance between the preceding concern and the novelty vs. familiarity factor—the uncertain may be novel. A look at our own experiences will reveal the attraction of novelty. Some teachers tend to ignore this factor as they become entrenched in the content of the lesson. Consequently, they may over use a particular modality—the most common display of excessiveness is with verbal expressions. Yet, in the interest of being innovative, the teacher who uses television or films excessively makes a similar mistake. A delivery which is attuned to the learning needs of the student that uses a mode to which the learner has become habituated may be ineffective.

Adding an element of complexity to a lesson and spicing it with *novelty* will do much towards soliciting attention from the learner. Of course, this success is contingent on displaying the information clearly. Stimuli that are not clear or two different stimuli that appear the same can quickly undo attempts to accommodate learners.

Another generalization from our real-life experiences is that we see in both general and specific terms. Our peripheral sight encompasses a global scene within which we focus on some detail. It is likewise in our experience with information;

we take in the whole scene as we fix on specifics. If too much information is displayed at one time the learner may flit from one stimulus to another without receiving the message. Information which is important must assume the most dominant part of the display.

Information that is displayed sequentially can be presented advantageously when arranged from general to specific ideas. The tendency to plunge the learner into the major idea of the lesson should be tempered by the realization that the learner may not be ready. Establishing a general setting for the critical idea to be learned will ease the student into the experience and provide a necessary background for reference.

A major factor that influences the design of instructional messages is the capacity of students to process information. Two factors appear to influence this capacity, namely, the mode of the stimuli and the learning style of the student. The flexibility of the auditory mode enables the teacher to provide an assortment of cues that may be helpful to the learner. The intonation of the speaker's voice can add emphasis. However, auditory presentations are linked to time—this display of information must be carried out at a precise moment. Of course, technology does provide a certain amount of flexibility that enables the presentation to be repeated.

In contrast, the visual mode may be relatively static thereby allowing the student to ponder the message. The combination of the visual and auditory display of information gives the learner another challenge. If particular attention is not focused on the design of both the visual and auditory displays, the learner may experience conflict.

When one display competes with another for the learner's attention, the conflict which results is called *stimulus competition.* In the case of the reading lesson on phonemes if you were to show a well designed display of "ch" as it appears at the beginning of the word "chair" and then discuss this grapheme as it appears at the end of the word "touch," confusion may result. The learner who perceived the speaker's voice as being important would come away with a different experience than the learner who perceived the visual as being important. To avoid this dilemma, design each display so that it complements the other.

Stimulus competition can occur anytime many stimuli exist. Thus, in a visual display parts of the display can attract the viewer's attention more than other parts. It is the designer's task to make sure that the important information is contained in the portion of the display which attracts the most attention.

The *capacity* of the learner as a function of learning style is not clearly defined. Although there seems to be considerable agreement that seven bits of information is representative of our capacity to process data, we probably should await more research on this topic before we generalize to teaching strategies. Some research findings have indicated that we can process four hundred words per minute of prose passages and pictorial presentations with 90 percent accuracy (Travers, pp. 74–83). Perceptual capacity is nevertheless an important factor to the design of instruction. Since the capacity to perceive information varies with the stimulus that the learner confronts, teachers who know this will be likely to consider different instructional materials in association with different perceptual tasks.

When students are confronted with verbal or visual materials, they tend to separate and group information as they seek meaning. Is there something that teachers can do to help the learner with this process? When one attempts to separate information, he searches for contrast. If the contrast is not apparent, the separation may not occur. Information which is displayed so that contrast is readily discernible will be helpful to the students.

Innumerable ways exist for providing contrast. One common one is with the use of color. Color has a strong attention-getting power. Certain colors are stronger than others—the red end of the spectrum is stronger than the blue end. Because color is such a strong cue, it is important not to mislead the learner's attention. When color is presented simultaneously with a verbal message, it has been known to attract the attention of the learner away from the verbal portion. Also, if all information is colored indiscriminantly, important information may be unimportant as it becomes subdued by the stronger element of the composition.

There are other methods of cueing information. Underlining words and providing direction with arrows are just a couple of possibilities. Arranging information spatially is a strategy for displaying verbal content; thus, we find paragraphs set off by headings. The spatial diagram of flow charts focuses our eyes on interrelationships. The concrete poet, breaking the tradition of left to right, places words on the page according to their meaning. Thus "up" and "down" are clearly discernible as contrasting ideas.

A common way of directing the learner's attention to differences is by providing examples. After this is done, the learner can establish significant associations that map out apparent differences. A means which is not common for assisting the learner with this separating task is to expose the nonexamples. How many times have our conceptualizations thrived on realizing what did not work?

A great deal of the learner's time is spent grouping similar information together. The exemplary lesson on functions in the previous chapter alluded to rules which account for certain groupings. The proximity or nearness of the elements often determines groupings. Therefore, the designer of instructional messages must be careful that he does not mislead the learner.

Attitudes often play an important role in determining what the learner separates and what he combines. Attitudes in turn can be affected by the culture within which one lives. Consequently, a film made in the United States for an American audience will carry a different message when viewed by Africans. The particular mental set which the learner carries into the experience will determine the outcome, and this can be influenced by the instructional designer.

Information Displays

Considering objective two (Distinguish examples from nonexamples of words that contain the six graphemes.), we will at-tempt to get a better grasp of the perceptual options available to you. Our concern in this reading lesson is with the following six graphemes: ch (mu<u>ch</u>), th (<u>th</u>at), th (ba<u>th</u>), ph (<u>ph</u>one), wh (<u>wh</u>at). Our task will be to help the learner master the unique characteristics of the graphemes. How does this assignment differ from the previous one? The previous charge was simply to recognize the letter combinations when they appeared. Objective two will expose the learner to different expressions of the six graphemes. An experience that might help the learner to meet the requirements of objective two is to ask him to select the correct examples of graphemes as identified by the underlined portion from the following list:

   I.   <u>wh</u>at
  II. heig<u>ht</u>
 III. mu<u>ch</u>
 IV. marc<u>hp</u>ane

The second and fourth choices have the correct letters, but they are in reverse order. So that he will be able to discriminate differences, the learner should be given the experience of selecting from correct and incorrect examples.

The chart below (List and Description of Perceptual Factors) represents a compilation of display possibilities and learning effects.

LIST AND DESCRIPTION OF PERCEPTUAL FACTORS		
Display	Description of Display	Learner's Perception
1. Figure & Ground	1. a portion of the display is in the foreground (figure) and a portion of the display is in the background (ground)	1. more importance is attached to the figure than to the ground

Display	Description of Display	Learner's Perception
2. Shapes	2. space contoured by lines	2. lines confining space determines shapes
3. Closure	3. incomplete display of information	3. tendency to fill in the blank spaces; often accompanied by a feeling of anticipation
4. Novelty & Familiarity	4. varied or constant modes of display	4. variation in display modes holds learner's attention; consistent display format habituates the learner
5. General & Specific	5. information may be presented in small or large units	5. there is an ease of processing information arranged from general to specific
6. Modes	6. the predominant presentation forms are visual, verbal, and auditory	6. the learner has a different capacity for processing each mode; the visual provides greater opportunity for including helpful cues
7. Capacity	7. one of the above six or a mixture of them	7. individual differences
8. Cues	8. color; mnemonics; spatial arrangement	8. attracted toward cued information; if wrong information is cued, message may be distorted; color is a strong cue
9. Separation	9. any one of or a combination of the above	9. attempts are made (depending on the display) to separate information
10. Groupings	10. any one of or a combination of the above	10. attempts are made (depending on the display) to combine information on the basis of similarities
11. Mental Elaborations	11. internal imagery: pictorial, visual, graphic, spatial diagrammatic, phonetic	11. learner generates images which serve as a key to the retrieval of information

The array of perceptual considerations that are expressed in the chart represent the display treatments from which one can make an appropriate selection. If we consider objective two, the targets are that the learner will be able to recognize the six graphemes when exposed to examples and that the learner will be able to recognize incorrect examples of these graphemes.

The requirements for this learning experience are covert in nature; that is, a large percentage of the students' time will be spent searching for the correct examples which will not be expressed until a choice is made. The learner selects and rejects information, or from the standpoint of the perceptual list, he separates (examples from nonexamples) and groups information (examples).

Verbal stimuli must be provided if the expected learning function is to be performed. Although the verbal stimuli are seen by the learner, they are not displayed in the manner that we consider to be a visual option on the stimulus dimension. Rather, the verbal symbols are graphically displayed—they are devoid of the real-life cues that one sees in pictures. The visual option as we will use it is pictorial in nature.

If you will refresh your memory with the model presented in chapter one (p. 16) which depicts the learner as a processor of information, you will see that the process which has been described fits the requirements of this model. Information that can be encoded easily will be more retrievable. Emphasizing the spatial difference between the grapheme and the other letters of a word is one example of such encoding. Cueing the graphemes provides the learner with another memory link. When the learner encodes this information, the mnemonic helps the retrieval process; thus "THat" is more helpful than "that."

Up to this point, little distinction has been made between graphemes which are spelled the same but appear at different ends of words, e.g. "their" and "bath." This task would be difficult for the learner to accomplish if we limited the display to a verbal treatment. It might be helpful to the student if the instructor added the auditory stimulus dimension to his instructional approach. It is now time to consider pronouncing the letter combinations (phonemes)—at least those that are spelled the same but appear at different positions within a word.

You might wonder why we did not pronounce the phonemes sooner. We could have provided the verbal and auditory treatment simultaneously; however, the assessment we have of the learners indicates a need to provide as much guidance as possible. Breaking the learning task into different processing functions (verbal and auditory) will hopefully make it easier for the student to learn and provide greater assurance that what has been learned will be retained.

The grapheme arrangement of "th" as it appears in "that" will sound differently than the "th" in "bath." This phonetic treatment will provide the cue to distinguish between the same letter combination as two different phonemes. The target in this case is to alert the learner to the relationship between phonemes and their position with other letters in a word.

A relatively new concept, imaging mental elaborations, is a form of internal display which aids the student's efforts to retrieve stored information. Differences in learner achievement can often be attributed to differences in the sophistication of internal processing (Snowman, pp. 1–10). That is, some learners achieve better because they employ more effective and efficient processing strategies. Although this ability may be acquired by some learners without their knowledge of it, it may be taught.

The application of the internal processing treatment may depend on the activation of a visual approach. The grapheme "ph" might be presented with a picture of a telephone. The picture may serve as a visual memory peg to which the grapheme is associated when the learner is asked to imagine these letters together. Establishing such a linkage has been proven to be a satisfactory method for inducing retention.

Consider other ways in which we might help students to learn the lesson. In the course of presenting words which contain a representative sample of the six grapheme/phonemes, we could present incomplete words and ask the students to provide the missing graphemes. The practice of forcing closure provides a direct involvement with the grapheme portion of the word. A modification of this means of displaying information could require the student to provide a complete word which contains one of the six letter combinations. Of the two display types, it seems that inducing the learner to handle the grapheme directly as indicated in the first approach is more in accordance with the objectives of the lesson.

Novelty as a factor of perception may be displayed when variety is used in the instructional strategy. Alternating approaches may attract the attention of the learner. Demanding both constructed and selected responses may provide novelty.

Novelty can also be provided by simply presenting the information differently. For example, instead of presenting words with the grapheme appropriately cued, the graphemes could be presented first and then associated with the words. This combination can be projected on a screen with an overhead projector (See chapter 7). Students can pronounce the phoneme as it appears and subsequently pronounce the phoneme again as it appears in a word.

There are several other ways that this lesson can be communicated. Students can formulate a word with the proper grapheme when given a felt board (physical stimulus option) and the appropriate letters, or the letter combination can be presented with a Language Master using a card on which the graphemes are displayed (see chapter 7). Media can be used to provide an element of novelty when transacting the lesson. However, it is not the use of media which creates novelty but, rather, alternative uses of media.

A few words should be devoted to the role that cues play in instructional transactions. Information displays vary as to the amount of knowledge to be communicated. When the display consists of information that varies in its importance to the lesson, it becomes necessary to guide the learner's attention. Some of the information may convey the major point of the lesson whereas other information may be supportive. Helping the learner to discern the differences is one of the responsibilities of teaching.

Color is one of the most effective ways of discriminating differences. In the exemplary lesson, just the graphemes can be presented in color. It is important to realize that displaying all of the information in color may only embellish the message. Displaying the major idea (grapheme) in color and not the rest of the word supports its importance.

A note of caution should be exercised with the use of color as a cue. Eventually, the learner will have to confront letters in their normal state (black on white background). Evidence has shown that when the transition is not made from color to black and white displays, a decrement in learning may occur when the learner faces the latter situation which may occur in the next grade with another teacher.

The greater the amount and complexity of information, the greater the need is for helping cues. In addition to color, cues may be provided in several other ways; exaggerating shapes or altering spatial relationships in an unusual fashion may serve to attract attention—cartoons exemplify this approach. An arrow or some other mnemonic pointing to a particular area of a display or words which are underlined or italicized are selectors of attention. The movement displayed in motion pictures and three-dimensional displays provokes the learner's attention.

Designing Materials for Stimulus Requirements

Consider the physical side of displaying information. In addition to being appropriate for learning expectations, the lesson must communicate. This means that some evidence should indicate that the message was received in the manner intended. Often so much time is spent considering the content of a particular lesson and its composition that the actual physical design of the lesson is overlooked.

We will elaborate on the preceding possibility from the standpoint of two stimulus options which are used frequently: visual and verbal. Design and a visual mode seem to go together, yet occasionally an important part of the composition is left out.

The pattern of a visual stimulus is not a random one; it is planned and purposeful. Achieving a balance so that the competition between elements is not excessive is definitely a must. For certain lessons, an amount of tension may be desired. This may be accomplished by placing the important part of the visual in a position so that the other elements of the design converge toward it (see Figure 6–2). The communication value of a message depends to a large extent on how the information is displayed. It is a good habit to check a

FIGURE 6–2   Tension in Movement: Circles tend to float in space and yet are securely tied by the interconnecting lines (Garret, p. 122).

visual display for its communication value before using it.

A problem exists with designing verbal displays because we are not in the habit of associating design with written formats. If the intent is for the display to teach, we must design what we have written. The exception to this occurs when we expect some intervention from a person who assumes the teaching role, i.e., the textbook format as opposed to programmed texts.

The trend toward individualized instruction has sufficient momentum to warrant our sincere attention. If this is the case, verbal displays must not only be written but programmed as well. When a particular display of information is expected to teach, it should be facilitated by the design. Effort must be expended to provoke interaction between the content of a lesson and the learner. Making one's writing interesting and clear is an important part of the process. In addition to good writing, programming a response throughout the display is essential.

Several models of programming can be described. Programmed instruction was given impetus by the efforts of three major contributors; each of them viewed learning differently but concurred that teaching and learning do not always depend on the human teacher. From the efforts of Pressy, Skinner, and Crowder, and the legions of proponents that followed, the recommendation that stimuli be presented in a controlled fashion and that it be directed toward interaction emerged (Lumsdaine & Glaser, pp. 118–56).

Programming depends on an understanding of the learning function. It is true that efforts to explain the programmed instructional approach will cite such characteristics as small steps, confirmed responses, redundancy, and other common attributes. However, an allegiance to these elements breeds a display of information that distracts from the important desire to provide good writing.

Often it is the learning function which dictates the characteristics selected; thus, it is important to hold the learning priority at the highest level. For instance, if you subscribe completely to a constructed response advocated by the Skinnerian approach, you overlook the desire for students to discriminate between several attributes. When the learning function stipulates that the learner is to select, that should be the nature of the learner's response. On the other hand, recall experiences suggest that the learner should construct an answer. Asking the learner to select the best answer in this case is to leave him short of the intended goal. In some cases, it is possible that both response demands are appropriate.

If we consider the learning function as an essential factor in the design, we can look at other information that is important. If there is a strong emphasis on interrelationships and if discrimination is of major importance, visual panels should be considered. Visual displays have a high cue factor which assist the communication value of a lesson. It is desirable to incorporate such displays into the design when programming a lesson. The determining factor is the learning function and its particular need.

Probably the most noticeable effect of considering the learning function is the reduced tendency to worry about the size of a particular information format. With learning function as the highest priority, whether there are small bits of information or large displays of information is of little importance. The question of whether or not the design helps the

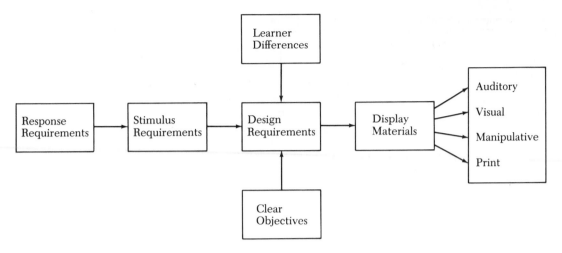

FIGURE 6–3 **The selection of display materials depends on a consideration of instructional requirements, learner assessment, and content as expressed by clear expressions.**

learner achieve the learning objective is far more relevant.

Lessons that are verbally displayed can teach providing that they are not just written. A well written lesson is one that communicates without compromising the learner's interest. If learning is expected to take place, the information must be mediated by a teacher or the information must be designed to mediate itself. The latter type of self-teaching approach is commonly called programmed instruction. The name, however, is descriptive of the programmed learning experience rather than the accommodation it affords self-teaching or individualized learning desires.

Selecting Resource (Display) Materials

Display materials represent the resources mustered together by a teacher to communicate the lesson. The selective process is the deliberate result of careful planning. The plan has been the essence of these six chapters; that is, an assessment of the learner is made; information is expressed clearly; learning behavior is described; responses are determined; stimulus options are considered; and design requirements are specified. Each of these areas contributes information which spells out certain requirements foɪ the design of instruction. As Figure 6–3 indicates display materials emerge from a consideration of these requirements.

The display options fall into four major categories: auditory, visual, manipulative, and print. These materials should be selected on the basis of their appropriateness to the requirements.

Display materials come in assorted packages. We can make the right choice by constructing a criterion that reflects three important considerations. Figure 6–4 suggests that a display material is ap-

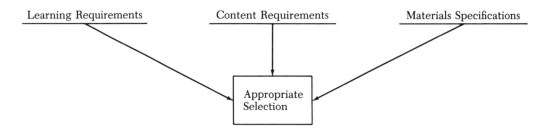

FIGURE 6–4   **The appropriate selection of display materials depends on a consideration of each criterion level.**

propriate only if it satisfies the requirements of all three criterion levels.

We have discussed in great length learning and content requirements. However, little would be accomplished if the limits of display materials remained unknown. Extending the use of display materials beyond their range of effectiveness is often practiced, and a lack of knowledge about the effectiveness of such materials may be the major contributing factor. Considering the strengths and weaknesses of display materials is one way of preventing such an overextension.

SPECIFICATIONS FOR SELECTING RESOURCE MATERIALS

Display Format	Strengths	Weaknesses

1. Auditory	a. enables one to perform several response functions
	  –realistic sounds
	  –words
	  –inflections in syntax
	  –multi-codes can be transmitted
		a. temporary in design—
		easily erasable

	b. cues can be provided without adding information
	  –amplification of sound
	  –omitting sound
	  –meaningless sound (attention getting)
		b. machine required—
		all recordings rely on a machine for conveying a message

	c. redundancy can be provided –words can be repeated for emphasis	c. rigid display format— tape is the material on which recorded information must be placed

Display Format	Strengths	Weaknesses
	—synonyms are possible —total messages can be repeated —context can be repeated (i.e., same setting) —sounds can be produced that will further identify meaning (verbal description followed by natural sounds) d. great capacity for information —information can be produced with verbal and nonverbal treatment —other codes are possible (music, words, natural sounds, and abbreviated codes) e. sounds can be reproduced —recordings can be made of realistic sounds —multi-copies of recordings can be made	
2. Visual	a. strong cueing potential is evident —colors have a high attention-getting value —spatial arrangements can add to the meaning of messages —consonance with perceptual functions (depth cues, figure and ground)	a. demands full attention —difficult to attend to something else at the same time and receive the message of the visual
	b. flexible display format is possible —several modes are available (e.g., pictorial, renderings, line drawings, cartoons) —information may be displayed in several ways (e.g., slides, filmstrips, photographs, motion films) —several perceptual dimensions are possible (e.g., 2-D, 3-D)	b. redundancy is difficult —requires time, money, and expertise

Display Format	Strengths	Weaknesses

	c. reproducible
	    –multi-copies can be made
		c. machine is required
		    –motion film
		    –unit is not needed with still photo

3. Manipulative	a. interactive
	    –students work directly with materials
		a. permanent physical structure
		    –cannot easily change or alter physical appearance

	b. high cue potential
	    –kinesthetic appeal
	    –three-dimensional appearance
	    –motor response demanded
	    –great spatial cue
	    –machine is not needed
	    –materials are handled directly
		b. low communication range
		    –not as versatile as some display options

		c. reproducibility limited –difficult to copy because of permanent physical structure

4. Print	a. reproducible
	    –multi-copies can be made
	    –several processes available (e.g., dry heat, wet chemicals)
		a. limited cueing potential
		    –code is abstract which limits cueing function

	b. cost
	    –relatively inexpensive
		b. rigid display format
		    –except for materials which accommodate information, little variance exists with presenting information

	c. machine requirements
	    –not necessary for individual presentations
	    –necessary for group presentations
	    –necessary for copying purposes	

	d. record durability
	    –relatively permanent
	    –easily disposable	

FORMATIVE TESTING

Most planning is based on assumptions; therefore, these plans should be checked against real-life demands. Checking these assumptions during the formative stage of instructional development will reduce errors.

It is possible to compare formative testing with entry level assessment. Both are concerned with gathering information— only the target is different. Our concern here is with those factors that compose the instructional design and the ability of this design to satisfy the demands of the lesson.

Formative testing occurs before the lesson is presented to the students. Who serves as the testing audience? Locating students who will provide the information needed is probably the most difficult aspect of formative testing. Students who are selected to provide the needed information should be the same age level as the intended audience. Students who have good, average, and low records of achievement will provide various levels of information to assessing the lesson. If a high achiever has difficulty, it is reasonable to assume that the low achiever might also experience a problem. Therefore, any error made by a high achievement student can alert you to alter the instructional treatment. Poor and average achievers can provide information which is relative to the communication ability of the lesson. A lesson that is altered to satisfy poor students may result from an effort to accommodate perceptual concerns.

Students are not always available for formative testing. If circumstances prevent you from applying the sampling procedure, it is important that some feedback be obtained before exposing the intended audience to the lesson. If no form of feedback is available, then consider the first exposure of the lesson to the students as a formative testing as well as a learning experience.

The intent of this testing experience is to provide information about the effectiveness of the instructional design. It is expected that the consequence of this testing experience will be to revise the instructional approach when it appears necessary. Revision is much simpler and void of the usual guesswork when this assessment follows a systematic process. If an objective is faulty, it will be readily apparent, and if a stimulus is not suitable for the task it will be evident.

Media Options

To help you manage the designing task, two planning methods will be discussed. The type of display will dictate to some extent the planning method that you should use.

If time is a factor of the design, a script is a reasonable plan to use. With an audio format, you use a narration script. Thus, when organizing verbal material which is to be presented on tape, the vocalizations are sequenced on paper. This provides you with an opportunity to assume the "other role" and experience what the audience will experience. It also allows you to revise the display before presenting it to your target audience.

A motion film also incorporates time into its design. If the film is silent, you still write a script. In this case, however, it will show the arrangement of camera shots which is called a shooting script. Writing your script beforehand will help you to maintain a continuity that is important to the final product. If you display your idea as a sound film, you will need both a narration and a shooting script. The time spent on this process will pay off from the standpoint of cost and quality. In contrast to scripting your ideas, a storyboard may be used. This is a method in which the visual portion is sketched whereas with scripting, the visual portion is described.

Management

The selection of information displays and the whole area of instructional design require a great deal of time. It may seem that little time is available in the average teaching day for such an activity. The selection of resource materials and the design of instructional messages are the culmination of an analysis process where certain requirements are identified.

It would be remiss to suggest that this process can be performed quickly. The identification of the design specifications and the organization of information do take time. Appraising these requirements with a realistic view of the constraints which face an instructor is definitely a part of the procedure. The presence of a fairly complete reservoir of design and display options is essential to success.

Look at each of these competencies with an eye toward managing this experience. The organization of requirements simply means arranging them in the order of importance and comprehending the need of each requirement. For example, we might question the importance of prerequisite testing prior to the lesson on phonemes. It may be your feeling that be-

cause of a previous experience with this group of students, the information you need is already available. Under these circumstances, you would probably forego pretesting, thus relegating it to a lower level on your scale of priorities for this lesson.

The teacher assumes the role of a decision maker who determines what requirements of entry level assessment, clear objectives, response, and stimulus needs will be treated. Encompassed in this decision-making task is the need for a clear understanding of each of these input categories. As indicated previously, it might be necessary to provide a visual treatment for a learning difference and concomitantly a verbal treatment because of the objective to be achieved. Accomplishing this task depends heavily on knowing the functions of entry level assessment and clear objectives as they pertain to the selection of the appropriate stimulus materials.

Our success with any task depends directly on the context of the situation in which we wish to implement our approach. Avoiding this issue is to reveal a preoccupation with theoretical concerns. Your circumstance is unique. Those requirements that will receive the most attention will vary from one classroom to the next. However, we should not rationalize our position to the point where ineffective instruction is defended. Pre/posttesting may be impossible because of time constraints, and this is a legitimate compromise. Yet, the void this creates in the instructional process is still undesirable.

A knowledge of resource limitations is also essential to the development of appropriate instruction. Each option has its advantages and disadvantages. A teacher who is interested in designing instruction for learning needs must have access to such information.

Instead of teaching the content of your subject the first week, the meaning of objectives can be presented. Students can then be taught to generate their own. The class could be divided into smaller groups according to their learning styles. With the proper guidance, students can develop their own information displays. The advantage of this approach is two-fold; the student has a learning experience while preparing the instructional treatment, and the teacher is given the necessary assistance that makes the offering possible.

Summary

Faced with an array of performance requirements on the learner, the content, and the interaction of one with the other, the teacher is ready to compose an instructional strategy. At this point, the gathered information is put to use.

The design of instructional messages represents the climax of instructional preparation—here the methods and the means of providing for the learner are selected. Not only the information gathered about the proposed transaction between learner and lesson but also how the information is received is considered important. The idiosyncrasies of information processing are taken into account when the design is chosen. The specifications of the design interwoven with the pursuits of learning compose the structure of information displays.

REFERENCES

Fleming, M. L. *Perceptual Principles for the Design of Instructional Materials.* Bloomington, Ind.: Indiana University Press, 1970.

Garret, L. *Visual Design: A Problem-Solving Approach.* New York: Reinhold Publishing Corp., 1967.

Lumsdaine, A. A., and Glaser, R. *Teaching Machines and Programmed Learning, A Source Book.* Washington, D.C.: National Education Association, 1960.

Snowman, J. "The Research on How Adults Learn from Pictures." *Viewpoints* (Indiana University) 49 (1973): 1–10.

Tibbetts, P. *Perception, Selected Readings in Science and Phenomenology.* Chicago: Quadrangle Books, 1969.

Travers, R. *Man's Information System.* New York: Chandler Publishing Co., 1970.

Chapter 7

Media Production

Introduction

Throughout this text, we have referred to media as a means of conveying instructional messages. The range of possibilities is extensive with each option exhibiting unique characteristics. We have suggested that media is a management tool. Media enables you to provide learning experiences that otherwise could not be considered. With media, we can exceed our limitations and, consequently, administer diverse instructional strategies simultaneously. Without media, it is unlikely that the notion of accommodating individual differences would be taken seriously.

It is important for every teacher to have a knowledge of media options. This involves not only a media referent but also an understanding of the limitations associated with each medium.

On more than one occasion, you will find that prepared materials are not appropriate for your needs. The possibility of

this occurring with adaptive instruction is multiplied by the emphasis it places on display formats and unique instructional designs. It is not unusual for media to serve as a means of displaying information; but when you are providing instruction to serve individual learning needs, media plays a key role.

Teachers who assume the role of managing the learning process will find certain media skills helpful. The following pages present a brief description of the most frequently used skills. This text does not attempt to give a detailed description of each area; however, enough information is presented so that you may attempt the process if you desire to do so. Several references will be provided that present a more in-depth treatment.

The following materials will be discussed in this chapter:

    I. Visual Materials

   II. Auditory Materials

Planning

Communication, whatever its mode of expression, will probably benefit from planning, and the chances of success are better for having expended the time and effort. When considering the difficulties experienced with efforts to accommodate learner differences, planning becomes essential. In this chapter, we are primarily concerned with selecting and executing skills which are necessary to the design of unique learning experiences. The planning process focuses on the following characteristics: modes of expression, communication codes, and conveyance. Modes of expression represent the range of stimulus options. Codes of communication refer to

response options. Conveyances refer to media which carry the display.

The type of mode selected (i.e., visual static, visual motion, etc.) will determine the type of planning format that you will use. A moment's reflection will reveal why this is the case. A static visual display (e.g., slide) requires a different type of interaction from a student than a motion visual display requires. Consequently, the stimulus conditions for each option will be different. One display has movement built into the design whereas the other relies on the suggestion provoked by the design. In one display, time is an integral part of the design, and in the other display, time is controlled by the user. Each selection contains its own set of priorities or requirements that must be satisfied.

If you choose slides to display the instructional message, it will be necessary for you to contend with a visual design and probably some verbal interaction—the verbal portion may be in the form of writ-

FIGURE 7–1   A storyboard frame consists of a visual, the narration, and any special treatment.

ten words or a vocal accompaniment. Because slides usually depict a pattern of sequences in which a series of pictures compose a message, it will be necessary for you to observe this sequence critically before the actual photography occurs. When combining auditory stimuli with the visual, it is of considerable importance that the ingredients of the composition complement one another. Stimulus competition always lurks behind multi-media presentations, and its presence is usually the result of careless planning. Preserving continuity between slides is important and may be accomplished by designing a visual story beforehand. Such a presentation is called a storyboard. After determining the objectives for the lesson, setting up the storyboard is the first step in planning the production of the slides.

Figure 7–1 reveals a frame of a story-board. There are three principle sections of the storyboard frame: the visual, the narration or caption, and the special treatment. The visual may be accompanied by a tape or written words. In either case, the area located below the visual portion of the frame is used for a verbal treatment. The upper right-hand portion of the storyboard is reserved for any special consideration (i.e., music and other special effects).

Imagine a series of fifteen slides which compose a particular sequence. If you express the visual and verbal information on 4" x 5" cards, you will be able to assess the layout of scenes before the actual production occurs. The placement of each card in its proper location, as illustrated in Figure 7–2, will provide you with a bird's-eye view of the total sequence.

After you have surveyed the sequence, you may discover that an important scene

FIGURE 7–2   Each frame of the storyboard is displayed in the order intended for viewing the proposed arrangement.

is missing or a scene you have included just does not fit. A knowledge of this information before photographing the scenes will save time and money in the final production cost.

Another advantage of preceding the production of slides with a storyboard is the opportunity it provides for testing your assumptions about the instructional treatment. After you have completed the sequence, the opportunity for feedback from another individual is possible; and if the individual fits the general description of your intended audience, your chances are better for determining the results of your plan.

You may be following this description with some reservation if artistic expression is not your strong suit. It is not necessary to be a Rembrandt, but certain basic skills are a definite advantage. Several

books are available that will prove helpful. One in particular, *Thinking with a Pencil* by Henning Nelms, is directed to the non-artist and is therefore very readable.

Although we have been considering static visuals which include slides and filmstrips, the storyboard technique may be used for visuals designed to show motion. Because of the difference apparent with the sequencing of frames, another planning technique is often used. A frame which represents a filmstrip conveys a segment of the message whereas a frame of a film represents one of several variations of a segment. In Figure 7–3, you can see the apparent difference between the frame of a filmstrip and the frame of a film.

Planning a motion visual may begin with the development of a script. In contrast to the storyboard approach, a script is more verbal than visual. A shooting script

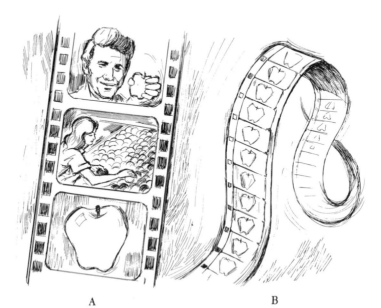

A   B

FIGURE 7–3   Each frame of a filmstrip (A) comprises a segment of the message. Each frame of a film sequence (B) represents a portion or segment of the visual message.

is comparable to a storyboard in view of its attention to the photographed scene. As indicated in Figure 7–4, a special vocabulary describes the three types of shots that film makers can use.

A CU indicates a closeup camera shot; a LS represents a long shot; and a MS refers to a camera position located between a CU and a LS.

The primary function of a shooting script is to maintain a degree of continuity between camera shots and to identify the scene to be photographed. Film makers recognize that camera angles and camera positions present a language of their own that can greatly influence the communication effect of the finished product. It is equally apparent to film makers that the projection of the finished film is important to its communication. A long shot followed by another long shot may create an awkwardness that is disturbing to the viewer.

In conjunction with a shooting script, another script can be developed for the auditory effects. Any narration, dialogue, or special sound effects can be accommodated by this effort. While the shooting script attends to the camera shot and the action, the audio script identifies the accompanying sound.

Without too much ingenuity, one can adopt either the script approach or the storyboard approach for motion film or static visuals. Each approach has its strengths and weaknesses. If you recognize these strengths and weaknesses, you will hopefully be able to select the appropriate format for the production you wish to accomplish. When it is important to plan a visual display, the storyboard format offers certain advantages. However, if motion is a consideration, a script provides more information by virtue of its verbal nature. Whichever format you choose, remember to plan carefully before you produce.

Your completed plan may consist of both photographs and art work. Seldom will you be able to film exactly what you want. If the limit of your range of compromises has been reached, art work may be

FIGURE 7–4 **(A) represents a closeup shot (CU); (B) represents a medium shot (MS); (C) represents a long shot (LS).**

the only answer. Whether you do the art work or solicit it from elsewhere, a certain amount of basic knowledge is necessary. Some visual conceptualization is needed to guide the art work and to assess the end result.

This concern was discussed to some extent in chapter six. For our purpose here, we will refer to some of these points again. It is especially helpful to the audience who must interpret your visual if the design combines information that should be united and separates information that is unique. Confronting a discrimination task which is too difficult will interfere with both the recipient's ability to understand the display and the recipient's willingness to attend.

Experience with seeing will alert you to the many cues which assist the eye in discrimination tasks. Incorporating these

cues into your display (as illustrated in Figure 7–5) is one way to guide the viewer's attention to the relevant aspects of the message.

One needs to be particularly careful when using color. As a cue, it is a powerful attention selector; unless color is used to emphasize the important information, it may do more harm than good. Color is an excellent means of helping the learner process information when it is used discriminantly. This is not to suggest that color displays communicate better than black and white displays. To the contrary, unless color highlights relevant information, it may not communicate as well as black and white.

From the standpoint of planning the arrangement of stimuli, the figure and ground relationship is an effective organizer. Whether we are talking about visual

FIGURE 7–5 The use of light and dark backgrounds helps direct attention to certain parts of this composition.

or verbal displays of information, this concept influences the way we process ideas. It is especially important that you display the critical idea as the figure portion of the message.

In the course of planning the features of the design, do not overlook the emotional considerations. The use of strong color hues and unusual contrasts can produce tension. Lack of conformity can create discomfort. Balance, on the other hand, tends to agree with our need for stability, thus leaving us with less discomfort. Effective use of these principles will build into your design a two-prong attack that will provoke the mind and stir one's emotions.

The visual interpretation should be appropriate for the intent of your message. Many researchers have bungled their findings because the visual expression they chose to use was inappropriate for the learning function being considered. A classic example of this problem is prevalent in much of the research on reading where different stimulus conditions are studied. Visual components are frequently used only to fill space; they add nothing of value to the display. Words projected on a screen may be considered a visual image and are tested as such; however, they are still verbal cues and demand different things from the viewer.

Production

The next step beyond planning is the implementation of your plan which we will call the production phase. If the foundation is well established with the mapping of your instructional strategies, the implementation phase will be more or less routine. The main challenge you will face is posed by the medium you wish to ac-

commodate. This is not to say that the message to be communicated does not offer certain difficulties but that these difficulties have been confronted during the planning phase and certain decisions have been made. Therefore, the requirements associated with the medium direct, to a large extent, the production process.

Visual Materials

Those materials which convey visual images are included in this section of the chapter. Although they differ in format, each serves in the capacity of an instructional aid. Each, in its unique way, contributes differently to the learning experience.

I. Types:
   A. Slides and Filmstrips
   B. Transparencies
   C. Photographs
   D. Motion Films

II. Advantages:
   A. Pictorial messages can be conveyed.
   B. Visual cues can be presented.
   C. Some formats require simple skills and can be produced inexpensively.

III. Disadvantages:
   A. Special production equipment is necessary for certain formats.
   B. Sophisticated skills are needed for certain formats.
   C. Visual information cannot be conveniently altered.

Because of the similarity between slides and filmstrips, we will consider both in the following discussion. Each medium uses the same size film. Filmstrips and slides can be photographed with a 35mm camera. When you make a filmstrip, you can use a half-frame camera or a standard 35mm camera; however, it is recommended that you use a standard 35mm camera. The film is processed and pictures are made of the slides by the processor into a continuous series of frames. If for some reason you are not sure of the arrangement of frames or if you want the sequence to be flexible, a filmstrip is not your best choice. It is true that the frames of a filmstrip can be separated from the sequence and projected as individual slides; however, since the frames are of the smaller variety, their size leaves much to be desired.

A case can be made for selecting filmstrips over slides when it is anticipated that the production will consist of several slides. The filmstrip format eliminates the need for several slide trays. Also, mass production can be handled better by a filmstrip format. Also, filmstrips can be stored in small containers which make them easier to shelve than slides.

Filmstrips are difficult to repair because each frame is an important segment of the message. One damaged frame can interfere drastically with the intent of the message. Yet, filmstrips are very popular with teachers because they are easy to store and relatively simple to use.

If you plan to produce slides or a filmstrip, you will need to know some things about cameras. It is suggested that you refer to the section on cameras in chapter eight before attempting to produce a slide or filmstrip.

As a production skill, overhead trans-

FIGURE 7–6 **The overhead transparency format enables the instructor to add more information when he desires to do so.**

parency making ranks high on many lists. You can use transparencies to provide students with insights that are difficult to convey in other ways. This display format is much larger than filmstrips and slides and can be directly manipulated by the user (see Figure 7–6).

The user can separate a concept into its components or develop a concept by using overlays. Overlays are most valuable for teaching concepts. Because of their design, information can be subtracted or added rather easily. One can build a concept or reduce a concept into its elements before the eyes of the audience. In addition, the ease by which color may be added to transparencies allows the designer to cue the information properly.

The user may mark on the transparency with a water soluble pen. This ability to write on the transparency while it is being projected adds to the communication po-

tential of this medium. After it is used, the transparency can be cleaned with a damp tissue and used again and it can be stored for an indefinite period.

Diazo film is acetate which is transparent. When the film is lifted from a protective envelope, it has a slight yellowish cast. One can handle this material without a darkroom setting because it is only sensitive to ultraviolet light. However, the film should not be handled carelessly for there is a percentage of ultraviolet light in florescent light sources and sunlight.

A picture can be made by simply placing an opaque object or design over the film and putting both on a window ledge for a period of time that can be determined by a trial-and-error procedure. Ordinarily, a photoprinter is used which incorporates a light source and an automatic timer. The film has a prescribed exposure time which is indicated by the manufac-

This student is demonstrating the Diazo dry photography process.

turer. Figure 7–7 shows the proper sequence for exposing the film. The corner of the film which is notched or cut off should face the upper right-hand corner of the printer's stage.

Figure 7–7 illustrates the correct arrangement of light, master, and film. Light penetrates the lighter areas of the master, burning off certain chemicals held in the emulsion of the film. The darker areas on the master will, of course, protect the film. After this phase of the operation, the film will have a pattern of light and dark areas. When the film is exposed to ammonia fumes that emanate from a sponge located in the bottom of a large, widemouthed (pickle) jar, the chemical that remains on the film couples with the ammonia and produces a colored dye. This resulting color depends on chemicals which are determined when the film is manufactured and appears only when the film is exposed to ammonia fumes. If you were to place a sheet of film that had been unexposed into the pickle jar, it would turn the color that it was chemically designed to produce.

The following steps describe the procedure for making a diazo transparency:

I. Use translucent materials (vellum) for the master.

II. Select the film color (indicated on the protective envelope) you want.

III. Place the notched corner of the film in the upper right-hand position.

IV. Place the master over the film.

V. Place a glass plate over the master and film to prevent the cooling fan of the printer from separating the film from the master.

FIGURE 7–7 The master to be printed is always located between the light source and the film.

VI. Place the master and film into the printer with the master facing the light source.

VII. Turn the timer dial to the proper setting.

VIII. When the timer indicates that the exposure is finished, remove the master and film from the printer.

IX. Place the film into a large pickle jar. In a matter of seconds, an image identical to the pattern on the master will emerge.

At this stage, the transparency is ready to be projected on an overhead projector. However, the transparency is a flimsy medium which may react to the heat of the projector by curling up. To prevent this from occurring, tape the film to a cardboard mount designed for this purpose.

Tape the transparency to the back of the mount so that it appears right side up when the mount is reversed; the tape will be hidden, giving the transparency a professional look.

Assume that something went wrong. We observe background color around the image. If this should occur, it is an indication that you did not expose the film long enough to the light source. If the image is too light, we can assume that we have exposed the film too long. This excessive exposure causes some of the chemical to be burned off the film even though it is behind the opaque portion of the master.

A knowledge of the materials which are used for transparency production is essential for the achievement of a good end product. The vellum resembles tracing paper but, unlike tracing paper, has the appropriate translucency for this production process. Any pattern which is placed on the vellum should have the necessary

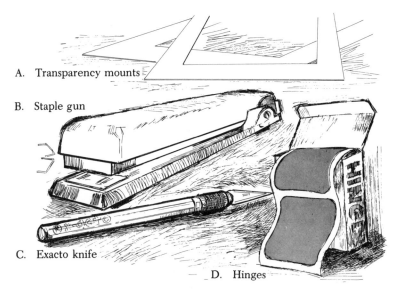

A. Transparency mounts

B. Staple gun

C. Exacto knife

D. Hinges

FIGURE 7–8 These materials are used to produce transparencies.

density to prevent the light from burning off the image. India ink and a host of opaque materials taped onto the vellum with transparent tape will provide sufficient density. It is important to realize that you cannot improve the opacity of the master with the processing function. Therefore, the density you start out with will determine the quality of the end result.

If lettering is difficult for you to do, there are press type letters which you can transfer to the vellum with any pointed object (e.g., pencil). The results appear very opaque and give the transparency a professionally designed look. Also, there are many patterns (e.g., stippled, hatched design, etc.) that you can transfer to the vellum.

You can add colored transparency materials with adhesive backings directly to the developed transparency. These embellishments should be used sparingly as directed by the principles of communication that we have discussed previously. These materials come in an array of colors. Care must be exercised when applying them because of their tendency to hold onto trapped air which causes air bubbles to be projected onto the screen and interfere with the message.

Figure 7–8 shows an array of materials that are used in the process of transparency making. The knife is used for cutting intricate areas of your design. You would use this instrument to cut the material mentioned above.

The hinges are placed on the finished transparency so that a large area remains to accommodate the staples (see Figure 7–9). Extremely adhesive, the hinges must be folded with care; once adhered, they cannot be easily separated. The staple gun is used to fasten the transparency to the mount. The transparency is lined up as shown in Figure 7–9, and two heavy sta-

FIGURE 7–9   Hinges attached to the acetate enable the user to add information by placing overlays over the base drawing.

ples are placed through the hinge and mount. The hinged transparency that can now be placed over another visual is called an overlay. It falls over the base visual, adding further meaning to the design (see Figure 7–10). The mount has four sides; therefore, it will accommodate four overlays.

It might be necessary for you to accommodate more elements than the overlay approach can handle successfully. When this is the case, another option is open to you: a reversal technique. As the term implies, a reversal alters the figure and ground—the figure (image) is made light and the background is made dark. It is like a negative in conventional photography.

You can use two production techniques to achieve a reversal. The technique you choose to use will depend on the nature of the design you have created and the effect that you wish to communicate. If the design is intricate and you wish to add color

to it, making a reversal with a reversal film is a better approach. This is accomplished by placing the reversal film beneath the vellum and exposing it for the prescribed length of time in the photoprinter. Instead of placing the reversal film in the pickle jar, it is gently immersed in water for one to two minutes. A sepia (brown) image, which is very opaque, will appear. The result is often spotty, because this is not the end product; this spotty condition is not important.

After it dries, the reversal film serves as a substitute for the vellum master—then the image on the reversal film is reversed from what you see on the vellum. The reversal film and film color you choose is placed in the printer for the time designated. The film is then placed in the pickle jar where the ammonia develops it to the color desired. If you choose a double-coated black (more opaque) film, pieces of transparent, colored material can be

FIGURE 7–10 Concepts can be built up gradually during the presentation by using overlays.

taped to the back of the finished transparency. Because the double-coated black is so dense, the tape will not show through; thus a multi-colored transparency can be made without the use of overlays.

You can project portions of the figure separately (as indicated in Figure 7–11) by cutting pieces of cardboard to the dimensions of the area to be covered and hinging these cardboard pieces to the mount (see Figure 7–11). This technique allows you to project the elements of a concept separately, in the same manner that is possible with overlays, without being limited by the mounting area.

You can also make a reversal by cutting out opaque materials and taping them to the vellum master. Where you do not want light to pass through, you cover the vellum with the opaque material. In Figure 7–11, you can see that the opaque material includes windows where the figures

will appear. The vellum, with the opaque material taped to it and figures sketched or not sketched into the window portions, is placed with a piece of transparency film into the photoprinter and subsequently into the pickle jar for processing. The option you have as far as the figure portion of your design is concerned is either to sketch a design into the window portions or to add information after the transparency has been developed—it all depends on the design you have chosen. Although this approach may appear easier to do than the reversal film approach, your choice to use it depends on how detailed your design is; you are somewhat limited with this approach because in many instances it will not be possible for you to cut out the design.

We have identified the following techniques for making overhead diazo transparencies.

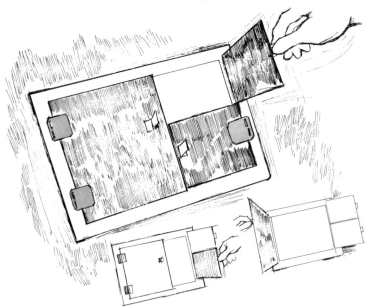

FIGURE 7–11 Cardboard gates enable the user to present information sequentially.

I. Positive Approach—dark image with a light background; uses ammonia processing.

II. Reversal Film Image—light image with dark background; uses reversal film and water development.

III. Reversal Cut Out—light image with a dark background; uses ammonia processing.

Each of these options has unique characteristics which will influence the choices that you make. When making such decisions, keep in mind not only the message you wish to communicate and the degree of impact desired but also acknowledge the user by making the end product easy to manipulate.

Another process for making transparencies requires the use of heat as a developer. This approach is much quicker than the diazo process. The original and a piece of acetate are fed together into a machine; and in a matter of seconds, the acetate is ready for projection. Depending on the film used, the result may be (1) black on color, (2) black on clear, (3) color on a negative background, or (4) clear on a dark background.

One of the restrictions with this process is that it will only copy information such as newspaper print, typewritten material, and pencil written material that has been printed with a graphite base.

Most schools have the machine to accommodate this process because it also makes opaque copies and ditto masters. The availability of the machine and the quickness of the process make this approach very attractive to teachers.

Imagine that you have seen a picture or an article in the newspaper that you would like to share with your class. This process will allow you to make a transparency quickly ready for projection. This eliminates the need to verbalize something which can be visualized better.

Although we have been talking about originals that consist of a single sheet, it is possible with the heat process to copy a page from a book. The opaque copy may be made into a transparency which can be projected. This approach uses two types of film; one is placed against the original and one is fed with the first film into the machine. This two-step process is very quick and also produces an acceptable result.

Other processes are available for making transparencies. Xerox machines use an electrostatic process which produces good quality transparencies. And, of course, you can make a transparency by coloring directly onto acetate with watercolored pens. In contrast with the other processes, however, the direct approach to transparency making is less permanent.

The remaining visuals, photographs, and motion films are discussed in chapter eight under the "Cameras" heading.

Auditory Materials

In this section, we will discuss auditory productions that can be developed in schools. Such materials are used to facilitate aural learning and enrich instruction.

I. Types:

    A. Audio magnetic tapes

    B. Language Master cards

II. Advantages:

    A. A minimum number of skills are necessary to produce auditory materials.

B. Information can be removed easily and replaced by new information.

C. No sophisticated equipment is required.

III. Disadvantages:

A. Sound control is required for recording purposes.

B. Information can be easily erased.

C. When producing an audio recording, a redundancy of information may be necessary to offset the time constraint built into this material.

One of the most important factors associated with tape recording is the current use of microphone techniques. These techniques are discussed to some extent in chapter eight under the category of microphones. Therefore, only a few salient points will be mentioned here. The problem of unwanted, ambient noise on tapes is always a threat and can be resolved by the selection of the proper microphone. Recording in a location which is acoustically designed to complete the recording is an important consideration. Extremely soft materials absorb sound and very hard surfaces reflect sound; each contributes a condition which can interfere with the balance desired in recording.

Often, the tape recorder will have more than one speed. The slower speed may give you more mileage on the amount of tape you need to use; however, when the slower speed is used for recording music, the highs and lows are compromised. Stretching your tape in this way may be at the expense of the quality you seek to capture.

Language Master cards come in a variety of sizes ranging from the 3" x 5" index size to the 8½" x 11" jumbo size. They are available in prerecorded or blank forms. Prerecorded cards may also include visuals displayed on the card to correspond with the topic. The cards consist of a strip of audio tape fastened to the base of the

Displayed from left to right are a cartridge audio tape, a cassette audio tape, a reel audio tape, and a disc record.

card and a display area for verbal or visual information.

When producing Language Master cards, the only recording technique you can use is to speak directly and closely into the built-in microphone. This is a highly directional microphone designed to keep out extraneous noise.

The size of the Language Master card will determine the length of your recording and also the amount of verbal and visual material you wish to include. This device requires a vocal response from the student. Although some may argue that a learning experience of some value can be conducted without such interaction (i.e., student's response), not using the advantages offered by a particular medium may suggest that another selection would be more appropriate.

Visual materials attached to the card should be taped or cemented to a backing; they should not be dry-mounted. Placing the card into a dry-mount press would undoubtedly destroy the attached magnetic tape.

In the next chapter, you will find a further discussion of recording as it relates to equipment use.

Interactive Materials

These materials directly involve the learner both physically and mentally. The interaction of learners with instruction is accomplished in a way which is unique with each material, thus satisfying different behavior needs.

Displayed from left to right are a picture series, an instructional game, and a simulation game.

I. Types:
   A. Instructional games
   B. Simulation games
   C. Picture series
   D. Programmed instruction

II. Advantages:
   A. Student involvement is assured.
   B. No sophisticated equipment is necessary.
   C. All are relatively inexpensive.
   D. Self-instruction is accommodated.

III. Disadvantages:
   A. Certain materials require sophisticated skills.
   B. Student's learning behavior is restricted by the assumptions of the instructional designs.

Instructional games are popular with students because their interactive feature is further complemented by their knowledge of the outcomes of the experience. When you design learning experiences in a game format, it is important to keep in mind the learning function for which the game is designed; otherwise, the game dynamics become the end rather than a means to the desired end. If the experience is to be a relevant one, some consideration must be given to the special characteristics of the audience for whom the game is designed; the game should appeal to those characteristics.

In simulation games, the players always assume roles that are patterned after real-life circumstances. Because of this feature, simulation games enable one to develop some appreciation for other roles and perhaps understand better their behavior patterns. When producing simulation games, it is essential that one fully understand the nature of the roles that have been designed into the game.

A picture series, as the expression implies, is a sequence of pictures designed to involve the student with a concept that he discovers through interaction. Dry mounting and laminating are two skills which are important to the use of photographs and other pictures for instructional purposes. In the production of a picture series, these skills are especially helpful.

The equipment for dry mounting materials must generate heat; therefore, a dry-mount press and tacking iron are required. In Figure 7–12, both of these devices along with other materials are indicated. The following procedure delineates the appropriate techniques for dry mounting:

I. The small toggle switch located on the top of the press should be turned to the on position and the temperature scale should be adjusted to 225°. Heavier materials may require a high temperature, and colored prints may require a lower temperature (180°).

II. Grasping the large handle, you should close but not lock the press. When the correct temperature has been reached, the green light will go off; a red light continues to flash once every second.

III. Place the material that is to be mounted into the press, and allow it to remain there for approximately twenty seconds in order

D. Dry-mount press

E. Tacking iron

C. Straight edge

A. Dry mounting tissue

B. Exacto knife

FIGURE 7–12 **The above materials are essential to the dry mounting process.**

to remove the moisture in the material and to flatten it.

IV. Cut a sheet of dry-mount tissue to the exact size of the material to be mounted; in the case of over-sized materials, combine several smaller pieces of tissue.

V. Place the dry-mount tissue on the back of the material to be mounted and touch it in several places with a tacking iron (medium temperature).

VI. Position the material over the mount board and tack each corner to the mount with the tacking iron.

VII. Fold a clean piece of paper under and over the material, and place it into the press.

VIII. Push the handle of the press all the way down and lock the materials into the press for a period of

five seconds. The red light will flash once every second.

IX. Remove the material from the press, and place it under a large weight to prevent it from curling.

X. When you have finished using the press, turn the switch off and leave the press open.

If you desire to protect the finished product, another technique that utilizes the same equipment but a different material can be used. This process which is referred to as laminating requires a slightly higher temperature (i.e., 270°) than dry mounting. The laminating tissue is wrapped with the dull side facing in around the material which you have dry mounted. The tacking iron is used once again to tack the tissue together in a couple of spots. The combined materials are then placed into an envelope of clean paper and put into the dry-mount press. The material should be left in the press for twenty seconds, turned over and left in the press for another twenty seconds. When the process is finished, the excess tissue can be trimmed off with scissors or a paper cutter.

With these techniques, pictures from magazines and other sources can be mounted and preserved for repeated use. The picture series medium is accomplished in this manner. It involves students with sequential concepts, allowing them to organize materials in linear and thematic arrangements. With this medium, students are able to make their own arrangements or discover what was intended in a previously arranged picture series. Because of its nature, a picture series lends itself very well to small group instruction and independent study situations.

We considered the programmed instruction technique as an instructional strategy in a previous chapter. Our concern here will be directed to the particular skills which are necessary for the production of a program. When you apply these skills, it is important that you remain aware of the purpose of programmed instruction. Because it attempts to perform all of the teaching functions, precision in the development of a program is crucial. It is the process of interaction between program and learner that is instrumental in affecting learning performance rather than an exposure to instruction. For example, a concept may be treated as an item of information in a textbook which someone in turn translates, rearranges, explains, or applies. In contrast, the same concept when programmed provokes immediate interaction (either covert or overt) between information and learner

which occurs directly without intervention from another source (e.g., teacher). Therefore, how information is displayed is the key to the program's success.

An important point to remember at the very outset of applying a programming technique is that you must communicate. This means applying the communication model we have discussed throughout the text. Therefore, a heavy emphasis on one display format (e.g., print) may result from ignoring basic communication principles. Also, an allegiance to one programming format (e.g., linear) ignores a communication principle. Any priority that forces a compromise of the learning function will cause a program to falter in its effort to teach.

One skill that is necessary to the writing of an effective program is the ability to recognize the learning functions which are being treated and to consider them to be the prime target. For example, if the response expected from a student is recognition, the experience provided to the student should be discrimination. In the following two examples, notice the different experiences the learner will confront.

SAMPLE PROGRAM ONE

I. Programmed instruction, whatever its format, exhibits a universal tendency to hold the user responsible for only the critical idea. This requirement necessitates that the programmer prevent other ideas from competing for the learner's attention. When writing a program, the author attempts to communicate certain ideas that are critical to the lesson. These _____ ____ are im-
   (critical ideas)

portant to the terminal behavior change expected of the learner.

II.   It is therefore important that these ideas be protected from becoming too embedded in the descriptive material that also serves a function within a P _ _ _ _ _ _ .
(program)

III. One way of keeping the _ _ _ _ _ _
(critical

_ _ _ to the forefront of the
idea)
learner's awareness is to build interaction between the desired understanding and the learner.

IV.   Demanding that the learner respond with the critical idea is a form of _ _ _ _ _ _ _ _ .
(interaction)

V.   Prominently displaying the critical idea is a type of _ _ _ _ _ _ _
(interaction)
oriented toward perceptual concerns.

VI.   Repeating this treatment to affect learner _ _ _ _ _ _ _ _ cre-
(interaction)
ates an element of redundancy that maintains the _ _ _ _ _ _ _
(critical   idea)
at the learner's level of awareness.

VII. If a confirmation is given to the learner each time he responds, that alerts him to the _ _ _ _ _ _
(correct)
answer, little confusion will intervene on the learner's part.

VIII. A knowledge of the correct answer will provide the learner with important feedback as to

where he presently is in the lesson.

IX.   This _ _ _ _ _ _ _ _ of the correct
(knowledge)
answer, frequent _ _ _ _ _ _ _ _
(interaction)
with the critical idea, and _ _
(re-

_ _ _ _ _ _ exposure will better en-
peated)
able the learner to ascertain the intent of the lesson.

X.   If this technique is applied only to the previous response that has been confirmed, the sequence of interaction will fit a logical pattern. Thus, information gained from the previous frame is used to stimulate the learner's _ _
(re-

_ _ _ _ _ _ in the following frame.
sponse)

XI.   Identify three techniques that will help retain the critical idea at the learner's level of awareness.
Answers:

A.   interaction
B.   redundancy
C.   confirmation

SAMPLE PROGRAM TWO

I.   Acknowledging the correctness of a response and provoking repeated interaction between learner and the critical idea of the program are techniques that will help the learner maintain this idea at a high level of awareness. Select those terms from the following list which identify techniques that prevent competition with the critical idea of a lesson.

   A. small bits of information

   B. redundancy*

   C. syntactical prompts

   D. terminal frames

   E. sample objectives

   F. formal prompts

   G. interaction*

   H. priming

   I. confirmation of response*

II. Select those terms which identify techniques that prevent competition with the critical idea of the lesson.

   A. reinforcement

   B. copy frames

   C. knowledge of results*

   D. multiple choice questions

   E. repeating content*

   F. involvement*

   G. branching

III. Identify three techniques that will maintain the critical idea of the lesson at the learner's level of awareness.
Answers:

   A. knowledge of results or confirmation of correct answers

   B. interaction or involvement

   C. redundancy or repetition of content

Notice that the final frame of both sample programs indicates that the lesson is

*Correct response

the same for both techniques. Yet, the learner's involvement with each program is quite different.

In the first program, the learner experiences the critical points of the program by responding to a series of prompted statements. As the learner progresses through the program, the level of difficulty increases until the learner is able to draw the desired knowledge from his repertoire. Throughout this interaction, there is a heavy emphasis on overt responding. The learner must express a response in each frame except the last one. The response in each case is constructed; that is, an idea is completed or created.

In contrast, the learner interacts with the second program almost entirely on a subjective basis. In the first frame, a statement which prompts the main ideas of the lesson is offered. The learner is directed to identify these ideas from an array of possibilities. To accomplish this task successfully, the learner compares the prompted statement with each of the items presented—in the case of the first frame, nine possibilities exist which the user will peruse for the correct answers. In the second frame, the prompted statement is removed and the learner compares his concept of the critical idea with seven possibilities. Altogether, the ideas desired in the lesson are used on a comparison basis sixteen times before the terminal response is given.

The major difference between these two programs appears to be in the type of interaction the learner confronts. Which of the two programs provides the learner with a greater opportunity to select and reject possibilities? If you answered that the second program does, we agree. From the very outset of the lesson, the learner is forced to subjectively search for a suitable response. Although meaningful associations were established in the first program which exposed the user to the nature of the understanding desired, the emphasis was on constructing a response rather than on the selection and rejection of information.

To understand the techniques of programming, it is necessary that you recognize the influence of learning theory on programmed instruction. Basically, the notion that learning involves a stimulus-response relationship is a pervasive factor in programming. The variance in programming formats is a matter of emphasizing either the stimulus or response point of view rather than denying either.

Most programming efforts fall into an extrinsic or an intrinsic pattern. In the extrinsic pattern, the response is an integral part of the learning process whereas in the intrinsic program, the response is used to evaluate the learner's progress. The extrinsic program usually follows a linear format and demands a constructed response from the learner; on the other hand, the intrinsic program generally requires a selective response and includes a branching style. However, it is possible to have any of these characteristics in each of the programming patterns.

Extrinsic programs are systematic in design with little tolerance for error. To the extrinsic programmer, errors signify error in the program design. The intrinsic programmer, on the other hand, anticipates error on the learner's part and provides remedial treatment when necessary. Therefore, in intrinsic programs, you find branches that are designed to attend to the wrong answer alternatives. This difference in priority is manifested by the treatment that each format accords the learner's response. In the extrinsic pro-

gram, each subsequent frame is built on the correct response which was confirmed in the previous frame. In an intrinsic program, the wrong responses are treated with an assortment of remedial branches. An example of an intrinsic program is Robert Mager's book, *Preparing Instructional Objectives*, on writing behavioral objectives.

The process for developing a program is similar to the pattern described for designing learner-based instruction. After the content has been selected, an assessment is made of the learner's characteristics. Objectives are specified, and a criterion test is generated for testing each objective. The criterion test provides some insight into the selection of the appropriate format. When you write programmed instruction, it is especially important that you associate the levels of learning difficulty with each objective.

The frames are designed to accommodate the desired learning function. It is a good idea to use cards for the development process in much the same way that one would use a storyboard to produce a filmstrip. Cards will enable you to arrange the frames of a sequence in the most appropriate order. You can respond to a revision step which testing indicates should occur with ease because of the flexibility with which cards can be rearranged.

We will consider some of the techniques which are used to develop a program similar to sample program number one. The progression of frames in this sequence is from simple to complex. How does a programmer put these frames into the correct sequence? A look at the first three frames of the program will provide an answer to this question. The first frame is a copy frame—all the learner needs to do is copy the key words (i.e., critical ideas). In the second frame, the learner is given formal prompts. The word is not present to be copied but the indefinite article "a" offers a cue and the letter "p" with the number of blanks provides additional prompting. In this frame, little learning takes place because of this heavy prompting. In the third frame, the learner is given thematic prompts. The third frame requires that some meaning be present in the learner's repertoire; that is, the learner has to comprehend that the desired response "critical idea" is synonymous with "desired understanding." Although more learning is required in this frame, there is a formal prompt. Can you find it? "Critical idea" appeared as the response requested in two frames before; therefore, the correct response may be influenced by a demand for the response in a previous frame. We call this assistance a sequence prompt; and if a programmer is not careful, it will be working much of the time in lieu of the expected learning. Requesting other responses from the learner before presenting the third frame will help alleviate this problem.

You can see that it is important for a programmer to know when to use the preceding types of frames. Each has a legitimate place in a program; it is simply a question of selecting which one is appropriate for the learning function.

Notice that the final frame (i.e., terminal frame) does not have a prompt. This frame should resemble a test question in design. Although some programmers include the correct number of blanks for the response, this too is a prompt which dilutes the evaluation; it will be a better terminal frame if the blanks are not included.

My experience with programming has indicated that more than one terminal frame is needed to foster retention. Nothing prevents you from testing the learner more than once. A terminal frame can occur after the intervention of new information as well as at the end of the sequence. The terminal frame may be worded differently each time it is presented. The value of assessing the learner more than once throughout the program is that you use the interference of new information (which has a detrimental effect on retention) to your advantage. The additional information that you receive from this type of testing will enable you to redesign some of the sequences to assure that retention will occur.

From this brief encounter with some programming techniques, it is probably apparent to you that a considerable amount of time is spent determining the proper blend of prompts and the particular pattern that is appropriate. Programming is as much a factor of design as it is an effort to communicate. Frequent exposure of your assumptions to a sample audience during the development stages is necessary so that you will know learner reactions to your program.

Intrinsic programs present some special problems that demand special skills. Because an intrinsic program makes no attempt to prevent errors, the programmer must give some attention to remedial training. Therefore, programmers must spend time and effort anticipating alternative answers. Writing an intrinsic program involves not only constructing right answer frames but also wrong answer frames. This often presents a problem if the designer cannot think of more than one wrong answer.

Alternative response possibilities lead the learner through the program. Sometimes, the learner will skip information which is designed for those who selected the incorrect choice. The programmer seeks to find out if any learning has occurred—if no learning has occurred, the user is provided with another experience that has the same learning function.

The following format is recommended for writing an intrinsic program:

I. Right Answer Frame:
  A. Confirm the response given
  B. Present new information
  C. Ask new questions

II. Wrong Answer Frame:
  A. Confirm the response given
  B. Provide an explanation or remediation
  C. Ask new questions or have the learner return to the original question

Write all of the right answer frames for a sequence. Then anticipate the wrong answer and write a frame for each. Intrinsic programs can also have a variety of designs. The learner may be required to return to the previous frame where he would confront the same questions again. New questions may be generated and a correct answer at this point may direct the learner back into the main line of the program.

If you let the learning function dictate the design of your program, you will probably mix the two formats which we have been discussing. In addition to providing appropriate learning experiences, this approach would add an element of novelty to the learning experience. The boredom that students experience with many programs is the direct consequence of holding fast to one format throughout the program.

In our final view of programming, it will be helpful if we consider how to assess a program that has been designed commercially or otherwise. As a prospective teacher, you will undoubtedly be faced with the need to appraise a program. You will find few good programs in the instructional materials market. One of the reasons for such a scarcity is the programmer's neglect of certain priorities. Many programmers frequently ignore the critical idea principle we alluded to in a previous section. Check the program to determine if the critical idea is communicated in each frame. Also check to see that a logical relationship exists which links the critical point of each frame with other frames and with the critical idea of the lesson.

Neglecting the learning function of a frame for structural characteristics (i.e., small bits of information) can dilute the effectiveness of a program. When you select a program, look carefully for such considerations; and while you search out the flavor of the author's efforts, check to see if the publisher has exceeded the intellectual limit that was intended. The desire to stretch a publication across a large audience is good business, but it can render a program ineffective. This condition is often the prime reason for exclamations that the program either turned off the better students or was too difficult for other students.

Programs are designed for specific audiences and certain objectives. Therefore, you should have this information in a form that you can interpret. If you know what the programmer expects of the program, you can better judge the program's worth. Request information that will indicate the characteristics of the audience for whom the program was designed. Before purchasing any program, you probably should try part or all of the program yourself. Programs are difficult to judge and what may appear to be an inferior program may in fact prove to be a good one.

Programs do not necessarily have to be print oriented, although many are for various reasons such as economics. A print mode might be inappropriate for certain learning functions. The techniques used to program print materials are applicable to other display formats. If you look at programming as one of several design techniques which can be implemented for the purpose of guiding the learner's progress through a lesson, you will not have a tendency to stick to one format. Mixed media presentations employing the techniques of programming are possible and may add an interesting dimension to your instructional efforts. We are not referring to mixed-media formats that are systematically

designed for individualized instruction but rather mixed-media formats that are systematically designed with the inclusion of programming techniques.

Display Materials

The materials described in this section display ideas. These materials may be used to portray information only, or they may be used to involve students with the instructional materials. One may view each of the displays directly without the aid of a projection device.

I. Types:
    A. Chalkboards
    B. Feltboards
    C. Magnetic boards
    D. Peg boards

Magnetic and porcelain on a steel surface to which rubber and metal magnets will adhere accommodates wet markers which dry instantly and wipe off completely.

FRIDAY TESTS

FEB.	READING 1	8	15	22	SPELLING 1	8	15	22	MATH 1	8	15	22
ARNOLD	73	76	80		80	95	86		92	X	82	
BECK	75	64	80		81	X	75		65	71	81	
GARDNER	85	74	X		63	84	74		63	65	X	
HARRIS	85	84	93		X	91	74		X	73	84	
HUGHES	X	74	73		X	71	74		X	54	71	
JACKSON	76	63	85		90	72	74		54	75	73	
JOHNSON	75	85	73		80	82	X		90	96	93	
JONES	85	96	84		94	78	83		X	87	88	
KELLY	64	63	73		84	77	69		74	7		
MANN	97	93	82		87	80	76		77	86		
THOMPSON	84	85	85		95	94	87		93	87	83	
TIMMS	90	93	95		91	93	97		85	89	96	
WILCOX	70	67	83		90	76	X		87	84	84	
WILSON	77	X	66		X	61	78		66	76	84	

Hook N' Loop® surface with silk-screened gridiron squares is displayed.

E. Hook N' Loop® boards

F. Models

G. Mock-ups

H. Dioramas

II. Advantages:

A. No sophisticated equipment is needed.

B. Minimum skills are required.

C. Students can perform learning tasks through manipulating materials.

D. Materials are relatively inexpensive.

III. Disadvantages:

A. Materials are exposed; therefore, they are vulnerable to abuse and environmental conditions.

For years, the chalkboard has been the old standby of teachers. With the influx of various, sophisticated audiovisual devices, the chalkboard waned into the unpopular category of being old fashioned. However, it never became obsolete like so many other areas of technology with similar histories. Perhaps this is because the chalkboard has modified its appearance somewhat in tune with instructional trends; it still serves with considerable satisfaction certain instructional needs.

If you want to present an idea verbally, graphically, or pictorially, the chalkboard will provide the means. The chalkboard does not require a projection device, and information can be easily removed and replaced by new information.

Although we could at one time refer to the chalkboard as the blackboard, this is no longer an accurate description. The chalkboard may appear in a light shade of green or other shades which are suitable for accepting a projected image. You can use watercolor pens and may put magnetic objects for three-dimensional displays on some chalkboards.

If you are interested in the direct involvement of students with materials which can be manipulated, there are several devices that you can use to accommodate this need. The primary difference between each of these devices is the

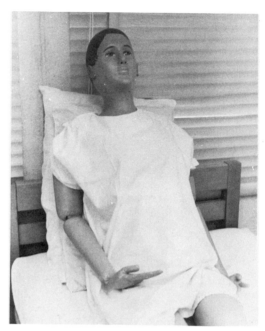

A mock-up is displayed.

materials used. For example, a feltboard uses cloth materials which the student can manipulate into a pattern, whereas a magnetic board uses magnetic materials. We also have Hook N' Loop® boards and pegboards which the teacher and students can use to display ideas.

Models, mock-ups, and dioramas all provide different spatial learning experiences. Creating a model or manipulating the parts of a model places the learner in the position of interacting with the real-life features of the concept. While the student is involved with the production of a topographic map, references to real-life features are made. When the student works with a mock-up of a gas engine, real-life characteristics of the working parts are considered. Real-life characteristics can also be portrayed by dioramas in which three-dimensional subjects are

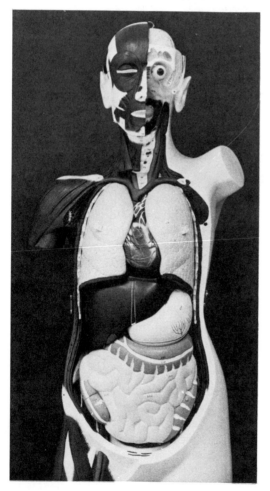

A model is displayed.

blended with two-dimensional pictures of real-life scenes.

Multi-Sensory Materials

In this category, we are concerned with the combination of display materials which together communicate a topic. A basic requirement of media mixture is that each medium while serving a unique function combines with another medium to contribute to the total learning experience.

I.   Types:
    A.   Instructional kits
    B.   Self-instructional modules

II.   Advantages:
    A.   More learning objectives can be accommodated.
    B.   May combine local materials with commercially prepared materials.
    C.   Certain learning differences may be accommodated.

III.   Disadvantages:
    A.   Appropriate selections may require too many instructional devices.
    B.   Sophisticated production skills may be necessary.
    C.   May be expensive.

Multi-sensory materials, as the expression implies, refers to a combination of

FIGURE 7–13   Diorama: Three-dimensional scene of a natural setting.

materials. Their success depends on involving the learner in more than one sensory dimension. A student might be involved with listening to a tape while looking at a verbal-visual display that also includes some manipulative materials. Instructional kits often include a variety of materials which challenge the different senses of a person.

If we select the appropriate media and combine our selections properly, we may have the most powerful of instructional offerings. However, a major problem which you should try to avoid when combining materials is the factor of interference. The student may become confused if the same idea is treated differently by different media.

The involvement of students with the production of a mixed-media approach to a topic may result in a profitable learning experience and contribute an end product which may improve future instructional offerings. The class could be divided into teams, and each team could assume a responsibility for a component of the total package. Of course, the selection of materials may be limited to materials that do not require sophisticated production skills.

Multi-sensory materials refer to the stimulation of more than one receptor of information. It is not the stimulation of more than one sensory factor that makes it a desirable learning experience; rather, it is the appropriateness of this stimulation to the learning function being performed that is important. The indiscriminate mixture of materials may lead the student away from the intended learning goal. Therefore, the techniques for producing such experiences depends to a great extent on why the selection was made.

Summary

Planning assumes a position of considerable importance in this chapter. Two techniques have been discussed in depth. Both the storyboard and film script can save the producer of instructional materials time and money. The major point of this discussion is to emphasize that planning is essential to production and to avoid it is to invite some serious problems.

In this chapter, we explored areas that assume a major role in the provision of instruction. Each material requires something different from the designer and producer. An effort has been made to highlight these differences and describe the minimal requirements associated with each. For example, the production of transparencies requires skills that are quite different from the abilities necessary to produce a picture series.

Viewing each of these materials from the position of realizing not only their description but particularly the advantages and disadvantages associated with each will give you a set of options that should help you select instructional materials. A knowledge of the inherent weaknesses as well as strengths is one way of determining what materials are appropriate.

REFERENCES

Mager, R. F. *Preparing Instructional Objectives.* Palo Alto, Calif.: Fearon Publishers, 1962.

Nelms, H. *Thinking with a Pencil.* New York: Barnes & Noble, 1964.

Markle, S. M. *Good Frames and Bad.* New York: John Wiley & Sons, 1964.

Chapter 8

Selecting and Using Equipment

Introduction

In this chapter, we will consider equipment, particularly those devices which will help you provide instruction of benefit to learners, that you might find available in schools. This is not a comprehensive study of instructional devices; rather, it is an expression of certain points that are important.

In some instances an in-depth discussion of certain equipment is presented while only a few highlights are mentioned for other equipment. The intricacy of the equipment dictates to some extent the amount of explanation given. Also, the extent to which the equipment contributes to instruction is another factor of influence. A certain level of proficiency is assumed to be sufficient for instructional purposes. We avoid any discussion that appears to be technically beyond the scope of teacher-student interaction with the equipment.

The format of this chapter was selected to acquaint you with the advantages and disadvantages of the equipment, as well as certain characteristics of the equipment. In most cases, a reference is made to those techniques which will help you use the equipment better and in the most appropriate situation.

The following types of equipment will be discussed in this chapter:

I. Cameras
II. Television Equipment
III. Still Film Projection Equipment
IV. Motion Film Projectors
V. Audio Recording Equipment
VI. Support Equipment
VII. Computer Equipment

Cameras

Cameras can be divided into two main categories. Still film cameras capture information in a static visual format. Motion film cameras capture information in a motion visual format.

I. Types:
  A. Still film cameras—Reflex cameras
     —Viewfinder cameras
     —Polaroid
  B. Motion film cameras—Super 8mm cameras
     —16mm cameras

II. Advantages:
  A. Students can be involved with the instruction.
  B. Instruction can be visualized.
  C. Large quantities of information can be stored on film.
  D. Motion and spatial cues can be presented to the learner.

III. Disadvantages:
  A. The equipment is sensitive.
  B. Accessory equipment is often needed.
  C. Special skills are required.
  D. Most of the film used requires darkroom processing.
  E. Film materials are expensive.

If you plan to produce slides or filmstrips, you will need to know some things about cameras. Generally speaking, still film cameras fall into two categories: the reflex camera and the viewfinder. As illustrated in Figure 8–1, you look directly through the lens of a single and double reflex camera; on the other hand, with a viewfinder camera you look through a window located above and to the side of the lens.

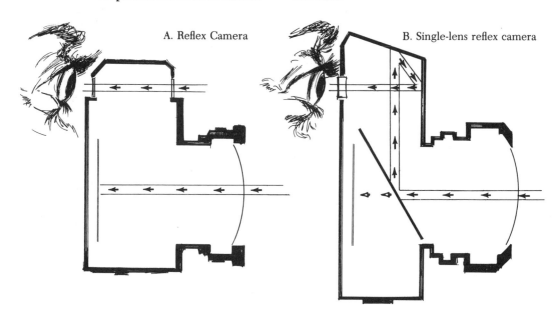

A. Reflex Camera

B. Single-lens reflex camera

FIGURE 8–1   A reflex camera enables you to see the subject through the lens.

From the standpoint of accuracy, sighting directly through the lens offers certain advantages. This factor is particularly important with closeup photography because with a viewfinder camera, one sees the image slightly differently than the camera does. Consequently, there is a difference between the image projected onto the film and the image which the photographer sees in the viewfinder. This problem does not occur with a reflex camera because the camera sees what you see. Naturally, you pay for this benefit in the expense of the camera.

A reflex camera has another feature that makes it desirable. When the shutter is not engaged, it covers the opening of the camera, thus protecting the film. This feature enables you to remove the lens when the film is in the camera without exposing the film. Exchanging a regular lens for a telephoto or a wide-angle lens is a simple function with this feature.

For the purpose of our discussion, we will concentrate on the use of a single-lens 35mm reflex camera. This camera is frequently used for copy work. As indicated in Figure 8–2, the lens is adjustable and operates somewhat like a telescope or a microscope. The lens is turned until you see the subject come into focus.

The single-lens reflex camera offers the flexibility one needs for most still photography situations. Such a camera will enable you and your students to develop amazingly good visual materials. It may appear to be very complicated when compared to fixed lens cameras. Actually, because of a logical relationship between the camera's parts, this apparent complexity is deceiving. So, before resorting to a simpler camera, consider the single-lens reflex camera.

Much of the adjusting that is done with a camera is done to accommodate changing light conditions. An understanding of these conditions will help you understand the camera's functions. The problem of lighting conditions is minimized considerably when artificial light is provided be-

A. By turning the outer ring, the lens can be focused.

B. By turning the ring containing the F stop settings (inner ring), the aperture is altered.

FIGURE 8–2

cause some consistency can be maintained. However, with natural light, the conditions are continuously changing, thus placing more of a demand on the photographer's ability to adjust. The photographer can produce the correct exposure by coordinating the proper F stop of the aperture with the proper shutter speed.

In Figure 8–2, observe the aperture (lens opening) through which light passes to the film. By turning one of the rings that surrounds the lens, you can alter the size of the aperture. The ring, as indicated in the diagram, displays a scale of numbers commonly referred to as the F scale. Each stop or number on the scale indicates a particular aperture setting. When you turn this ring to the higher F stops, the aperture gets smaller. Thus, F11 is a smaller opening than F8. (F8 allows twice as much light to enter as F11; F5.6 allows twice as much light to enter as F8; and F4.5 allows twice as much light to enter as F5.6.) The aperture setting range varies from camera to camera; the more expensive cameras have a greater range.

It is probably obvious to you that the aperture regulates the amount of light that will enter the camera and expose the film. Therefore, when light conditions are poor, the aperture is opened wider; when an excessive amount of light prevails, the aperture is closed. For example, would you adjust the F scale to a higher or a lower number at noon than you would at dusk? If you said the higher F stop, we agree because at noon the amount of light is greater and you need to compensate for this by reducing the size of the aperture (i.e., moving the scale to a higher F stop). The texture of materials (i.e., how well

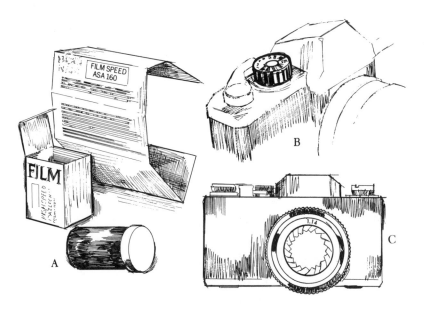

FIGURE 8–3   Film speed (A), shutter speed (B), and shutter opening (C) are all important to determining the correct exposure.

they reflect light or absorb light) alters the amount of light entering the camera. A device designed to help the photographer with this variance in conditions is called a light meter; this device will be described later in this chapter. For now, we will concentrate on the conditions that affect the art and science of photography.

Another factor that is associated with light control is the speed at which the shutter opens and closes. The faster the shutter opens and closes, the less the amount of light that is allowed to enter the camera. Therefore, another way we can compensate for changing light conditions is to regulate the speed by adjusting the shutter opening.

In Figure 8–3, we can see the shutter which controls the length of time that light is allowed to pass through the lens. The faster the shutter speed, the larger the aperture opening needs to be.

Calibrated in units of time, a shutter speed scale may reveal a range of time intervals that extends from 2 minutes to 1/500 of a second. This same scale also accommodates the variances in movement by the subjects you are photographing. If you consider the fast rate of a moving jet, the slow pace of a walking subject, and the range of possibilities in between, it becomes apparent that some means of compensation is necessary. This, of course, is one of the areas in which cameras that have limited shutter speeds and less efficient apertures are weak. If you set the lens speed to photograph a still subject, a moving subject in the same scene will be blurred.

A shutter speed of 1/125 of a second is suitable for most daylight situations. However, the time may come when you wish to photograph a scene in a situation in which 1/125 of a second is unsuitable (e.g.,

late afternoon with existing daylight conditions). In this case, both the aperture and the shutter speed may need adjusting. You may have to leave the aperture wide open and adjust the shutter speed way down to accommodate the little light that exists. A light meter reading would indicate to you how much light you would need. It would be well for you to know, however, that when the shutter speed is reduced below 1/30th of a second, a tripod or firm tree is necessary to steady the camera. At that particular speed and slower speeds, the shutter moves across the opening slow enough so that it is affected by the photographer's vibrations as he holds the camera.

Look at the data sheet which comes with each roll of film. You will notice on the data sheet the F stop settings and shutter speeds that are recommended for varying light situations. For example, faster shutter speeds and higher F stops are needed to compensate for snow or beach scenes in bright daylight. In the absence of a light meter or a camera with an electric eye (built-in light meter), you can use the information on the data sheet to obtain well-exposed pictures. You will also notice first that your film is rated with an ASA (American Standards Association) number. This rating varies with different films and refers to the chemistry of the film emulsion. The higher the ASA number is, the faster (or more sensitive) the film emulsion. Both the aperture and the shutter speed are linked to the ASA number. Therefore, what is appropriate for one film may not be satisfactory for another film.

Another factor of importance to the attainment of a good photograph is the focus. Is the subject blurred? Focusing is relatively easy with a single-lens reflex

Model 420 Polaroid Automatic Land camera with flash attachment is shown.

camera. Just turn the outer ring until the subject is in focus; if you need to know the distance between you and the subject, you can locate the distance on the barrel of the lens opposite a small triangular index (see Figure 8–2).

The shutter speed, the aperture setting (F stop), and the focus are the big three of photography. The interplay of these three factors along with the ASA rating contribute to making a good photograph (see Figure 8–3). Of course, good subject matter and composition are also key factors. Because of the importance of these functions, it is recommended that you do not leave their relationship to chance.

One of the principle advantages to using a motion picture camera with a copy stand is that you can create two visual effects which are of value to instruction. By using still objects and manipulating them in a pattern, you can produce an animated film. Each time you change the pattern, photograph a few single frames. The end result conveys an illusion of

movement when it is projected on the screen. Providing a learning experience using this technique is an excellent way to get students involved with instruction.

You can also create the illusion of movement with still pictures by using a motion picture camera and a copy stand. You can use this technique to carry the viewer through a wide span of time with the transition of cues provided in a fast sequence. Still pictures are photographed on four or five frames; when these pictures are projected on a screen, they remain on the screen long enough for the viewer to recognize them. The effect produced by this technique is that a considerable amount of information can be conveyed in a short period of time. Enough information is produced to cause an acceptable transition from idea to idea. The viewer is forced to provide the closure necessary for conveying the meaning. Consequently, one can view the plight of the American Indian over a time span of many years in just four or five minutes. If you use a camera

Instamatic viewfinder camera with fixed lens is shown. Courtesy of Eastman Kodak Company.

equipped with a zoom lens, you can add the effect of moving toward or away from the subject, thus providing additional dramatic appeal.

With this technique, you can use inexpensive materials (e.g., pictures from magazines, newspapers, etc.). History lessons and literature experiences can be treated with this technique in a way that will attract the student's interest. The poor achiever who does not respond to passive experiences may show amazing progress when directly involved with the composition of such a production.

A camera function that is often used and seldom with good results is a lateral shot of a moving subject. The difficulty which many photographers experience with this type of shot (pan) is the tendency to move the camera too fast or too slow in relation to the subject. The movement of the camera should be slow to avoid a jerkiness in

Instamatic reflex camera with adjustable lens and automatic exposure control is displayed. Courtesy of Eastman Kodak Company.

the finished film. The problem appears to be one of forcing the scene rather than letting it emerge naturally.

If your camera is equipped with a zoom lens, one that allows a range of points of focus, you can experience a continuum of shots from long to closeup by simply turning a ring on the lens barrel. Zoom lenses are of particular value when you wish to photograph a subject that is some distance away. Duplicating the function of several telephoto lenses without having to change lenses has a certain amount of appeal. The same statement can also be made with respect to a closeup lens; that is, one having varying focal points can eliminate the need for several separate lenses.

A function similar to zooming is to dolly toward or away from the subject. This is accomplished by transporting the camera on a vehicle which carries the camera in the direction desired—the camera remains stationary. When performing this technique, it is necessary to change the focus of the lens. The end result, when projected, gives the viewer the feeling of passing through space; that is, the viewer experiences a dimension of depth.

When you juxtapose scenes, take care to move smoothly from one sequence to the other. Creating the right transition for a particular sequential gap is an interesting challenge. Let us, without being overly technical, consider some of the possibilities.

You can gradually fade one scene out and fade a new one in. One way of accomplishing this task is to close the aperture slowly on the old scene. When the new scene is ready, open the aperture gradually to a predetermined setting. Another possibility is to change the focus, thus blurring the old scene, and refocus on the new scene.

There are many special effects (e.g., fades, overlaps, and dissolves) that can be used to combine images. However, these effects are beyond the technical capabilities of most teachers; therefore, we will leave these embellishments to more in-depth writings on this subject.

Frequently, scenes are photographed out of sequence. The unavailability of a particular scene at a certain time and a host of other reasons can cause this to be more the rule than the exception. Actually, the film is made after the scenes have been shot. This may sound strange, but the final composition of sequences is where much of the creativity comes into play. This editing stage is where the out-of-sequence footage is put together; and for the first time, the film maker can see whether his assumptions were correct.

Often, much footage is discarded. In large productions, the ratio of film re-tained to that discarded runs as high as five or ten to one. For your purposes, however, careful planning and a realistic approach will probably provide reasonable results. A length of film remains after cutting, splicing, and viewing; this length of film which remains is called a working print which, because of its many splices, is not intended for use in a projector. The film is processed once again for the purpose of eliminating splices, and if your budget allows, certain special effects may be added.

Television Equipment

Television equipment captures visual and audio information which can be later displayed for viewing and listening. Such information can be recorded on magnetic tape and played back immediately, or it may be stored for later use. Television pro-

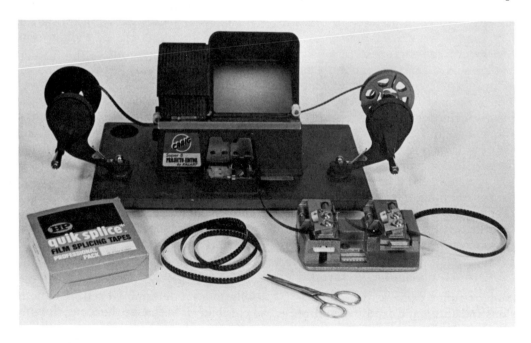

Film editor and film splicer for Super 8mm film is shown.

grams may be transmitted over an open circuit via commercial or educational channels; they may also be transmitted over a closed circuit to a limited audience.

I. Types:
   A. Studio
   B. Video tape
   C. Cartridge

II. Advantages:
   A. Immediate feedback of visual information can be provided.
   B. There is no chemical processing stage.
   C. Visual and audio information may be replayed as desired.
   D. Recorded information may be erased when desired.
   E. Students can be involved with the instruction.
   F. Other visual and audio formats (e.g., motion film, slides, transparencies, etc.) can be conveyed by television.
   G. Instructional offerings can be enriched.

III. Disadvantages:
   A. Equipment is relatively expensive.
   B. Some technical skills are necessary to operate and maintain the equipment.
   C. FCC (Federal Communications Commission) clearance is necessary for certain television delivery systems.
   D. Equipment is sensitive to misuse.
   E. Recording equipment is sensitive to climatic conditions (e.g., smoke, humidity).

Television as an instructional tool has been on the educational scene for several years. However, it was not until the advent of video tape that teachers were able to realize the full potential of this medium. Many of the problems that prevented educators from making good use of television were resolved when recording pictures as well as sound became a possibility. The scheduling of programs, for instance, was always a bone of contention between the educational television station and the classroom. With video tape, it is possible to record programs and play them back at some other time. The tape can be played as often as desired, thus allowing students who were absent an opportunity to view the lesson.

Because of its versatility, television is viewed by many as a threat to the job security of teachers. For the teacher who refuses to match progress with improved competence, the threat may be a real one. It need not be, however, for no medium has yet been able to replace the transactional role that exists between teacher and student.

Many texts devote large portions of space to the sophisticated closed circuit television approach. Certainly, if the budget permits, a television studio that can transmit its programs into rooms throughout the school offers both teachers and students great instructional dimensions. However, most schools do not have such a luxury. We will, therefore, confine our discussion to the range of instructional possibilities available for the use of video tape. We will especially focus on the skills you need for the proper use of this medium.

First, look at Figure 8–4 where you will see a typical video arrangement. In this configuration, the monitor, the video tape recorder, and the camera are interconnected. The camera which records live action performs all of the functions you would expect of a camera. Light control and all of the interrelationships between shutter opening and shutter speed are similar to the optics that we associated with motion picture cameras. The main difference between a motion picture camera and a television camera is the medium base; the motion picture camera uses film while the television camera records on magnetic tape. For this reason, the camera is linked to the video tape recorder where the visual and audio impressions are recorded on tape.

The video tape recorder is connected into the television monitor which is sensitive to signals that are being recorded. This configuration enables one to see what is being recorded at the precise moment that the signal is placed on the tape. This immediate feedback of information is unique with the video tape medium and offers instruction a dimension formerly not available. It is unfortunate that this feature is not used more in television programming. Subject areas in which skills are taught could benefit greatly from the use of this unique characteristic.

Suppose you are a science teacher. Periodically throughout the year, you may devote several hours to setting up a demonstration; however, some students usually have trouble seeing your demonstration. From the standpoint of efficiency, this is not the best use of your time, especially if there is a video tape setup available to you. Such a medium enables more

A studio television camera with a monitor is shown.

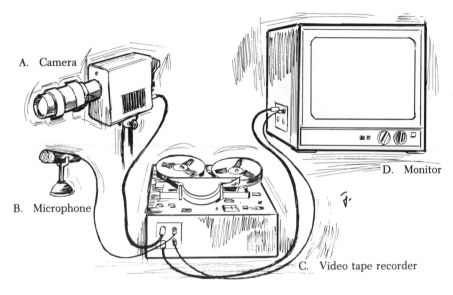

A. Camera

B. Microphone

C. Video tape recorder

D. Monitor

FIGURE 8–4 The proper linkage of the above components form an audio video taping system for recording and playback purposes.

students to see what you are doing; a student may see the actual demonstration or the image of it on the television screen. At the same time, you can record the demonstration onto video tape for future use. Not only can the video tape be used in place of the actual demonstration the next time this event is scheduled but it can also be used by students as the need arises.

Let us take a closer look at the physical nature of this medium. The tape is similar to any magnetic tape, although it is wider. The widths of the magnetic tapes currently used are 2", 1", 1/2", 1/4" and 3/4". Of these widths, the 1" and 1/2" are most commonly found in schools. Because state governments have helped fund the purchase of audiovisual equipment, they often determine the format to be used (state contracts provide schools with reduced costs). Consequently, a school system in one state may use a 1" format whereas

schools in another state may use a 1/2" format.

The larger tape machines and tape are usually more expensive. The 1/2" tape is most suitable for public school needs. Commercial television stations are regulated by the Federal Communication Commission (FCC) which requires them to use the 2" format. The primary reason for this requirement is the better quality of the larger format. The 1/4" tape is relatively new; supposedly, the electronic features built into the recorder compensate for any quality loss due to this smaller format.

Tapes run in length from one-half to one hour in duration. Because the tape composition is basically the same as audio tape, it can be erased and used over again.

The usual care must be administered to video tape as with any magnetic composition. Magnetic materials can erase the

Video tape cassette player/recorder unit is displayed.

tape, and dirt interferes with the recording function of the tape head. The tape head is the most critical part of the tape recorder for it places information on the tape. It should be cleaned frequently with alcohol which is placed on a small cotton swab.

In Figure 8–4, you will notice a television monitor which resembles a standard television set. The basic difference between these two pieces of equipment is that a monitor can accommodate a tape recorder input signal whereas a television set can only receive incoming signals generated from a television station. A monitor can also receive incoming signals generated from a television station; thus a monitor enables one to view pictures transmitted directly from a TV station as well as pictures transmitted from a recorder.

Although in our example the picture was being transmitted from the video tape recorder into the television monitor, it should be realized that the picture could be transmitted through an amplification and converting system directly to the television monitor. This occurs where live action is transmitted directly into the televi-

sion monitor. However, our concern is with the three-way arrangement of recorder, camera, and monitor mainly because it readily lends itself to classroom teaching and learning situations. Look at the interrelationship which exists in Figure 8–4 once again. Note that the monitor also feeds signals into the video tape recorder. With its ability to present programs that are being transmitted from television stations, the monitor serves as another source for recording programs on tape. Any program that the monitor can pick up clearly can be recorded on tape by this arrangement. From the standpoint of

This man is using a portable video tape recorder (PVTR).

instruction, this feature extends educational offerings beyond the scope of the classroom. Once the programs have been viewed, the information should be erased for reasons of integrity and copyright considerations.

The skills involved with using television equipment are similar to those required for motion picture photography. A knowledge of these skills and an understanding of the potential of television are essential to the effective use of this medium. Video tape as an instructional tool has more to offer than photography. Possibly one of the most obvious advantages of video tape over photography is the fact that no processing time is necessary before viewing a picture. A close second to this is that the tape can be used over again. Both of these features have appeal from an economical standpoint. In addition, the delayed and immediate feedback features provide the teacher with certain options that would not be available in any other way. For ex-

ample, the science teacher can bring ecological information into the classroom. Before this, the student could only experience such information through the words of the teacher or textbook author or perhaps through a film. Video tapes can be used to provide student interaction with the instruction. A social studies class, for instance, can develop a production that portrays a particular era of history; while the students are attending to the requirements of this production, they are actually learning.

As suggested in Figure 8–5, the portable video recorder unit has its own power source which enables the user to move freely about as one would with a conventional camera. The camera is connected into a taping device which records approximately one-half hour of programming. The tape can be placed on a video recorder linked to a television monitor for viewing. Some cameras are equipped with a miniature television monitor that allows

FIGURE 8–5   The portable video recorder enables the user to capture remote information on tape.

the user to play back the recorded segment in the camera for the purpose of assessing the quality of the end result. Science teachers, physical education teachers, business education teachers, and others can add a new dimension to their instructional program because of the range of this medium.

Certain tapes are incompatible with certain machines. Therefore, you need to exert care when playing tapes back on a recorder that is different from the one that it was recorded on. It is gratifying to note, however, that this problem is being resolved with the advent of a new taping format. This format can be used on all machines that have been adapted.

I. Types:

    A. Slide projector

    B. Filmstrip projector

    C. Opaque projector

    D. Transparency overhead projector

    E. Microfiche and microfilm readers

    F. Microprojector

II. Advantages:

    A. Large and small groups can be accommodated.

Still Film Projection Equipment

Static visual information can be projected, with or without the accompaniment of sound. Visuals may be displayed from a front or rear view screen projection angle.

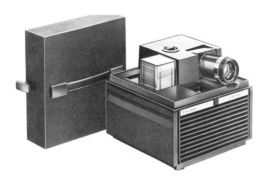

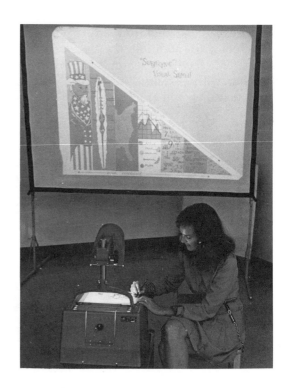

35mm automatic slide projector is displayed.

The instructor is using an overhead projector.

B. Self-instruction can be accommodated.

C. Three-dimensional as well as two-dimensional materials can be projected.

D. Microscopic information can be projected.

E. Students can operate equipment.

F. Equipment is easy to maintain.

III. Disadvantages:

A. Student interaction is limited.

B. Light control is essential for certain equipment.

C. Spatial and motion cues are difficult to convey.

D. Some of the equipment requires that the user have certain technical skills.

E. Film can be damaged by a malfunction of the projection equipment.

Although slides and filmstrips are made from the same size film, their finished form is quite different. Consequently, the projectors which convey these two visual formats are different. Conspicuous by the large circular or elongated trays which carry the individual slides, slide projectors are generally more difficult to use than filmstrip projectors. Filmstrips, in contrast to slides, are rolled into a small plastic container or threaded directly into the projector. Both projectors must be used in a dark or dimly lighted room. Remote controls extend the flexibility of using these projectors for instructional situations. Small rear screened, self-contained units can be used in self-instructional situations.

Another projector which must be used

Autoload filmstrip projector with remote control is displayed.

Microfilm reader is displayed.

in a dark or dimly lighted room is the opaque projector. This projector is unique in its ability to project two- and three-dimensional objects. With ease, it can project a page from a book or a mineral laden rock. Because of this capability, the opaque projector is bulky in size and difficult to handle.

The overhead projector projects an image from a transparent sheet of film. One can make these transparencies with a chemical, heat, or electrostatic process (see chapter 7). Also, sheets of film such as X rays can be projected with this device. A very attractive feature of this projector is that it can be used in front of your audience without reducing the lights drasti-cally—only those lights directly over the screen need to be dimmed. Facing the audience, the user of this machine can point to items on the transparency which is conveniently exposed on a glass stage. Once the machine has been properly focused, there is no need for the user to refer directly to the screen on which the image is being projected. Comparatively speaking, this projector is probably easier to use than the others for it contains only one switch and a focusing and elevating mechanism.

Two other types of projectors have found their way into the libraries of many educational institutions. They are the microfilm and microfiche projectors which

The opaque projector can enlarge photographs, specimens, and other opaque objects.

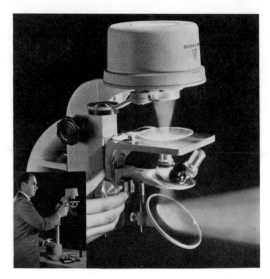

The microprojector can project wet and dry slides of microscopic organisms onto a screen.

Microfiche reader is displayed.

convey large amounts of information for convenient perusal via a rear-view projection screen. Consequently, old documents, periodicals, newspapers, and other sources of written information can be stored conveniently on rolls or sheets of film and made available to students.

Microorganisms can be mounted on a slide and projected onto a screen with a microprojector. This equipment has made it much easier for the instructor to identify certain features which are difficult for students to locate through the microscope. Like a filmstrip projector, it too requires a dark room.

Motion Film Projectors

Visual information can be projected for instructional and entertainment purposes. Film may be contained on a reel or as a continuous loop within a plastic cartridge.

Both sound and silent motion films are available.

   I. Types:
      A. 8 mm and 16 mm reel-to-reel projectors
      B. Silent and sound Super 8 mm cartridge projectors

  II. Advantages:
      A. Conveys real-life cues.
      B. Inexpensive Super 8 mm format can be produced by students.
      C. Cartridge projectors are relatively easy to use.
      D. Projectors can be used for small and large groups and also for self-instructional purposes.

 III. Disadvantages:
      A. Unless rear-view projection

Super 8/Regular 8mm film projector is shown.

16 mm autoload film projector is shown.

is used, light control is essential.

B. Student interaction is limited.

C. Some of the equipment requires that the user have certain technical skills.

D. Film can be damaged by a malfunction of the projection equipment.

Until the introduction of Super 8 mm film, film usage in the classroom was restricted to 16 mm films prepared by commercial producers. Now, because of the less expensive 8 mm format, it is possible for educators to involve students with film production. We now find more film usage than ever before on the educational scene.

We also find films being used in a variety of group sizes. Previously, films were used mostly with large groups. Now, with the

advent of rear-screen projection units and the compactness of Super 8 mm projectors, small groups and self-instructional needs can be accommodated. The Super 8 mm cartridge is small enough and has the proper optics to be used in study carrels.

Another noticeable change in motion film use is that films can be shown in lighted rooms because of rear-screen projection. Consequently, teachers can more easily preview films since they no longer need a dark room for this purpose; all they need is a section large enough to house the projector-screen unit.

Film content is no longer restricted to the presentation of large amounts of information; it is now possible to have a film less than eleven minutes long. Now, it is not unusual to find two- or three-minute films available on a single concept. Also, open-ended films designed to provoke discussion are produced in this short sequence format. Open-ended films are purposely designed without a definite ending; it is hopeful that after discussing the issue, the viewer will provide the ending that he considers appropriate. Multi-learning kits may contain a short cartridge film. The student must no longer wait for the teacher to show a film because cartridge films are now available in the instructional materials center.

Teachers find that the availability of these films to students reduces the time they normally devote to instruction by reducing the amount of redundancy that is sometimes necessary. For example, a science teacher can have a closed loop Super 8 mm silent cartridge film projector available to students at some convenient location in the classroom. This film can depict a process that was previously demonstrated to the class. Students can view the demonstration as often as they like without disturbing the class. These projectors have a special stop-action button which can be used to isolate certain scenes.

Audio Recording Equipment

Sound is recorded on tape. Some audio systems provide for listening experiences

A continuous loop cartridge sound projector combined with a rearview screen unit form a compact projector and screen combination for small and large group showings.

Small group instruction can be accommodated easily by the technicolor silent cartridge projector because of its small size and short range focus capability.

only while other audio systems provide students with listening and response opportunities. Both the audio passive and audio active systems are used extensively in instructional situations.

I. Types:
   A. Audio tape recorders
   B. Language Masters
II. Advantages:
   A. Vocal learning tasks can be accommodated.
   B. Listening skills can be developed.
   C. Some of the equipment is relatively inexpensive.
   D. Cassette tapes have minimized operational difficulties.
   E. Appropriate for self-instruc-

tion as well as large group instruction.
III. Disadvantages:
   A. Listening experiences must be short to be effective.
   B. Problems may be experienced when playing a tape that has been recorded on a different machine, especially if there is a wide difference in the quality of the two machines.
   C. Reel-to-reel recording requires technical skills.
   D. Audio tape is sensitive to magnetic fields.

Tape recorders can be divided into two major categories: reel-to-reel and cartridge or cassette. Cartridge tape recorders are easier to operate because it is not necessary to thread the tape. The tape does not require handling by the operator because it is threaded in the cartridge as one continuous loop. Although cartridge tape recorders ease the handling of the tape, they do not provide the editing capability of reel-to-reel tape recorders. Marking the tape as it passes from reel to reel is much easier than marking and splicing the tape which is within a plastic container. One also experiences a problem when the tape within the plastic container breaks. Although it can be spliced, it is difficult to do.

Tape recorders are available with one and two magnetic heads. The latter feature allows the user to respond to instructions on the tape without erasing them. With such a feature, the student becomes actively involved. Of course, the added dimension of stereo sound is possible with this feature because more information can be added to the tape. Two magnetic heads

are available on cassette tape recorders as well as large recorders.

Some recorders are only available in a playback mode. These recorders are inexpensive and reduce the risk associated with allowing students to sign out tapes as they would a book.

With the advent of less expensive and easier-to-use tape recorders, there seems to be an upsurge of interest in the teaching of listening skills. For many years, this skill was left virtually unattended. Yet, we recognize the importance of this skill to learning. Several commercial packages have been produced for the purpose of teaching this skill.

Tape recorders have also been used as an audio input for skill learning. Certainly, listening to directions while performing a learning task (especially with a machine) is much easier than shifting one's eyes frequently from a machine to the written page.

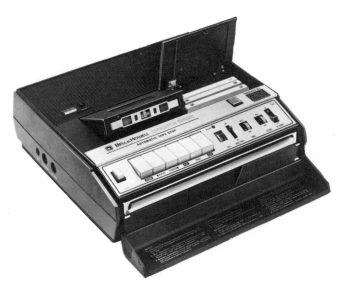

Portable audio tape player/recorder is displayed.

Language Master Recorder is displayed.

Language Masters allow the user to respond on tape as well as listen. This feature, in addition to the visual and verbal capability, makes the Language Master a desirable instructional device. It is especially suitable for self-instructional purposes, and the relative simplicity of its operation enables young students to operate the equipment without teacher intervention.

A sophisticated use of tape recording is demonstrated by language laboratories. Here, students have an opportunity to listen to a foreign language lesson or to interact with the instructor who monitors the student's aural performance. This enables the instructor to have a one-to-one relationship with students as well as a total group relationship. The potential of this technology to expose foreign language students to native speakers is an attractive feature of language laboratories.

Finally, an obvious use of tape recording is to satisfy a logistical concern. On occasion, students may miss a lesson which, if taped, could be played back to them at a later date. This would be especially helpful for students who are incapacitated by a long illness.

Support Equipment

Without the assistance of other types of equipment, the instructional potential of the equipment previously discussed would not be possible. Equipment which is necessary to the function of a medium but which is adjunctive to it will be discussed in this section.

I.   Types:
A.   Light meters
B.   Copy stands
C.   Lighting equipment
D.   Microphones

II.   Advantages:
A.   Equipment, with the exception of some microphones, is relatively inexpensive.
B.   Equipment does not consume a large amount of space.
C.   Equipment does not require much maintenance.

III.   Disadvantages:
A.   Equipment varies among manufacturers; therefore, there is a range of desirable and undesirable designs.
B.   User often overlooks the need to develop skills for using such equipment.

You will need a device called a light meter if you want to produce good, well-balanced photographs. Light meters, like cameras, come in assorted sizes and styles. Single-lens reflex cameras with built-in light meters are the most convenient to use. However, because of their expense, we will limit our discussion to the light meter as a single unit.

Figure 8–6 shows a typical light meter. You will notice a reference to the ASA setting which we have associated with the emulsion chemistry of the film. Setting the meter to the appropriate ASA rating is the first step. After this is done, the meter will register the light conditions that prevail. The exposure value of this reading is determined by rotating a movable disc until the number that equates the value expressed by the exposure needle appears in a small window. When you execute this maneuver, you are turning a disc that has an F scale calibrated on it. This scale is aligned to a corresponding scale which contains the shutter speed readings. Consequently, you have synchronized the F

scale setting with the shutter speed scale. For any shutter speed, you can read the appropriate F stop setting for this particular lighting situation and for this particular film (ASA rating). If you will notice the two scales in Figure 8–6, it is apparent that the faster shutter speeds correspond to the higher F stop numbers which represent the smaller aperture openings.

The light meter should be pointed toward the subject (see Figure 8–7). Changing light conditions will cause a corresponding change in the position of a hairlike needle which registers the intensity of the light in lumens.

A device called a copy stand supports the camera. It is used for taking photographs of pictures of art work. Two photoflood lamps are placed at an angle of 45° to the surface of the subject being photographed.

With a light meter, the F stop setting is determined. A neutral test card (a gray

FIGURE 8–6   A light meter is used to determine the proper camera settings.

FIGURE 8–7 The light reflected off the subject is recorded by a light meter and translated into camera settings.

card with 18 percent reflectance) can be used. This gray card has the reflectance of the average subject. After the F stop setting is established for the average subject and the camera is adjusted accordingly, the reading does not need to be repeated unless, of course, the material to be copied is excessively lighter or darker than average.

You will notice attached to the camera a cable release that allows you to shoot the picture without touching the camera. Therefore, the possibility of getting one's fingers in the way and jarring the camera is prevented. Also, slow shutter speeds, which are overly sensitive to camera movement, may be accomplished.

A copy stand contains a mechanism for raising and lowering the camera. The copy stand can be adjusted until the desired area is viewed through the lens of

the camera; it is then locked at this point. After the camera elevator mechanism is adjusted and the subject is brought into focus, the same setting can be used again for pictures of similar dimensions.

A few remarks can be made that will make your efforts at the copy stand more productive. Each time you sight the area to be photographed through the lens, make certain that you scan all sides of the viewing area. Many pictures have been ruined because unwanted information appeared in the scene. This defect is called a bleed and usually results from the photographer's concentrating too heavily on sighting through the center of the lens, thus allowing undesired information around the sides of the scene to go unnoticed.

In the course of doing copy work, you will undoubtedly have to change a photoflood light that has burned out. When this happens, both lights should be changed in order to prevent an imbalance of light intensity caused by the age differences between the two lights.

It is also important when using photofloods to position the lamps so that a 45° angle is made with the surface of the subject. Avoiding this adjustment can cause a "hot spot" (brighter area) that is disturbing to the end result. If you are using a single-lens reflex camera, you should be able to notice this difficulty directly through the camera lens and make the necessary adjustment. You will notice in a diagram that each photoflood is covered with a diffusion shield that will disperse the light over a wider area, thus reducing the possibility of bright spots.

Copy stands are often used to produce title frames. The first exposure that the viewer has of the finished product is the title frame. A good title frame can alert

the attention of the audience to the intent of your message. There are several display options open to you, and what you choose will be influenced by the nature of your topic and the expectations you have of the audience.

If you wish to provide your display with a certain amount of distinction, arrange a few textbooks concerned with your topic into an interesting composition. The A portion of Figure 8–8 illustrates such a composition. Your aesthetic sense will dictate the particular arrangement; nevertheless, give some consideration to keeping the arrangement balanced, simple, and clear.

The same diagram (Part B) offers another interesting approach to the composition of a title frame. The title is arranged at an angle to the photofloods so that a shadow is created. This gives the letters a dimension of depth. It is important that you take a reading with a light meter

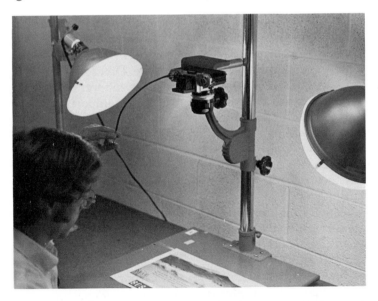

This man is using a copy stand with a 35mm single-lens reflex camera.

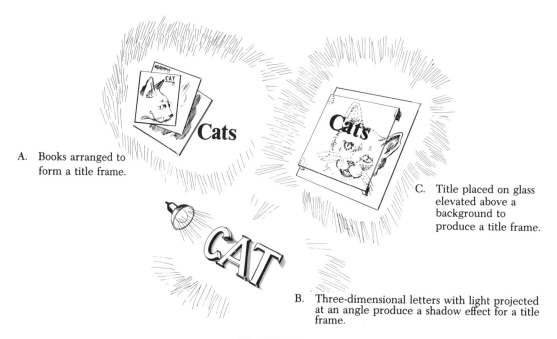

A. Books arranged to form a title frame.

C. Title placed on glass elevated above a background to produce a title frame.

B. Three-dimensional letters with light projected at an angle produce a shadow effect for a title frame.

FIGURE 8–8

whenever you make such an adjustment to ensure the proper exposure.

Part C of Figure 8–8 reveals another arrangement for a title frame. In this composition, a picture or pictures provide a background scene. If these pictures are placed slightly out of focus, they provide a visual reference that helps to introduce the message conveyed by the title. This composition is accomplished by placing a plate of glass in an elevated fashion over the background. Letters which are arranged on the glass serve as the principle point of focus. Arranging the lamps properly will eliminate any reflection from the surface of the glass. A nonreflective glass can be placed over the opaque materials, thus eliminating possible glare.

When using a copy stand for motion photography, the light control procedures are the same as they are for still photography. However, the end results will be different because of the differences between still and motion cameras. A slide camera photographs one frame at a time while a motion picture camera photographs several frames in the same interval of time. Different motion picture cameras register different shutter openings. It is, therefore, important for you to ascertain what the shutter opening is for the camera you are using. A rating of 180° will usually give an exposure of 1/50th of a second when the camera is run at 24 frames per second and 1/30th of a second when the camera is run at 16 frames per second. When using 8 mm silent film, the exposure is at 1/35th of a second when the camera is run at 18 frames per second (Pincus, p. 48). The instruction booklet that comes with your camera will provide this information.

In addition to photofloods, other artificial light sources can be used to provide the necessary conditions for a good photograph. Common artificial light sources are flash attachments which are available for even the most inexpensive cameras. When photography is conducted indoors, flash bulbs can provide the light needed for the particular film being used. On occasion, flash attachments will be used outdoors to supplant the extreme light and shadow conditions that might prevail. A common mistake made by the novice photographer is to overlook the limited distance at which a flash can be effective. This information is available with the film.

An electronic strobe attachment is convenient to have because it contains a potential for several flashes and, therefore, negates the need for flashbulbs. This attachment carries its own charge and some can be recharged by plugging into a household circuit. The strobe emits light which is equivalent to outdoor light; therefore, outdoor film can be used indoors without a lens filter. This attach-

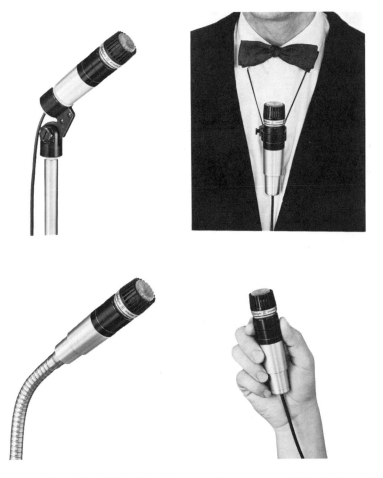

An unidirectional (unidyne) microphone especially designed for lavalier use can also be mounted or held by hand.

ment is available in an assortment of price ranges which makes it worth the consideration of amateur photographers.

Before completing our discussion of accessory equipment, we would be remiss in overlooking audio recording equipment, particularly the microphone. All microphones do not pick up sound in the same manner. Unidirectional microphones are designed to filter out unwanted sound; therefore, they are suitable for auditorium use where only the

speaker's voice is meant to be heard. Bidirectional microphones pick up more sound than unidirectional microphones but limit the coverage area especially around the sides of the microphone; thus they are suitable for interviews. Omnidirectional microphones extend the range of coverage in all directions, making them suitable for large group or classroom interactions.

Even when the proper microphone is selected for the recording task, many persons do not know how to use it. When the person is too close to the microphone, we can hear a popping sound with certain letters (e.g., *P*). When the person is too far from the microphone, certain letters are not recorded. A rule which is worth remembering that will help correct this problem is to speak about a paper's length

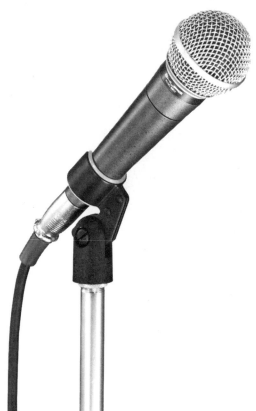

Unidirectional microphone with windscreen picks up sound from the front while suppressing sound from the back. It is ideal for close microphone usage (e.g., interviews).

Omnidirectional dynamic microphone picks up sound evenly from all directions. It may be hand held because of its outstanding noise isolation.

Bidirectional microphone picks up sound from the front and back while suppressing sound from the sides, top, and bottom. It is ideal for across-the-table interviews or dialogues.

(8" X 10") away from the microphone. Many worthwhile messages have been spoiled because the speaker did not know the proper technique for using recording equipment.

Computer Equipment

Computers can store, manipulate, and immediately retrieve large amounts of information. More schools are renting a computer terminal in order to provide individual learning experiences in the form of Computer Assisted Instruction. Many libraries are using the storage and retrieval capabilities of computers to provide better access to information. Many

guidance counselors are considering the use of computers as a means of providing career information.

I. Types:
   A. Teletypewriter
   B. Terminal
II. Advantages:
   A. Information can be upgraded when the need demands.
   B. Self-instruction can be provided.
   C. Large amounts of information can be handled at one time.
   D. A permanent display of information can be acquired for future reference.
III. Disadvantages:
   A. Equipment and service is relatively expensive.
   B. Certain sophisticated skills are necessary for computer interaction.
   C. Computer equipment is sensitive to climatic conditions.
   D. Because the computer interacts with other users at other locations, the incidence of computer breakdown may be rather high.

Small computers are being purchased by many schools. Their limited storage capacity makes them unsuited for anything beyond solving a problem. With this type of computer, programs are fed into the computer and left there only as long as the program is being used.

This student is using a computer terminal.

Computer terminals can be rented by several schools on a time sharing basis. The computer in this situation may be located miles away from the terminal. Yet, through the interconnection of telephone lines and the ability of the computer to process information rapidly, the impression is given that it is serving only one particular terminal.

Before you can use the computer, you must use a special language. This language must be one which the computer has been programmed to accept. Although there are several computer languages, computers are seldom programmed to accept them all. Your first step, therefore, will be to learn a language which the computer can accept. The newer computer language forms are easier to learn because they have been structured like conventional language.

Computer Assisted Instructional programs and teaching machines are labels that describe the same concept: the end product of applying a programming technique. They vary from a simple paper and pencil design to a computer terminal (see Figure 8–9). Programs that are conveyed by computers are referred to as CAI (Computer Assisted Instruction). Although the computer medium is sophisticated, the principle for programs and teaching machines remains the same as selective or constructive responses are confirmed during the course of student interaction in both cases. Even the outputs of CAI may vary, and a range of stimulus possibilities from print to video displays of information can be experienced by the learner. The extraordinary feature of CAI is the unique possibility it offers to instructional improvement. Every unanticipated wrong answer fed into the computer by the unwary user may be recorded for revision purposes. Thus, an instructional program can be adapted more easily to learner differences.

Another instructional use for which the computer is especially proficient is in the area of simulation games. Students can have an opportunity to learn basic economic principles by assuming the role of a ruler of a country; through interacting with the computer they can make decisions that influence the country's destiny. There are several simulation games available that deal with different areas of interest. This type of learning experience helps the individual develop empathy toward the roles of others as well as acquire certain knowledge.

The fact that computer programs can be upgraded because the computer records all student responses is probably one of its most attractive features. The improvement of instruction is a very difficult task in traditional situations; and unless stu-

dent-teacher interactions are video taped for critiqueing purposes, upgrading instruction may be compromised. With the student-computer interaction recorded, assumptions can be tested and the necessary program changes can be made.

It is evident that much of the interaction with computers involves the input of humans. Although it may appear that we are talking about a human-machine interaction, we are in reality considering a human (student)-human (programmer) interaction in which computers like any other medium serve the function of extending us beyond our limitations.

Summary

In this chapter we considered the devices which convey many of the materials that were discussed in chapter seven. First, we gave attention to equipment that handled visual materials. Still and motion

A. Programmed Text

B. Computer Assisted Instruction

FIGURE 8–9

film cameras were described in terms of their functions and features.

Television was approached as a separate category and its uniqueness was emphasized. Special consideration was given to the appropriate use of this medium.

Equipment that conveys still and motion visuals was given extensive coverage as we considered the large array of devices that fall into this category.

Reel-to-reel and cassette audio recorders were discussed in terms of their unique contributions to instruction.

A sometimes overlooked but always important category of equipment consists of those devices that play a supportive role. This equipment is used in conjunction with one of the major devices. Thus, copy stands, microphones, and other equipment were given the appropriate attention.

The last category gave us a view of the computer terminal which makes a significant contribution to instruction in areas such as CAI (Computer Assisted Instruction) and information storage and retrieval.

REFERENCES

Pincus, E. *Guide to Film Making.* New York: Signet, 1969.

Chapter 9

Evaluation

Introduction

We have considered the what, how, and when of instruction. We are now ready to ask if the instructional plan was effective. Often overlooked, this is nevertheless a crucial question.

It is not unusual for a teacher to hastily construct a test in an unsystematic fashion. A question skipped, however, may be an objective overlooked and an assumption unfulfilled.

Some critics are suspicious of the notion of quantification and the suggestion of measurement because they feel that some teachers juggle figures to suit their purpose. This point of view is given impetus when the teacher's role as a source of knowledge is predominant. In this context, all that is required of the instructor is an expression of profundities.

Most teachers have a tendency to be very lax in their efforts to evaluate their pupils. Educators do not seem to be in total agreement on the issue of what constitutes a good evaluation.

In an effort to find an acceptable approach, foremost among our concerns is the fact that evaluation was depicted as the final link of the proposed instructional system. Therefore, evaluation will be treated as a factor of design which will agree with other considerations that have been discussed.

In this chapter, we are concerned with the following question: How do we know that our assumptions have worked? The goal of this chapter is to provide a model for evaluating classroom teaching and learning experiences. Reaching this goal will be the culmination of your involvement with each of the following objectives:

I. Distinguish between assessment and evaluation.

II. Delineate the causes of student failure.

III. Stipulate succinctly the purpose of evaluation.

IV. Describe the exit level profile and how it equates with the entry level profile.

V. Interpret the end results of post-testing.

VI. Criticize evaluation practices.

VII. Defend the evaluative model, and apply it to a classroom circumstance.

VIII. Distinguish between developmental and field testing experiences.

Exemplary Situation

Imagine that you are a junior high school social studies teacher with a class of approximately thirty students. The class is a conglomerate of social backgrounds and achievement levels with the only consistent factor being that the students are in the twelve- or thirteen-year-old age bracket and that they are in the seventh grade.

One of the concerns in this class is current events. Interspace travel qualifies as a topic worthy of attention. Space travel has a history that emerged from the acumen of science fiction writing to the discipline of science, and from there into the real world. With this as a prime motivator, you have decided to provide a series of lessons on some aspect of space travel. The first lesson for this unit will be concerned with the topic of weightlessness.

Your goal is to bring each student to a point where he can discuss weightlessness as a factor of earth living as well as a condition of space travel, describing in the process psychological and physiological implications.

The following objectives represent specific aims of your instruction which will prepare students to achieve the goal:

I. Contrast the factor of weight with the earth's gravity.

II. Describe the influence of the earth's gravity on our mental and physical behavior.

III. Define weightlessness.

IV. Reveal how it is possible to experience weightlessness on earth.

V. Describe the adjustments space travelers must make when confronted with weightlessness.

Past performances of this class have indicated the presence of three distinct groups of learning styles. One group consists of students who do well with verbal experiences. Another group of students performs better when provided with visual stimuli. The third group requires some direct involvement with stimuli.

The first step toward accommodating the three groups will be to analyze the learning objectives and determine the target behaviors. The contingent behaviors that each terminal behavior is dependent on are as follows.

I. To contrast the factor of weight with the earth's gravity, the student must be able to

A. identify the distinguishing characteristics of weight and gravity

B. compare one concept with the other

II. To describe the influence of the

earth's gravity on our mental and physical behavior, the student must be able to

A. distinguish between mental and physical behavior

B. express the cause and effect relationship of gravity on human behavior

III. To define weightlessness, the student must be able to

A. identify the characteristics of weightlessness

B. compose these characteristics into a descriptive statement

IV. To reveal how it is possible to experience weightlessness on earth, the student must be able to

A. cite examples of simulating weightlessness

V. To describe the adjustments space travelers must make when confronted with weightlessness, the student must be able to

A. identify the effects of weightlessness on the human body

B. express the demands which the effects of weightlessness pose to the human space traveler

In this lesson, the learner is expected to recognize the elements of the concepts, comprehend these concepts, and with the fifth objective, generalize from the inferences made.

Before the learner can construct the desired response, all of the contingent be-haviors must be achieved. The stimulus conditions should be directed toward these specific contingent behaviors. The mode of expression for the responses, insofar as the goal is concerned, is predominantly vocal. However, visual and verbal responses will be expected for some of the contingent behaviors.

Before we can consider the stimuli we propose to use in our instructional strategy, some attention should be given to the three styles of learning that the class displays. For example, since one group is verbally oriented, this does not necessarily mean that the instruction should be void of other stimulus possibilities, but rather that a verbal approach will be the predominant one. Although the style of the learners is accommodated, the response in which students must express a competence is specified by the goal of the lesson; in the case of this lesson, it is vocal. Therefore, each group should be provided with a vocal experience before exiting from the lesson. Associations must be made between the stimulus modes and those that are demanded by the lesson.

How the content of the lesson will be displayed depends primarily on isolating the contingent behavior conditions and the learning styles. Therefore, each of the three groups will receive information pertaining to the contingent behaviors. There will be an effort to accommodate the learning styles. The experience is complete when each student has been brought to the point of complying with the demands represented by the goal of the lesson. We can call this demonstrable ability an expression of competence.

Visualize the interrelationships between the factors we have been discussing. Figure 9–1 shows a linear arrangement with each event occurring at a certain point which either precedes or succeeds another point. Whether or not the competence is demonstrated depends to a large part on the attention paid to each of these events.

First the functions are described which reveal the learning task and then strategies (methods and means) are selected for accommodating these functions. In other words, if a behavior dictates a selective response from the learner, the strategy to accommodate the demand will be to select the particular method (i.e., stimulus approach: visual) and the means (i.e., medium: transparencies) that is appropriate.

Throughout this process, assumptions are made, decisions are activated, and results are forthcoming. Are the assumptions accurate and do the decisions fulfill the expectations of the lesson? The answer to this question is the essence of this chapter.

Assessment and Evaluation

A linkage exists between this chapter and chapter one. Chapter one dealt with a process for estimating the characteristics of learners before the lesson is presented —we labeled this process entry level assessment. The end product of this effort emerged as a student's profile (see Figure 1–3). Such a graphic picture enables teachers to observe the posture of each student with respect to the lesson, thus making it easier to provide the appropriate instructional strategy.

In contrast, this chapter is concerned with results. How effective was the instruction? The student's record of progress can be represented with the same graphic expressions that characterized the entry level profile. Combining these two profiles reveals information of value to the instructor and the learner.

Although the terms assessment and evaluation describe a similar function (i.e., each is a form of estimate), in this text an important distinction is made. Assessment considers conditions before a lesson is presented; on the other hand, evaluation is concerned with the effectiveness of the methods used to accommodate these conditions.

The acceptance of this distinction will influence the manner of conducting both information seeking processes. Each process must hold at a high priority the level of accuracy of the information. Therefore, certain means must be employed to optimize the collecting process to assure the desired level of accuracy. The method of meeting this requirement with respect to entry level assessment is the essence of chapter one. There are requirements which we must also attend to in the evaluation process. Denying them may ad-

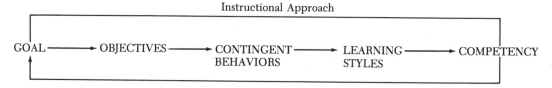

Instructional Approach

GOAL ⟶ OBJECTIVES ⟶ CONTINGENT ⟶ LEARNING ⟶ COMPETENCY
                         BEHAVIORS   STYLES

FIGURE 9–1   Competence to perform a goal may be the result of attention which is given to each of the above concerns.

versely affect our efforts to obtain accurate information about the effectiveness of instruction. The nature of these requirements and the strategies used to accommodate them is an important aspect of this chapter.

Student Failure

One way of discovering the requirements evident with evaluation is to probe the issue of why students do not succeed. Requirements, like functions, emerge from asking pertinent questions. Although similar in this respect, they are nevertheless distinct; and it will be helpful to recognize their differences. The key to distinguishing between requirements and functions dwells in the nature of the question. Questions which consider the how of the learning process unveil methods. How can learning be accomplished? Whatever the issue, the answer is an expression of some form of action. In contrast, questions which consider the what of the learning process unveil requirements. What is needed to satisfy a particular learning function? Here, decisions are more concerned with identifying what is needed rather than how these needs are satisfied.

Functions are not performed in isolation, but rather in respect to certain requirements. Functions are action oriented; requirements, in contrast, are descriptive. Through a consideration of both of these, one will be able to design learner-based instruction.

We are concerned with assessing our treatment of both of these characteristics, and we will oblige this concern by describing what appears to be the cause of student failure. The causes are many, but

most efforts concentrate on student achievement. The learner brings into the learning situation a host of reasons that affect his chances of success.

Contrary to common belief, the most important cause of student achievement does not necessarily depend on the pupil's attitude. Far more important are the abilities that the student possesses when he enters the learning experience. Most learning experiences presuppose the presence of certain competencies—often this assumption goes uncontested. The consequence may be a student who cannot cope with the demands of a particular lesson.

Student deficiencies that are not detected pose some serious difficulties to instructional efforts. Efforts to provide remedial instruction are also interfered with when the possible causes of learner errors are the result of excessive guessing on the part of the student. Few teachers will argue with the effectiveness of detecting and providing for this requirement. However, providing remedial instruction and regular instruction simultaneously seems impractical to many educators. The realization that matching student ability with instructional strategies is a requirement of most instruction and that denying this can cause student failure is of importance.

As we look at causes of student errors, we would be remiss if we did not include the attitude of the student. In some respects, this aspect is perhaps the most carelessly managed and the most critical as a factor in learning. Initial attempts to manage attitudes are sometimes nonexistent. Yet, the learner can, at any given moment, prevent the message of a lesson from reaching its destination.

Often neglected as a probable cause of student failure is inappropriate instruction. So much time is spent blaming the student for his failures that the failure of the instructor is often overlooked. This is understandable if the teacher is perceived as an imparter of knowledge and the student as a recipient. In this scheme, the burden of responsibility lies with the receiver—therefore, it is the student who must catch what has been delivered.

If the teacher's role is viewed as that of a communicator, it is impossible for one to overlook the importance of the presentation. The burden of responsibility in this framework rests securely with the communicator (i.e., teacher). The teacher and the instructional treatment, from this viewpoint, definitely influence student failure.

Finally, we cannot ignore the means by which we assess student behavior and evaluate student performance. Assumptions which are made should not remain untested. Who can argue with the premise that false assumptions do not lead to error?

Learning information for further use may provoke a particular instructional approach; however, assessing the effectiveness of this approach may deteriorate into a few spotty questions. When information revealing student progress is solicited regularly throughout the teaching and learning experience, feedback serves as an indication of teaching effectiveness. In this scheme, testing assumes a role which is equal in importance to teaching strategies, for it is here that specific responses are requested that spell out the requirement for further instruction.

Since individual learning deficiencies, inappropriate instruction, and inappropriate test questions may cause student failure, seeking information about each of these causes may be considered to be the prime goal of evaluation. Unless information is available in all three areas, a princi-

ple cause of failure may not be noticed. Evaluation is not only an information-seeking process; it also reveals to the learner and the teacher whether or not any learning has taken place. If the evaluation shows that a weakness exists with reference to the learner, the instruction, or the test, it will be apparent; and the necessary modifications can be applied.

Test Questions and Objectives

A good place to start constructing test questions is with the objectives. One of the things that test questions should do is to provide students with an opportunity to demonstrate their ability to perform the terminal behavior.

While objectives express what is expected of the learner, test questions induce the learner to react. These questions, if written in conjunction with the objectives, will stimulate responses which can serve as a criterion for assessing the learning performance. To illustrate this point, let us use the first objective on weightlessness as an example.

We have indicated the contingent behaviors to be the following:

   I.   Identify the distinguishing characteristics of the concepts of weight and gravity.

  II.   Compare the concept of weight with the concept of gravity.

Questions can be generated for each target behavior as follows:

   I.   Select those characteristics which are considered to be attributes of weight

A. pounds

B. contributes to gravity

C. product of gravity

D. unit of force

E. pull of the earth

II. Describe weight and gravity by citing at least two distinguishing features.

Each contingent behavior has been accounted for in these two questions, and in responding, the student demonstrates an ability or lack of ability to perform the terminal behavior.

We might consider the possibility of sampling the objectives when constructing a posttest. What would happen if we eliminated objective three as a source for a test question? We could reason that if a student had mastered objective four, he will probably be able to handle objective three. Look at these two objectives.

I. Objective three—Define weightlessness.

II. Objective four—Reveal a way of experiencing weightlessness on earth.

The solution to this problem is not quite as obvious when we view the objectives and the terminal behavior expected. When we probe beneath the surface of these objectives for the function that must be performed (contingent behaviors), it becomes apparent that accomplishing one objective does not necessarily mean that the other objective can be performed. The goal of the lesson will be only partially achieved if objective three is not mastered.

Perhaps a consideration of the contingent behaviors associated with objectives three and four will help.

Contingent Behaviors for Objective Three:

I. Identify the characteristics of weightlessness.

II. Compose descriptive statements about these characteristics.

Contingent Behaviors for Objective Four:

I. Cite examples of simulating weightlessness.

The following questions might be written for the preceding behaviors.

Objective Three:

I. Watch a short film loop of a person experiencing weightlessness and identify, in writing, at least two characteristics associated with this condition. (Avoid biological considerations.)

II. After watching the film, describe the characteristics of weightlessness.

Objective Four:

I. From the realm of everyday experiences, give two examples of weightlessness.

It is possible to identify differences of meaning between questions pertaining to each of these objectives. The first question that refers to objective three not only stipulates in specific terms what is desired but also reference is made to that which is not desired. It would have been misleading to the pupil if we had left this portion (i.e., avoid biological considerations) out of the question. The student might have approached weightlessness from a biological point of view (i.e., its effects on the human body signified by a loss of control) rather than as a phenomenon of gravitation. The stimuli and the responses demanded from the student to questions for objective three are highly selective in nature. The student is required to categorize information and reject information that is not pertinent.

On the other hand, answers to the question which pertains to objective four are dependent on the learner's ability to recognize the characteristics of weightlessness (objective three) and apply these characteristics to everyday life. Although this is also partly a discrimination task, the learner must cope with characteristics different from those experienced in the learning situation. To answer this question successfully, the pupil must associate the characteristics of weightlessness with a situation which was not presented in the instruction. Comprehension, as well as recognition, is required of the learner before he can answer the question.

A complete test for this lesson on weightlessness could consist of the following questions:

I. Select those characteristics which you consider to be attributes of weight.
   A. pounds
   B. contributes to gravity
   C. unit of force
   D. pull of the earth
II. List two characteristics of mental and physical behavior.
III. Write a mental and physical effect which is caused by the force of gravity on the human body.
IV. Observe a short film loop of a person experiencing weightlessness, and identify at least two characteristics of this condition without referring to the human body.
V. Describe the characteristics of weightlessness that you observed in the film.
VI. Describe a means of experiencing weightlessness which is available to most of us.
VII. Identify the point of motion which is critical to establishing a weightless condition.
VIII. Describe the possible effect of weightlessness on the human body.
IX. Describe what a space traveler must do to adjust to the effects of weightlessness.
X. State your opinion on the severity of this limitation to space travel.

A frequent question that arises when a posttest is constructed is whether the number of questions is enough and whether the questions are appropriate. To answer this question, we must consider the three areas about which we desire information (i.e., instruction, learning performance, and the test). As far as instruction is concerned, the number of contingent behaviors will dictate the number of questions—there should be no less than one question for each contingent behavior. The question is appropriate if the responses demanded of the learner correspond to the contingent behaviors. The learning performance of the student and the quality of the test will be reflected from an analysis of the test results.

When developing pre- and posttests, it is desirable to know the prerequisite levels of students. Remember from chapter three that target behaviors are obtained after entry level and contingent behaviors have been compared. Therefore, test questions should attend to those behaviors that the learner previously did not comprehend.

Since we have acknowledged that a student's attitude is a contributing factor to his success or failure, information pertaining to a student's feelings would be valuable. In the student profile in chapter one (Figure 1–3), attitude is divided into positive or negative feelings. Knowledge of these feelings prior to and following the lesson may help the instructor to influence a pupil's performance.

Information which is collected about students' performances, the effectiveness of the instructional approach, and the appropriateness of test questions is of little value unless it can be used to modify and revise the practices that were employed. A matrix such as the one in Figure 9–2 can be constructed to provide the direction necessary for revisions to take place (Designing Effective Instruction, pp. 143–54).

A convenient number of ten students and ten test items has been selected for our example. Each square of the matrix represents a pre- or posttest response of a student. A blank section of a square signifies that there was no response to the question. This is common with pretest results because the student is not expected to answer most of the questions. The numbers listed in the left-hand margin of the matrix represent test questions, and the accompanying letter represents the correct response to that question. For example, test question 1a is the first question of the pre- and posttest and the letter *a* represents the correct response. The right-

hand column indicates that three of the ten students could answer this question correctly on the pretest; on the posttest, ten students were able to answer the question correctly. The difference between these two performances indicates a substantial gain in learning.

Observing the pattern of responses to each of these questions reveals important information about student performance and the instructional approach. For example, the responses to the second question on the posttest were all correct. This score is only impressive if you do not take into account that 50 percent of the students were able to answer the question correctly on the pretest.

Question three was difficult for all of the students on the pretest. No one answered the question correctly on the pretest, and only two students answered the question correctly on the posttest. We might assume that the lesson was not taught properly. However, a closer look reveals that all of the incorrect responses were identical. In each case, the response given was the answer to question two. Apparently, a degree of confusion existed on the part of the students between the ideas represented by questions two and three. The same thing seems to have happened with question ten which appears to have been confused with question five. Analyzing students' responses in this way can reveal information about factors other than students' ability.

The lower area of the matrix records how each student performed on the pre- and posttest. Student D, for instance, achieved a perfect score between the pre- and posttests whereas student G gained only three points. It is reasonable to assume that the teaching approach does not agree with the learning requirements of student G. Perhaps, the student does not

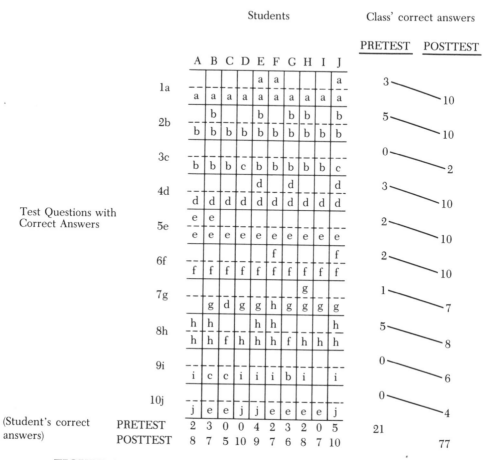

FIGURE 9–2   A profile of students' pre- and posttest performances with a lesson for which one question is generated per objective.

possess the skills to achieve these objectives. Such a finding might be substantiated if this student's performance was below that of the other students. The fact is, however, that other students did not show much improvement, i.e., students B, C, E, G, J. Therefore, we must conclude that for these students, the lesson was not taught properly and/or evaluated.

From an analysis of what the class as a whole did with each question, expressed on the right-hand margin of the pre- and posttest scores, some specific reasons for student difficulty are evident. The following data represent the performance of the ten students with respect to each question:

Question	Student Performance
1	reasonable performance gain
2	50 percent of the students knew the answer before the lesson was taught

3	poor question—confusion exists with question two
4	reasonable gain
5	reasonable gain
6	reasonable gain
7	reasonable gain
8	50 percent of the students knew the answer before the lesson was taught
9	poor instruction
10	ambiguous question

An analysis of the responses to these test questions reveals that only 50 percent of the objectives were managed correctly. We can also see that some of the test questions were confused with one another and that certain objectives were just not taught properly.

The Grade

Few educators will disagree with the criticism that grades play a questionable role in the prediction of student performance. The intent of grades is honorable since they attempt to give students some indication of how they performed. Yet, grades reflect only what the student did in response to certain questions. If a test simply samples the objectives of a lesson, then we cannot infer anything about the student's ability regarding the content which was not tested. If no attempt was made to assess students' performance prior to the lesson, we cannot infer that their responses are the results of teaching strategies. They may have known the content before the lesson was presented. If test questions do not correspond to the desired terminal behavior, we cannot infer anything of value from a grade. All we can say

about grades with any degree of certainty is that they represent a reward for which some students will work.

Is it possible to have a grade that will indicate something about the learning that has or has not taken place? For this to happen, the conditions we have described as being necessary to evaluation must be present. Rules for assuring the inferential ability of grades can be stated as follows:

  I.   All of the objectives of a lesson must be tested.

  II. Test questions must require responses which agree with the expected terminal behavior.

  III. The stimulus conditions in a test question should be appropriate for the behavior desired.

  IV. Test questions for each objective should be administered preceding and following the lesson.

If the fourth rule is considered, we will find a departure from the one grade approach. If a pre- and posttest is given, a grade can reflect the amount of gain the student achieved between the two tests (providing all of the other conditions mentioned above remain the same). A grade that reveals a gain from a score recorded prior to the lesson allows one to infer something about the effectiveness of the lesson.

Yet, there are certain limitations to this procedure. Suppose we have two students such as C and E in Figure 9–2 who have the same gain (i.e., C = 0–5; E = 4–9). In each case, we record a gain of five. Can we assume that both students have reached the same degree of accomplishment? Student C entered the lesson with no competence demonstrated for any of the objectives whereas student E had mastered four of the objectives prior to the lesson. Although each student has gained five, is their performance equal?

The answer is no if you agree that learning occurs from simple concepts to complex concepts. The chances are good that the objectives already learned by student E are less difficult than those not learned by him. This suggests that student E is functioning at a higher level of learning than student C. Therefore, students C and E are performing at different levels, and their gain is not equal. However, a record of their pre- and posttest performances suggest otherwise.

If, on the other hand, we consider what students C and E could possibly gain, the result would be 100 percent. Each student could have answered all ten questions correctly. Since student C did not correctly answer any of the pretest questions, he has a possibility of gaining 100 percent on the posttest; since student E answered 40 percent of the pretest questions correctly, he has a possibility of gaining 60 percent on the posttest.

Looking at the students' record from the standpoint of what they can possibly do compared to what they have done reveals the following useful information:

Students	Pretest Score	Posttest Score	Actual Gain
C	0	5	5
E	4	9	5

Students	Pretest Score	Possible Score	Possible Gain
C	0	10	10
E	4	10	6

Both students fall short of what they could have possibly achieved. We can illustrate this comparison by relating their actual gain (posttest score–pretest score) with their possible gain (100 percent–pretest score). Such a relationship is conventionally represented as a ratio:

$$\frac{\text{Actual gain}}{\text{Possible gain}}$$

The results of this computation is a modified gain score (McGuigan & Peters, pp. 23–34).

How will this additional information resolve the problem associated with comparing the achievements of students C and E? If we consider what each student gained compared to what they could possibly gain we find a difference, and thus, a more accurate expression of their performances. In the development of criterion testing, the instructor should consider the difficulty level of each question. When questions are associated with objectives, they cannot all be at one level of difficulty. This difference should be reflected at some point in the student's total grade. Questions which require more effort from the learner should carry a bigger reward than questions which require less effort.

When test questions are written for objectives which are at different levels of learning difficulty, it is a simple matter to assign the appropriate weight to each question. Each level of the cognitive taxonomy can be used to designate a numerical weight (e.g., the number 3 of level 2, or the number 5 of level 5). Combining this information with the number of responses required for each question will provide the value. For example, a question that demands five answers at level 3 of the taxonomy will carry a weight of 15. With this process, the student is rewarded proportionately for the amount of time necessary and the level of learning difficulty to accomplish the task.

Consider this approach using the exemplary lesson's test questions which are on page 186, and identify the number of items required and the difficulty level associated with each question.

Test Questions	No. of Answers	Level of Learning	Total Weight
1	3	4	12
2	2	1	2
3	2	3	6
4	2	4	8
5	4	2	8
6	1	4	4
7	1	1	1
8	1	2	2
9	2	2	4
10	1	6	6
			53

The total weight of the test is 53 points. If you wish to relate this value to 100 percent, the procedure is to establish the ratio 53/100 and equate it to the ratio of score/test grade. The result is expressed in the following formula:

$$\frac{Total\ Weight}{100} = \frac{Score}{Grade}$$

Therefore, a score of 30 will give:

$$\frac{53}{100} = \frac{30}{X} = \text{a grade of 56 percent}$$
$$\text{(approximate)}$$

A certain amount of subjectivity is apparent with this approach (e.g., number of items per question) as is true with most weighting procedures. The argument often given is that essay questions should count more than objective questions. In fact, such a breakdown does not apply to the system we are suggesting because it is possible to ask either type of question at various levels of learning difficulty. If it is true that a grade serves as a reward, it should be a just one.

Exit Level Profile

Both the entry and exit level profiles are constructed by the students and teacher working together. Given the necessary information, the students can develop the objectives portion of the profile from the test results. The teacher will need to provide information for the other areas of the profile.

While the matrix in Figure 9–2 provides the instructor with valuable information for the modification of instructional techniques, the profile provides the students and the instructor with a clear graphic representation of the student's performance. Both graphic representations display information necessary to the decision-making processes of the teacher and the students.

Developmental Testing versus Field Testing

There are two evaluative processes which can be used to test the design of an instructional system; one is known as developmental testing and the other is known as field testing. Developmental testing evaluates an instructional design in its formative stages. The extent of developmental testing depends on the particular design and on the degree of uncertainty in the design as perceived by the designer. For example, the technique of

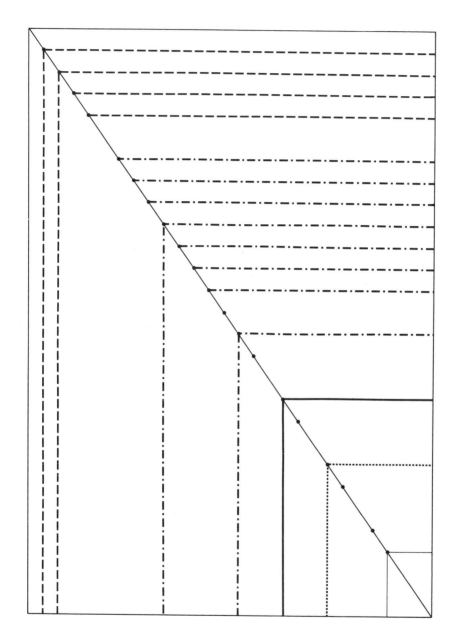

EXIT LEVEL

ENTRY LEVEL

FIGURE 9–3 A visual interpretation of a student's achievement with a particular lesson.

programmed instruction stipulates that one should overestimate the competency of the learner with the first draft (Markle, p. 185). This technique is tested in its developmental stage with some members of the group for which the program is designed. The first draft's difficulty level may be reduced as a result of the users' interaction with it. This procedure may be used several times before the programmer is satisfied. Field testing, on the other hand, is usually concerned with the end product of the instructional system and the involvement of the whole group. Depending on the medium, certain alterations are made on the basis of the feedback obtained from the field testing experience.

Like criterion testing, both the developmental and field testing experiences provide information which is relevant to the design of an instructional system. Unlike criterion testing, however, both of the evaluative processes occur after the content is treated and after the criterion test has been constructed; therefore, both the treatment and criterion test are evaluated.

Media Options

In the evaluation experience, the teacher desires a response from the pupil that will exhibit a mastery of knowledge. If the learner is to communicate this information effectively, the questions must be reasonable. Here, as in the teaching situation, a mode or medium for transmitting information to the learner may or may not be adequate.

Educators have a tendency to make most test questions verbal. Sometimes this is legitimate if the objectives suggest a verbal or vocal response. However, suppose objective four of the exemplary lesson (Simulate weightlessness on earth) is tested. In this instance, the learner must have an opportunity to manipulate certain stimuli, thus making word stimuli only partially effective. Providing a situation where the student can manipulate certain stimuli (i.e., parts of a visual, model, or mock-up) may enable the learner to apply the necessary principles.

There is a difference between designing a test question which communicates and designing an instructional display. In the former task, a response must be obtained from each student. The response requirement reduces the possible media options that may be used, but this does not necessarily mean that a verbal mode is the only resource. A film is a possible option, and from the standpoint of the many cues it offers, this mode is attractive. Yet, its availability is considerably less than some other possibilities. A transparency might be used with the request that the learner manipulate the information to simulate weightlessness. Of the various possibilities, a diagram is probably the least expensive.

Figure 9–4 presents a situation which could be arranged to describe a weightless circumstance. The problem that the learner faces here is one of arranging the elements correctly. When the learner places the swimmer at the peak of the dive, the correct answer is revealed because at this point, the upward and downward forces of gravity cancel each other out.

In another approach, you could ask the learner to select from several possibilites a combination of objects which could describe weightlessness when arranged. The following list is an example:

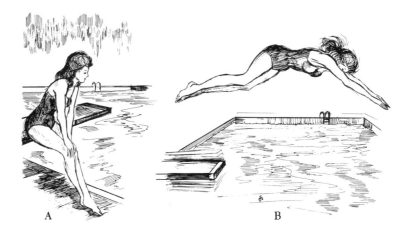

FIGURE 9–4   Arranging the elements of (A) as shown in (B) illustrates a simulation of weightlessness.

I.   diving board

II.   swimming pool

III.   road

IV.   bather

V.   airplane

VI.   driver of a car

VII.   car

VIII.   pilot

Six, three, and seven might be chosen. In this case a description of how a particular arrangement of these items simulate weightlessness would be necessary.

When constructing test questions, media can and should be used as discriminantly as in the teaching and learning situation. In some respects, it may be more important to select the proper media for this area when one considers that at this juncture of the learner's experience, the value of what has preceded will be determined. Certainly, if the learning experience consisted of a visual stimulus, then this stimulus should be used during the testing segment.

Management

The management of the posttest, actual gain, and modified gain scores may pose a problem to the teacher. Each of the three scores presents information with a slightly different meaning. Whereas the posttest enables the student to see how well he did in comparison with other students, the actual gain score shows his achievement from the beginning to the end of the lesson; and the possible gain score indicates how well he did compared to how well he could have possibly done. Each bit of information is important to the goals of evaluation, and each demands a percentage of time from the teacher.

The posttest is constructed by most teachers anyway; therefore, considering it as a management problem is not as critical. If display options other than verbal ones are considered this does require additional time of the teacher. This problem can be handled, in part, by using some of the same materials that were used to present the lesson.

Although it takes a considerable amount

of time to construct a matrix, it is an excellent way to view the performance of the class as a whole. It is of great value when the instructor is not satisfied with the students' performances on a particular lesson, and this situation might be the only time when it would be necessary to compose such a matrix.

Evaluation is not perceived, in the context of this book, to be an experience which lies outside of the teaching and learning sphere. Rather, it is an integral part of the whole instructional design. The concordant relationship between the reactions elicited by test questions and the expectations of objectives spells out the requirements necessary to establish the instructional design. For this reason, we recommend the construction of the criterion test at the beginning rather than at the final stage of the learning experience.

Summary

Evaluation is an effort to test those assumptions which influence the learning process, whether they are associated with the learner, the instruction, or the test. From each area, a set of requirements emerges that establish the conditions for learning. The unique characteristics of the learner specify certain conditions that must be satisfied. The instruction involves the learner with the content of the lesson. Through testing, the learner expresses whether or not learning has taken place.

In each of these three areas, assumptions can be tested through the medium of criterion testing, developmental testing, and field testing. Each of these tools contributes valuable information about the accuracy of the assumptions. This chapter deals with the interrelationships that exist between the three areas associated with learning and the techniques one might use to gather and use the evaluative data.

REFERENCES

McGuigan, F. L., and Peters, R. T. "Assessing the Effectiveness of Programmed Texts: Methodology and Some Findings." *Journal of Programmed Instruction* 3:23–34.

Markle, S. *Good Frames and Bad Frames.* New York: John Wiley & Sons, 1964.

"Designing Effective Instruction." *General Programmed Teaching* Unit 15:143–54.

INSTRUCTIONAL SYSTEM

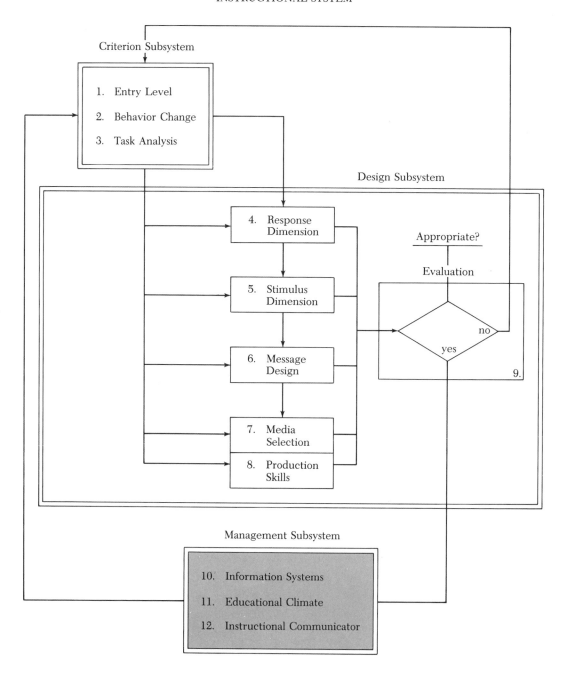

Part 3

Management Subsystem

Throughout this text, we have been cultivating a strategy for nurturing the learning process. The needs that have been identified and the requirements which have emerged serve as targets for our attention. Thus, the process for designing instruction concentrates on the assessment of learner needs and the fulfillment of their requirements. Each need influences the instructional design.

Faced with this situation, the teacher cannot avoid making endless decisions. Without sufficient information, decisions will be little more than guesses, and the law of chance will prevail. The cost of education alone dictates this to be an undesirable alternative.

Part Three is meaningful only as it relates to the processes which have nurtured it. So, before considering this section, let us be sure of the processes which were described in the previous chapters. Figure 10–0 presents a flow chart of the events which were discussed in depth.

Each step of the flow chart in Figure 10–0 describes an event that a designer of instruction will be expected to perform. Within each event are many activities and certain needs that will suggest the appropriate instructional strategies. With each function, there exist certain requirements that must be satisfied. With each function, there also exists the need for the instructor to decide which of several possible strategies is the most appropriate.

What emerges from this approach are discrepancies between what is required and what can be provided. These discrepancies compose the substance of your design problems. If you satisfy the need, the discrepancy is erased and the problem is resolved. If not, you should continue your search for the appropriate strategy.

The outcome of using this process is the

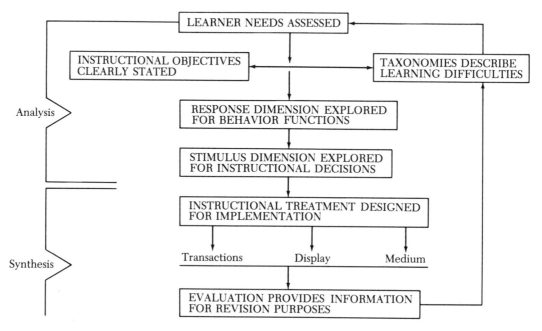

FIGURE 10-0

creation of an approach that is unique to the problem. Although the decisions which are made at this point are not without intuition, the amount of guesswork and the percentage of error is minimized.

The extent to which teachers are able to design learning experiences to accommodate learner differences depends not only on their recognition of the requirements that must be satisfied but also on the climate in which they must work. Unless the administration sanctions the instructional approach, the best intentions will not be realized. The teacher who is aware of the constraints prevelant within his school and the alternatives to these constraints will experience less frustration with his efforts to implement innovative strategies than the teacher who is not aware.

Many of these constraints can be minimized through the efforts of a resource person who, with teacher and administra-

tor, helps to provide better instruction. As a generalist, the instructional communicator helps the teacher to display and communicate the content of a lesson. Chapter ten will consider the information systems which are prevalent in schools and the transactions that occur within these systems as they relate to the design and composition of learning experiences. Chapter eleven will consider the climate which influences the teaching and learning situation. Particular attention will be given to the constraints that an instructor might confront. Chapter twelve will consider the role of an instructional communicator who acts as a resource person and consultant to the classroom teacher. From a realistic point of view, it may be this team effort that will succeed in managing the many variables associated with adaptive instruction.

Chapter 10

Information Systems

Introduction

Every learning experience emerges from a desire to teach something to someone. That something is the message of a lesson. It is the meaning that we attempt to communicate; and to a large extent, how well this meaning is conveyed depends on the treatment accorded the information.

The storage and retrieval of information refers to the accessibility of knowledge. It is a function which strives to fulfill the requirements of a variety of needs. It is a function which also greatly influences the directions of instructional design. It is a function which the teacher looks at during the initial stages of preparing learning experiences. Good learning experiences have been compromised because of the lack of critical information, and no learning experience can be described that is void of some transfer of information.

In this chapter, we will be concerned with the aspects of managing information within the context of classroom instruction. What system are we presently using? Is the system adequate? Can we improve the system? These questions and others will attract our attention, always from the viewpoint of designing learning experiences.

The location of information systems and why they are necessary will be discussed. We especially want to know where they fit into the scheme of classroom instruction and learning.

An area of importance is the availability of information to be presented and the variety of forms this information assumes. Is the information available at all? Is it available in more than one format? Is it available to students as well as teachers? A negative answer to any of these questions will alter the design.

The goal of this chapter is to present a case for the management of information as a system which consists of a variety of components that, if understood, can help you implement your instructional design. The following objectives indicate how we expect you to achieve this goal. At the end of this chapter you should be able to:

I. Identify an information system.

II. Describe the mission of an information system.

III. Compare different information systems in an educational setting, citing their strengths and weaknesses.

IV. Cite the important requirements that an information system should meet.

V. Recognize the relationship between information systems and the design of learning experiences.

What Is an Information System?

As living creatures, we spend a large part of our time weeding out the desired from the undesired, and the important from the unimportant. In each instance, the choice is initiated by us although we are not always aware of it. We refer to this effort as *processing*. Some information is selected; some is rejected; some is *stored* for long and short periods of time; and some is *retrieved* at a future time.

As a teacher, you will be responsible for managing information systems. Our efforts are geared toward promoting the transfer of skills, knowledge, and attitudes beyond the initial learning experiences. This concern with behavior modification and the transfer of learning prevents us from isolating ourselves from other areas in the organization. Information may be described as a factor of both our internal and external environments. Faced with the challenge of accommodating students, we need to be cognizant of how information should be displayed. Because of the complexities associated with this task, it seems reasonable for us to view both inter- and intratransactional possibilities. We can anticipate certain requirements for instruction from such a view. As you recall, the learning experience is depicted as a system (see Figure 10–1). We see certain characteristics in this model which can be generalized to other system models. One in particular is the transfer of information that moves in and out of each event. This

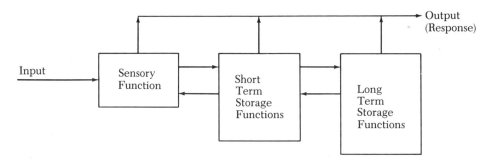

FIGURE 10–1 Our information processing system is composed of interrelated parts in which one part contributes to the function of the other.

dynamic interactive function suggests rather strongly that instructional design is an ever changing process.

Realizing the importance of this pattern of interrelationships will prevent the tendency to look at the function of one part as being independent of the others. This happens when a teacher presents a lesson adequately but fails to inform the student that the message is worth keeping. This also happens when lessons are presented consistently with the same display mode. Seldom does a teacher have the luxury of considering any factor in isolation. Throughout this chapter, we will support this conjecture and show the consequences of ignoring it.

Teaching and Learning as an Information System

Given the possibility that certain actions which occur in a school organization can be viewed as a system, what does one observe that is useful? The most common event a student or teacher will undoubtedly find is a teaching situation. Is this an example of an information system?

The answer to this question lies in part with the issue of whether or not the situation involves interrelated parts. Every teaching situation includes a teacher—this is obvious. But what else? Someone is the recipient of this teaching. Not so obvious, however, are the various processing stages which the lesson must pass through before these two elements are satisfied. There is a relationship between the teacher, information, and the student, and this is clearly expressed in the functions performed.

The teacher retrieves information from a variety of sources, both covert and overt.

From a textbook, past experience, and other displays, the information composing the lesson is conveyed. The selection of this information is based on assumptions made about the learner's needs. In other words, the needs of the student influence the teaching. The transaction is response oriented. The information is altered on the basis of how the student performs.

Let us get this into some perspective. Imagine that you are a commercial math teacher with thirty students. How to correctly write a check is the goal of your lesson. This decision is the result of an assumption that this skill would be beneficial to your students. The lesson is taught in what appears to you to be the best way. The students respond to your effects, and on the basis of their actions, you vary the lesson. If you are at the end of the lesson, your alternative may be to move on and hope that sooner or later those who are experiencing difficulty will catch on to the intended message.

The preceding example is a typical situation. The transactions between teacher and student run a rather consistent pattern. In an effort to see the advantages of viewing this situation as an information system, we will concentrate on two factors; namely, the needs to be served and the functions to be performed.

One can assume from the previous example that the actual need may differ from the perceived need. The teacher may perceive the primary need to be teaching so that a student will learn. However, the functions indicate the primary need to be more logistical, i.e., presenting the lesson so that the student will learn in a constrained period of time.

We have described a system as need oriented. Therefore, in that sense, the teaching situation is a system. Conflict may arise in determining which of the two needs is legitimate. Herein lies one of the advantages of looking at the teaching and learning situation as a system. You are forced to look at the need as a functional concept. Once identified, all of the functions to be performed strive to serve this need. With this approach, the dilemma of unwittingly serving a need that was not intended is not possible.

Another advantage of regarding the teaching and learning situation as a system is that the desired functions are easy to delineate. Only those functions that serve the need are considered. Because the need is stated clearly, it is not necessary to spend endless amounts of time decoding what is desired. Information selection and presentation strategies will subsequently concentrate on accommodating the desired end.

In the case of our exemplary lesson, the desired end may be described in the following way: Students will be able to use a recommended format for writing checks. Students who are not able to perform this task at the end of the scheduled time cannot be considered finished with the lesson. They would not be expected to go on to the next lesson, especially if success in the

next lesson assumed their mastery of this particular skill.

Needs, like schedules, are real; but oscillating from one need to the other does not necessarily bring forth the desired solution. It would be better if those needs that interfere with the desired needs were considered a special type of requirement which we will call constraints. For example, schedules are viewed as competing factors which must be satisfied but not at the expense of fulfilling the learning needs of the system.

Compromise is not foreign to educational circles because there are times when effectiveness must be traded off for reasons of efficiency. The point we are making is that constraints are normal, and compromise is natural; both can be managed more effectively when instruction and learning are viewed as a system.

As a system, instruction displays a pattern where the teacher directly influences the end result (see Figure 10–2). Information is processed by the teacher and transmitted to the student for storage and retrieval purposes. The process is initiated by the teacher regardless of the outcome. This type of instruction is prevalent in classrooms today.

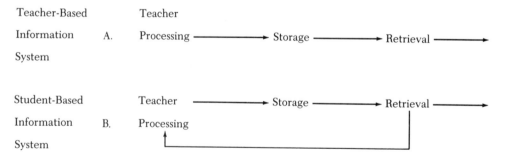

FIGURE 10–2 **Teacher-directed instruction assumes two patterns of information transmissions.**

STUDENT-DIRECTED INSTRUCTION

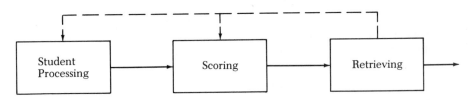

FIGURE 10–3   In student-directed instruction, the processing of information is done by the student who stores it for later retrieval.

There are two variations of this model as presented in Figure 10–2. The (A) portion of this flow chart describes a system in which the teacher imparts knowledge to his students; although the student is asked to retrieve this information, little variation in the teacher's approach results.

In contrast, the (B) portion of the diagram describes a system in which information imparted by the teacher is modified by the student's performance. Yet, in (B) as in (A) the teacher serves as the main source of knowledge. An example of the (B) version is evident when teachers solicit participation from their students whereas the (A) version is demonstrated when a teacher lectures to his students with little or no class participation.

In both of these transactions, the student needs to be provided with experiences that will enable him to store information for the purpose of retrieving it at a later time. The flow back of information depicted by arrows to the processing and storage functions suggests an awareness on the part of the teacher and student to the learning performance. In (A) the teacher's appraisal disregards the student's performance, and in (B) the teacher uses feedback to alter the instructional conditions.

An alternative pattern to the preceding one is portrayed when a student directs the instructional process (see Figure 10–3). In this approach, the student assumes a dual role—he performs as the teacher and the learner. In the case of our exemplary lesson, a student will be given the intended goal of the lesson; he then assumes the responsibility for achieving the goal. Instructional devices and sources of information are selected by the student. In such a situation, the student requests the services of a teacher as one would choose a book or some other suitable medium (Ofiesh).

Reactions to this type of information system vary from total acceptance to total rejection. The teacher is threatened by the effect this role will have on his job security. The student is threatened by the risk of having to make such decisions. Yet, the consequences of this system could be fruitful for both teacher and student. The teacher would assume the role of a consultant and evaluator, both of which place him in a better role for influencing the student's learning behavior. The student becomes involved with the lesson from the very outset.

It should come as no surprise that students are not overwhelmingly in favor of student-directed instruction. The thought of change for many of us is in itself threatening, especially when the proposed change interferes with a successful routine. Teaching has been the function of a professional, and there is some resistance to suggesting that it be otherwise. As Gagne has pointed out, those of us at the terminal position of formal education have succeeded rather well with teacher-oriented instruction, and for that reason, it survives—the lecture approach continues because it works (Gagne, pp. 1–2).

Of course, as Gagne points out, it works because the level of difficulty revealed by the prevailing learning experiences allows many students to succeed. Although there is some merit in the notion that student-directed instruction will better prepare students for problem-solving situations, individual differences cannot be ignored. Students who are outwardly influenced may experience considerable difficulty with this approach. Yet, if our desire as educators is to promote self-actualized individuals, then tolerance of external control is less defensible (Maslow, pp. 135–145).

Although the teacher-based emphasis has been considered a result of teacher-directed instruction, one might see its emergence in student-directed systems (see Figure 10–3). Since the student assumes the role of the instructor during the course of selecting materials for processing, it is possible for him to select inappropriate information displays. This situation is more likely to occur if learning as a process is ambiguous. In an effort to prevent this possibility and the inevitable consequence of reduced knowledge, the teacher can guide the student's decision-making processes. The establishment of a criterion to measure success with ob-

jectives is one way to control this problem.

If we compare the three different information systems, what do we find? The chart below makes such a comparison:

I. Consequences of Teacher-Based Instruction

A. Teacher is a purveyor of information.

B. Authoritative approach is used.

C. Content assumes an important role.

D. Instructional materials are selected indiscriminately.

E. Students are not very involved with instruction.

F. Objectives may be ambiguous.

G. Evaluation samples objectives.

II. Consequences of Student-Based Instruction

A. Teacher is a manager and designer of learning experiences.

B. Teacher and student assume partnership roles.

C. Instructional materials are selected on the basis of appropriateness.

D. The identification and satisfaction of learning requirements is important.

E. Students are involved with instruction.

F. The objectives are written clearly.

G. All objectives are tested.

III. Consequences of Student-Directed Instruction

    A. Student decides on the nature of the instruction.

    B. Student uses the teacher as a consultant.

    C. Instructional materials may be selected discriminately or indiscriminately.

    D. Process or content may be important.

    E. Student may or may not experience a wide range of involvement.

    F. Objectives may or may not be written clearly.

    G. Testing is usually controlled by the instructor—all objectives may be tested or sampling may occur.

As you can see, each system brings forth a different set of consequences, and your attitude as a teacher will determine the direction to be taken.

As a commercial math teacher who uses a *teacher-based* approach, you will present the lesson differently than a teacher who uses the other two options. A certain amount of time will be spent gathering information about writing checks if you are inexperienced with this particular lesson. If not, you probably will continue to do what you have done before, unless of course the results were not satisfactory. You will be conscious of the possibility that students might ask questions, and you will direct them to an information source if you are unable to answer their questions. Your main responsibility will be to present the information on writing checks clearly without assuming the student's responsibility for learning.

In the classroom, you will assume an authoritative role. This attitude is rather important, and to emphasize the importance of this priority, you might stress your demands the first day that students are with you.

The content of the lesson is the most important feature of your instructional design. You may give the lesson to students directly, or you may provide them with some information and ask them to search for the rest. The manner in which they get this content is of little concern to you unless cheating is evident. As stated previously, it is the students' responsibility to get the lesson and your responsibility to present it.

The materials selected for presenting this lesson will probably be those that you have found successful in the past. If, on the other hand, audiovisual materials are available, you might use them. The choice will depend on how much time has been allotted for the lesson.

You will keep the students involved by asking them to respond to questions. For example, you might ask a student to come to the chalkboard and label the various parts of a check. Of course, all students could not be involved because of the time constraint; but hopefully, those who do not participate will be encouraged by watching their peers.

Naturally, you will alert the students to the nature of the lesson to be presented by assigning them pages to read in their text which cover this particular topic. You might even ask them to write answers to certain questions posed by the author.

Periodically, to keep students alert you will give unannounced quizzes. In addition to asking students questions posed by the author of their text, you will test them at the end of the lesson. In the case of this lesson, you might ask them to label the parts of a check. You will vary your questions so that a good cross section of the content is covered.

If you use a *student-based* approach, you will present the lesson differently. On the basis of information gathered about the learner, the difficulty of the lesson, and the objectives, you will select, create, and provide the appropriate experiences. In contrast to the previous approach, your experience will not be a deciding factor in the selection of an instructional strategy; instead, you will be interested in the variance between this group of learners and the group of learners that was exposed to the lesson at a prior time. The question that you will consistently ask is, does the selection provide the most appropriate learning experience?

Because this approach is based on an assessment of each student's needs as well as the demands of the lesson, the materials which you select to perform instructional functions will be varied. Therefore, the expectation that students be able to write a check correctly at the end of the lesson suggests the need for you to recognize all the parts of the recommended format and comprehend their functions.

The student has accomplished the goal of the lesson when he demonstrates an ability to write a check correctly. If the student can label the important parts of a check, this is only an indication that he recognizes the important parts. Necessary? Yes, but it is certainly not a demonstration of the competency expected (i.e., the actual writing of a check).

Displaying the information visually will help the learner recognize the different parts of a check and how they interrelate.

A transparency would be ideal for this response because the individual parts can be added one at a time to the total checking format while the lesson is being presented.

For students who need to be more directly involved, the transparency can be projected onto a chalkboard. When each part of the cycle is projected, a student can write the desired information on the board. Providing the student with this opportunity during the course of teaching the lesson gives him an active role in the instruction.

If several students have similar learning styles, you can use a Language Master. Periodically, a vocal response will be required from students as a visual and auditory display of the lesson is presented.

In contrast to teacher-based instruction, this approach is more concerned with communicating the lesson. Although you will attend to the lesson's content by expressing it clearly in terms of expected learning behavior, you will also concentrate on how this particular content and its various levels of difficulty will be communicated so that the objectives will be achieved. How the lesson gets from you (or selected teaching devices) to the learner should be your major concern.

One can easily see with this approach that the student is exposed to a variety of experiences. A single medium will seldom be enough because each medium has certain weaknesses and, thus, a limited range of effectiveness. The resulting media mixture depends, of course, on the varience of the lesson's difficulty and the variance in learning styles among students.

As a teacher using the student-based approach, your first task will be to specify in behavioral terms what it is that you want students to do with the content of the lesson. Great pains should be taken to assure that the objectives specify the levels of difficulty at which the learner is expected to perform.

Test all of the objectives—for to deny one is to label it as unimportant. At least one question is asked for each objective, thus feeding back important information about the instructional treatment. Evaluation will be a means of gathering a maximum amount of information about the instructional approach and the learning performance.

As a teacher using a student-directed approach, you would function primarily to help students make the appropriate decisions. It will be your job to help the student stay on course—to make sure that he is moving in the direction that was intended. The student chooses an instructional means from an array of options. The teacher is just one of several possibilities. The teacher is therefore a consultant and a part-time teacher.

The extent to which students discriminately select instructional materials in this system depends somewhat on the degree to which they are advised. This is not to say that unadvised students will not make good selections but that the possibility for error is greater. Most of us are not able to be objective about ourselves and our needs. The rigor that is sometimes associated with learning makes this approach a risk, for the tendency to opt toward less resistance is always a temptation for the student.

Whether the learner becomes more engrossed with content or the process of learning is another case of ambivalence. Either is equally possible, depending on the extent to which the learning process is ambiguous in the mind of the learner. If you devote sufficient time to this issue

prior to the student's indulgence in student-directed instruction it will prove helpful to him.

As a teacher assuming the role of such a partnership, you need to be aware of the demands placed upon the learner when assuming his role. There are certain skills and knowledge with which the learner must be competent. Certainly the student must know the techniques clearly stating objectives and specifying how to arrive at such a destination if he is to be successful in his decision making. It is crucial that he comprehend the idiosyncracies of the learning process and its range of difficulties. The techniques of looking at a problem in terms of its many constraints and alternatives will prove valuable to a student functioning in this system. Finally, a conceptualization of the range of human behaviors (i.e, affective, cognitive, psychomotor) must be among the learner's repertoire of competencies.

It is likely that the students will become involved in a wide range of learning experiences. Most individuals have a natural desire for variety and find routines adverse. However, the power of media can be persuasive and one can imagine a student's over indulgence with one presentation mode (e.g., television) whether or not it is the most appropriate for the learning task. Student-directed instruction offers no guarantee that the learning experiences will be more effective than those offered by either of the other approaches. Certainly, the student's comprehension of instructional methodologies and their inherent strengths and weaknesses is crucial to success. It is probably evident at this point that a strong suggestion is being made to provide students with a training experience before entering into a student-directed system.

Systems and Change

At several points in our previous discussion of instructional information systems, we referred to accommodating variance. This was particularly true of the student-based and the student-directed approaches. Viewing the interactions between teacher, information, and student as a system affords one the opportunity to relate such transactions to change. For example, if we consider what each system is attempting to satisfy, we can recognize where change will have the greatest impact. A teacher-based system has been described as being content and teacher oriented; therefore, a variance in these two areas will probably be accommodated unless one happens to threaten the other. A student-based system, in contrast, will be more sensitive to changes among the students. With this system, we can expect to find adjustments occurring to accommodate learning needs in both teaching techniques and content areas. While a student-directed system ideally would be more like the student-based approach, it has the potential for polarizing toward either of the contrasting systems. Therefore, one would not be able to predict the changes that may occur in this system. However, viewing student-directed instruction as an information system enables one to ascertain to some degree of accuracy the effect of change.

Changes in society and in consumer needs are often met by lethargic conservation; this is demonstrated by a conspicuous educational lag. Perceiving transactions that occur in the school organization as information systems will help the observer better understand the prevailing practices.

The difference between how things appear to be and how they are is subtle, and yet, if the difference is not perceived, the fraud continues unchallenged. The concept "system" helps to untangle the web of ambiguity that surrounds so many educational practices. Educational transactions viewed as information systems will, if nothing else, enable the observer to understand why certain practices prevail.

STORAGE AND RETRIEVAL INFORMATION SYSTEM

One important and popular area of the school organization is the library. Possibly the most active area in schools, it is also one of the most controversial. Few educators agree on its intended function. Is it a reservoir of knowledge? Is it an educational market that exists to serve students' needs? Are its contents in print, nonprint, or both? Is it a place to browse, or is it a data bank waiting to respond immediately to any request? Are those who manage this facility librarians or are they media specialist, and what is the difference between these two roles?

Let us focus on the function of libraries as a possible system. First, in terms of attributes associated with a system, do we find these evident in library transactions? There appears to be little question that libraries serve a need. Problems that arise stem not from evidence of no need but rather a universal expression of that need. Thus, it is not unusual to find the recipient of library services and the administrator of these services at different positions of agreement.

Are libraries sensitive to interventions which strive to alter prevailing practices? How one views systems is definitely a part of these transactions. Let us look once again at the relationship between these

INFORMATION SYSTEMS WITHIN
LIBRARY OPERATIONS

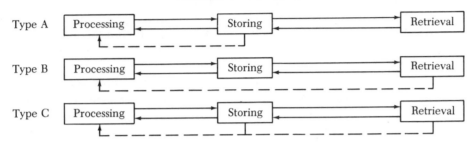

FIGURE 10–4 **Although all three of the same functions interact within a library organization, the emphasis shifts from one function to the other as
depicted with the feedback (broken arrow)
symbol.**

functions of a system, but this time look at these functions within the context of possible library practices (see Figure 10–4).

Can one perceive a goal to which libraries should strive? Certainly, there would be little disagreement with the notion that they house large parcels of information. What is done with this information (i.e., how it is managed) are specifics to which opinions will differ. Essentially, there are several goals toward which a library may function, and they may differ from one facility to another.

The total operation of a library is the result of several areas working together; at any rate, this is the hopeful quest. Information is processed and stored for use. The main commodity is information, and the transactions which occur in libraries center around this factor. The nature of these transactions may differ from one facility to the next. However, the three characteristics associated with information processing are universal practices in library operations. They are all involved with the function of processing information, and one would imagine this task to

precede the storage of information. The *processing* operation consists of preparing the materials for display. The shelving of materials is considered a *storage* function. After the materials are coded and placed on shelves, they are ready for use by the consumer—this is a *retrieval* operation. Included in this operation is further processing; the diagram shows such interaction as arrows move in both directions between the three characteristics.

A library which places emphasis on storing information demonstrates this to be a priority function. Of course, all libraries will attend to some extent to all three functions as depicted in Figure 10–4. However, as diagrams A, B, and C indicate, the emphasis may vary.

Where storage is the primary goal in a library, we will find considerable emphasis on processing information to accommodate storage requirements. More concern may be given to the display of information on shelves than the use of this information. The administrator of this facility experiences frustration if the shelves are not occupied. Storage in this system inadvertently becomes an end in itself. The use of a facility with this system may be sparse and some degree of resistance is experienced when consumer demands become too persistent.

If the library you are using is a type A system, you can expect your needs to be of less importance than the storage function. Knowing this situation does not necessarily mean that you can change the conditions. Perhaps, however, understanding the operation will ease your frustration, even to the extent of improving conditions—especially if you choose to reinforce the conflicting priority. On the other hand, if you choose to impose a different priority (i.e., your needs), intimidation will not be a total surprise.

A contrasting picture is presented by type B of Figure 10–4. Retrieval is the most sensitive function in this relationship. Lack of fulfillment in this area will influence other functions in the operation to the point of modifying their processes.

In a library of this type, you would expect to find more usage than with the previous type. That is, the needs of the user are paramount with this type of library, and one would perceive this to be an encouraging factor. However, one could argue that serving the retrieval priority excessively may result in a compromise of the other two functions, thus diminishing the desired service. This argument is easily refuted when one considers that a reduction of the storing and processing functions, to the point where they interfere with retrieval, will alert the system to the need for alternatives in these two areas. In essence, feedback would alert one to the problem before it reached disturbing proportions.

If you use the student-based approach to learning, the necessity for a library operation similar to type B becomes quite evident. The management and design of learning experiences do not occur in a vacuum. Support from several areas throughout the educational institution is necessary.

The ideal situation, you might think, is presented in diagram C of Figure 10–4. Each area is equally sensitive and each area is of equal importance. However, in practice, the consequence of this approach is constant change with few beneficial results. The instability of this system inhibits the benefits one realizes from change; in this system, change becomes an end in itself.

One could even argue that if each function had a minimum standard of operations below which it would not tolerate, beneficial results would be realized. However, when this is done, a hierarchy of standards results and the function with the least tolerant level becomes the most sensitive and the highest need of the system; then you have a pattern similar to type A or B.

When one experiences erratic results from using the library, it is most likely an example of type C. At times the code used in the processing stage leads you to the book; at other times it leads elsewhere. The book is at a certain place one time and a different place at another time.

Recognizing a library as a type C will better enable you to gauge your expectations accordingly. Frustration is generally experienced when we are at a loss to explain why something happens. One advantage to viewing library operations as a system is that it partially answers the question why. This places you in a better position to contribute to the functions of the library facility if the opportunity should present itself.

LIBRARY INFORMATION SYSTEMS

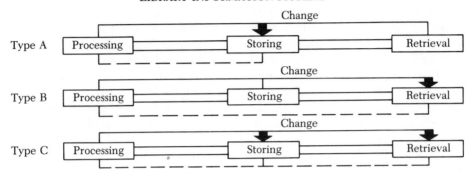

FIGURE 10–5 Change disturbs the balance of a system. Attempts to restore equilibrium are directed toward the function which is perceived as the greatest need (depicted with the heavier arrows).

One of the challenges presently facing libraries in educational institutions is the realization that educators are now aware that information may assume several display formats. The library as a system is sensitive to changing priorities and needs. The degree of this sensitivity depends on the type of system (i.e., A, B, or C) being used.

A change in attitude toward libraries on the part of the teacher or the learner can be perceived as a form of intervention which will disturb in various ways the balance of the library operation. Figure 10–5 illustrates how intervention can influence the three different library systems. With a library system of type A, the change will influence each of the three functions, but how this interferes with the storage priority is the major concern. If including different display formats means drastically altering the storage practice, the proposed change may be rejected.

Although using nonprint materials as well as print materials in learning experiences is accepted practice, libraries are still predominantly print oriented. This condition seems to corroborate the existence of library systems which do not hold the consumer at the highest level of priority. It almost appears as if the decision to accommodate this change rests on the condition that print and nonprint materials seem to be incompatible. Viewing one mode in competition with the other favors the status quo; thus with a type A library, print remains protected. A different picture presents itself with the type B system. Here, the question is whether or not the change interferes with retrieval. If one considers retrieval to be a function of consumer use, then obviously this change left unfulfilled will deny the consumer.

If information in nonprint formats serves a different need than print materials as far as teaching and learning are concerned, it will need to be processed and stored differently. Print and nonprint materials will be scrutinized, selected, and prepared for shelving. New storage configurations will be investigated for shelving these materials for access by the user.

Does this happen in reality? The emergence of instructional materials centers and computerized operations attest to the existence of this type of library system.

Library system type C which has no defined or apparent primary need retains its instability in the advent of change. These impingements stir to a degree all of the functions within a library operation so that no apparent change is evident. The lack of any defined goal removes a point of compromise from existence.

It is interesting to note that we are in effect describing two types of balance or equilibrium: one is a balance of change, and the other is resistant to change. System types A and B will be in a continuous state of flux (although for different reasons and toward different ends). Type C, in contrast, is static; change is a threat to its balance.

From this standpoint (i.e., type C), one would expect any proposed change to result in a rigid front of resistance. Advocates of this type of library will be rather vehement in defense of their rigidity, and the omnipotence of tradition will be cherished. A user in this situation will often find not only a deficiency in materials but few reasons, if any, given for such a void.

In the interest of crystallizing the differences in behavior between these three types of library operations, we will quickly consider one more intervention of change and see what can be expected from each system. Educators are currently being challenged by a deluge of new knowledge. This condition has been expressed so profusely that the term "knowledge explosion" is a cliché. The librarian is deluged by requests for new knowledge which cannot be fulfilled. Here is a classic example of change intervening with present library operations.

On the basis of our previous discussion and the diagrams in Figure 10–5, how would you expect libraries A, B, and C to respond? If you said that library type A, whose primary need is storing information, would be most severely challenged, we agree. More information means that the present processing and storage practice will be disturbed. How are we to accommodate more? is the classic cry. The result, however, will often be the utilization of space to the highest degree.

New formats such as microfilm and microfiche have greatly alleviated this storage problem. Microfiche can be encompassed within traditional library structures. Microfilm readers do not require an enormous amount of space. Coding and other preparation procedures remain basically the same. Consequently, microfilm and microfiche satisfy a high priority as a means of storing information.

Microfilm and microfiche accommodate the demands of retrieval as well. It is therefore little wonder that these innovations have been adopted by libraries in general. The concern expressed here is to make the new knowledge available. Unless it can be readily used, it is of little value to the consumer.

Will the more effective use of the facility and the adoption of different storage methods be sufficient to fulfill increased demands for new knowledge? The answer, of course, rests with whether or not these alternatives will make more knowledge available to the consumer when he needs it. It is possible that new knowledge can be made available but not readily accessible. The category of reserved books represents a classic example. Microfilm that is available but which cannot be transported to another location for viewing may not be readily accessible.

Solutions that are acceptable to a library like type A that does not consider the retrieval of information a high priority may fall short of consumer expectations. Only a limited amount of new knowledge is accommodated under this system and that information which is available is not always easily attainable.

Libraries which focus on the consumer would go beyond these solutions and consider altering both the processing and storage functions to the extent that retrieval is possible. This may mean incorporating drastic changes such as the use of computer technology to extend the library's capability beyond its present limitations.

ADMINISTRATION AS AN INFORMATION SYSTEM

Another area of the school organization with which a teacher has a strong working relationship is the administration. It will be to your advantage to know what prevails as a pattern of operation. As you survey this area, it will become apparent to you that here also information is a major consideration. Information is processed, collected, categorized, and prepared for use. It is filed and eventually channeled to affect decision-making processes throughout the institution.

Administration is an area where the teacher's ideas may be expressed or halted abruptly. An understanding of the decision-making pattern which is prevalent in the administrative sector may determine the extent of your professional future. Knowing how information is managed does not enable you to change conditions; however, it does enable you to work with this area in a more effective way.

What type of variance can we expect to find among administrators? Unlike the teaching and learning situations and the preceding library situation, all administrators seem to consider the retrieval function as a high priority. Information that is collected and stored is expected to be used.

Information that is received from parents and board members who represent the community influences the school's operation. Information collected about students dictates class schedules and other logistical considerations. Promotions for both student and teacher are the result of using the collected information in a certain way. The intent in each case is to make this information serve a meaningful purpose. All information appears to have a useful destiny in the administrative setting. However, the *for whom* part of this destiny gets different interpretations from different administrators. In other words, one administrator will exhibit a different priority than his colleagues when it comes to serving a particular consumer. Consequently, each variance in consumer satisfaction causes a difference which can be noted in the administrative operation.

The consumer, in the context of an educational setting, is anyone who benefits from the results of education. There are few in our society who do not fall into this category. Consequently, everyone believes he has a vested interest in the educational process, and everyone assumes a decision-making role. Although each role may see his sphere of influence differently, each wields a sufficient amount of power to provoke change.

This involvement is expressed in the form of five distinct roles that we will consider a cross section of consumer inputs. They are student, parent, board member,

ADMINISTRATION AS AN INFORMATION SYSTEM

Consumer Bias	Processing	Storage	Retrieval

Type A   Consumer Bias: Student

Type B   Consumer Bias: Teacher

Type C   Consumer Bias: Parent

Type D   Consumer Bias: Board Member

Type E   Consumer Bias: (all roles)

FIGURE 10–6   **At any given time, an administrator may formulate a decision that will benefit A through D of the above consumers. Over a period of time, administrators may reveal one of the consumers to be more worthy than the others. This is not to suggest that the administrator is consciously biased toward one of the roles or that it is a consistent practice but rather that over a period of time such a position is taken.**

teacher, and administrator. Students are, of course, the principle targets of education. Their influence has been realized in recent years as they have actively pressed educators to make instruction more relevant to their needs. Parents have made their feelings known by voting against proposed school budgets. Teachers have shown their discontent through protesting overtly with decision-making. Board members are elected to represent the will of the people, and they accomplish this purpose through broad policy-making powers. Administrators assume responsibility for implementing the established policy and, depending on the level of the role, influence the policy.

The administrator works toward satisfying all of the consumers' educational needs. However, since this is a lost cause, a polarization toward one consumer role will occur. The end result is illustrated in Figure 10–6.

In Figure 10–6 one basic information system is described. What happens in each of these three functions (i.e., processing, storage, retrieval) depends on which particular bias an administrator exercises. The following situations illustrate how this process might work.

An administrator surprises his faculty by announcing, "Commencing this school year individualized instruction will be adopted as a major approach to teaching and learning." The fact that no effort is made to prepare those involved for different roles suggests that neither students nor teacher is a main concern. Introducing such an innovation may suggest an effort to keep up with the times. Perhaps it is an effort to show superiors (i.e., board members) that their school is moving with progress.

An administrator rejects the idea of individualized instruction because he feels that control would be compromised. He might respond, "Students would be in the parking lot," or "Bedlam will result." This consequence would, of course, bring the wrath of consumers B, C, and D to the administrator. It is evident here that learning is a secondary concern.

An administrator rejects a teacher's request to implement individualized instruction in his class because it will distract other teachers. Some of the older, more traditional teachers will complain. The possible benefit of this approach is compromised for the well-being and concern of other teachers.

The ideal administrator is one who can satisfy all members of the decision-making team; such is the case with type E of Figure 10–6. This proves to be an impossible dream because attitudes are seldom the same, and the end result is that no one is satisfied.

The type E administrator will experience difficulty in making up his mind about change (i.e., introducing individualized instruction). Perhaps, this issue will be discussed and committees may be formed to study this new approach; but for some reason, the issue ends at that point. The administrator who uses this pattern is characterized as a friend to all. The administrator's reluctance to risk alienating one of the consumer roles is very evident by his predominance of a rather noncommital attitude toward issues. What appears to some administrators to be the ideal path becomes for many a dead end to a promising career.

What does all of this have to do with you, a potential teacher? Let me respond to this question by asking you to imagine yourself in a real-life teaching situation. You wish to do something about the wide variance in performance that a particular class has been displaying with respect to previous lessons. Having seen a class at another school functioning on an individual basis, you feel this approach is a possible solution to the problem. You approach the principal with a request to provide students with an individualized program in which students will be doing different kinds of things and going in different directions during the course of the class period. They would also assume some of the responsibility for their own instruction. The principal listens patiently with a condescending expression and a sympathetic ear, but his answer, although somewhat camouflaged, is a definite NO!

Everything that we have described as strategies for designing appropriate learning experiences will be in vain if the result of the preceding confrontation is a complete acceptance of a refusal. Such transactions between administrator and teacher are rather common, and the consequence, of course, has little effect on either but a rather strong impact on the learning performance of students.

A knowledge of the principal's mode of operation may result in the teacher approaching the principal with an alternative or two in the event that a refusal is anticipated. If, for example, the principal is strongly influenced by his teaching staff, a suggestion of an alternative that appears more controlled and thus less threatening to other teachers may be more palatable to him.

For instance, if you suggest that the class be individualized into three groups rather than on a strict individual basis, you will be given in part what you desire and the principal will be given less of a problem. You may focus on certain learning styles which the group has generally exhibited (i.e., analytical, impulsive, visual, verbal, manipulative, etc.). In each of these groups, different learning experiences can be conducted by media, students, and teachers.

Although this is a compromise compared to what you originally intended, it certainly is far better than to abort your idea completely.

Summary

We have looked at different areas of an educational organization. It is possible, as you have seen, to view such areas as systems where information is transacted between the teacher and other members of the organization.

When viewed as a system, these transactions assume a variety of patterns, yet each consists of a process that is common to all. Information of some form is being processed for possible storage and anticipated retrieval. The success of these transactions depends to a large extent on the need displayed by the behaviors of those involved.

Each system has its own array of strengths and weaknesses which reflect its primary needs and the function (i.e., storing or processing) that provide for these needs. Therefore, processing functions vary from one system to another in an effort to serve changing goals.

Although each area (i.e., teaching-learning, libraries, administration) displays a dynamic quality in their business dealings, there exists a noticeable pattern. This pattern will orient you to the transactions which occur of which you will be a part. A knowledge of such patterns provides you with certain insights that will add to your capabilities as a manager-teacher. As a decision maker who must reckon with the sometimes awesome task of facilitating the learning process, such insights are invaluable.

REFERENCES

Gagne, R. "Learning Theory, Educational Media, and Individualized Instruction." Paper presented 1967 at Seminar Educational Media, University of California.

Maslow, A. *Toward a Psychology of Being.* 2d ed. New York: Van Nostrand Reinhold Co., 1968.

Ofiesh, G. "University without Doors." Lecture presented March 1972 at University of North Carolina.

Chapter 11

Educational Climate

Introduction

Throughout our discussions, we have expressed a bias toward learner-based instruction. An emphasis on developing lessons to accommodate learner needs was strongly suggested. When one views this intent in contrast with other instructional approaches, it becomes apparent that a large challenge is presented by learner-based instruction. In this approach, the teacher assumes the role of both a generalist and a specialist. The teacher's success in this dual role is contingent on the nature of the climate within which instruction and learning are transacted.

In this chapter, we will explore some of the constraints prevalent within the educational organization that influence to a large degree the three areas of interaction we have been discussing (i.e., teacher-student interactions, teacher-librarian interactions, and teacher-administrator interactions).

If we view each of these areas as a system within which information is transacted, we will find that certain conditions must prevail for these interactions to be successful. For example, it would be extremely difficult for a teacher to conduct learner-based instruction without a scheduling system that would accommodate the flexibility inherent in this approach. It is also equally difficult for teachers using this approach to compose learning experiences when evaluative information includes descriptors that are of little value to the process being employed.

Logistical considerations are definite constraints when they are not recognized, and they can prevent the system from functioning properly. It is our intent to discuss with you the nature of these constraints. The process of providing learner-based instruction is a total experience—all facets of the school organization must be supportive. Although we will avoid a stringent analysis of all of the necessary inputs, we will give close attention to those conditions that are most critical to teacher-learner transactions.

The goal of this chapter is to make you aware of those conditions which are essential to the successful implementation of learner-based instruction. To achieve this goal, you are expected to accomplish the following objectives:

I.   Recognize conditions that are critical to transactions within classroom instruction, libraries, and the administration.

II. Indicate a relationship between the climatic conditions identified and the implementation of learner-based instruction.

A Dilemma: The How of What?

Textbook after textbook tells prospective teachers what they should do, but they often fail to tell the reader how to do it. The result is that only a very small percentage of good suggestions are ever implemented by teachers.

However, sooner or later, the prospective teacher leaves the textbook and enters into real-life situations. Therefore, it is to our advantage to pit new techniques against the conservatism of real-life situations.

When one looks at interactions as a system, the answer to the question of how to implement a program becomes a natural by-product that cannot be avoided. In concert with this practice is an equal emphasis on those constraints that may interfere with the implementation of an instructional design.

If, for instance, you look at the prospect of attending to the individual learning styles of students not only in terms of merit but also in terms of what functions are involved and how they may be accommodated, certain constraints will emerge. You cannot avoid this. The priorities of other teachers will be a concern. The bias of the principal will be considered. You will also give attention to the reactions of students and parents.

Determining these reactions before deciding to implement an innovation will help you prepare the best possible strategy for accomplishing your mission. Expressing a willingness to consider the *how* question at such an early stage necessitates that you be willing to compromise.

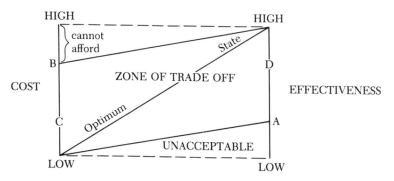

FIGURE 11–1   The above diagram describes a model for rational compromise (trade off) (Banathy, p. 73).

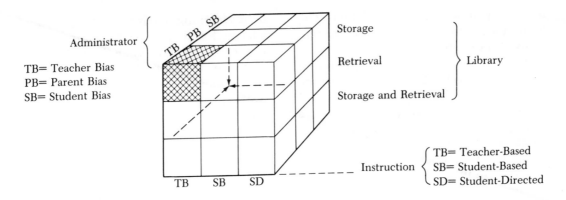

Administrator
TB= Teacher Bias
PB= Parent Bias
SB= Student Bias

Storage
Retrieval
Storage and Retrieval
} Library

Instruction {
TB= Teacher-Based
SB= Student-Based
SD= Student-Directed

TB   SB   SD

FIGURE 11–2   Each block of the cube depicts a different interaction of the three systems. The dark block shows a system which has a teacher-biased administration, a teacher-based instructional strategy, and a storage-oriented library. The arrows point to a hidden block that illustrates a system with a parent-biased administrator, a teacher-based instructional strategy, and a retrieval-oriented library.

This is not to suggest that giving in is a total experience but rather that a certain amount of give and take is necessary in all transactions.

Banathy suggests an approach to the problem of how much to compromise (see Figure 11–1). You will notice in Figure 11–1 that a conflict may exist between cost and effectiveness which necessitates a form of compromise. The optimum state occurs when a degree of compromise is expressed on both sides of the confrontation. There is, however, a point beyond which compromise is unwarranted; that is, it is either too expensive, or its low state of effectiveness makes it undesirable. Rational compromise may be a reciprocal expression at any point within the two extremes designated in the diagram as being below B or above A.

The successful implementation of an idea depends to a large extent on one's ability to perceive clearly the major interrelationships that exist within an organization. From the standpoint of a public school system, the three areas we discussed in the previous chapter each have different priorities. The attempt to implement an innovation in a school with a principal who is teacher-oriented, instruction that is predominantly teacher-based, and a library that is storage-oriented will render different results than the attempt to implement an innovation in a school where the principal is parent-oriented, the instruction is teacher-based, and the library is retrieval-oriented.

In Figure 11–2, we can see these interactions. The first combination previously suggested is represented by the hatched section of the cube. Thus, each block of the cube is a particular interacting combination of the three systems. The limitation strategies will vary with the patterns of interaction.

If you were to recognize the different biases associated with each of the combinations in the cube, you would realize that each block of interactions presents a different challenge. A knowledge of such information places you in an advantageous position when considering the implementation of an instructional innovation.

The approach of looking at interrelationships does not diminish the effort required to implement change. What it does do, however, is prepare the instructor to carry on the transactions better with others who will be affected by such a change and whose sanction is often the determining factor. From time to time, we have referred to the teacher as a decision maker; what we are now discussing is a tool that will help with the decision-making processes.

THE PRESENCE OF ALTERNATIVES

Most teachers desire to complete a teaching day in which successful transactions have occurred. Most teachers, however, complete a teaching day not knowing what, if anything, of value happened. Part of the reason for this is that many systems place an emphasis on teacher-content instruction. Another problem which interferes with a teacher's realization of what occurred is his uncertain perception of what role a teacher should play. Even in the decision to implement learner-based instruction, there exists some confusion as to how a teacher assumes the role of consultant, teacher, and manager. The option and opportunity to move in this direction does not necessarily answer all questions.

Instruction that is oriented toward student's learning needs suggests the role of a facilitator. If you have taught in another role or if you have been strongly conditioned in favor of the teacher assuming the dominant position in a classroom, you are confronted with the immediate problem of unlearning. For some, not being the center of attraction will be an unwilling compromise and for others, a most difficult one.

A teacher in this role must manage the learning experience in such a way that the student is assisted throughout the various stages of learning. This means that the relationship between teacher and student should be a harmonious one. This kind of relationship is dependent, in part, on the teacher's sensitivity toward a student's behavior and the climate in which it is conducted.

Ofiesh feels that designing learning climates is a responsibility of the teacher (Ofiesh). One has only to reflect on the plight of a student who is easily distracted to realize that in a large group situation such a person has a definite disadvantage which no amount of reproach will alter. The teacher who is sensitive to such needs will have in his grasp several possible configurations.

Variances in teaching and learning configurations are important. To assume that one particular configuration is ideal is to deny the many variables that make lessons unique. A large group of students is not a typical configuration that students will be likely to confront in real-life situations. Most of our communications with people are on a one-to-one basis. Yet, to restrict classrooms to this configuration will drastically reduce the amount of interaction that students may experience as members of large groups. Independent study with a teaching machine is completely unrealistic when considered from the standpoint of real-life experiences.

Some thought will reveal the strengths and weaknesses of each possible configuration; therefore, even here the factor of appropriateness is a consideration. The teacher who assumes the role of a communicator is constantly involved with decisions which include choosing the appropriate configuration of teacher and learner.

The nature of the teaching and learning system will determine to a large degree the transaction that occurs during the involvement of the learner. A student who is subjected to a teacher-based instructional system will spend a great percentage of time listening to the instructor. Those who adopt this approach consider the lesson's content to be the most important part of the learning situation.

On the other hand, if a learner-based instructional approach is used, the major factor will be the level of learning difficulty at which the instructional objective is presented. For example, if you present a lower level task to a group of young learners, it might be necessary to provide them with more rehearsal time than would be necessary for older children. Rehearsal time refers to the time that a student repeats a learning task. Also, this same circumstance might cause you to build more redundancy into the lesson which will add substantially to the learning experience. Redundancy refers to repeating certain parts of the lesson in a different manner or in other display possibilities.

The desire that the student be able to apply what he has learned requires that he be given the opportunity to do so. One of the reasons that programmed instruction is a desirable instructional technique is

that it demands an active response from each student. To some extent, the nature of the medium used to convey the instructional message plays a part in determining the kind and frequency of student involvement with a lesson. In contrast to programmed instruction, a film requires very little, if any, active overt responding from the learner. Other media (i.e., simulation games, slides) fall somewhere between these two extremes in terms of the amount of time the learner will spend involved with a particular lesson.

The type of terminal behavior change expected of the student also influences his amount of involvement. Affective changes may occur in the student over a period of time as a result of some very subtle strategies. The extent to which the learner is actively involved depends on the attitude to be expressed and the reason for expressing it. For instance, trying to alter the learner's attitude would differ considerably from the desire to have the student react to an attitude expressed by someone else. The former reaction could undoubtedly occur only after a period of time had passed while the latter reaction might be immediate.

Psychomotor behavior, in contrast with affective and cognitive behavior, demands the greatest amount of active responding. In order to learn a skill, the learner must be given an opportunity to apply the skill. Cognitive goals, on the other hand, may range from considerable involvement (analysis) to comparatively little involvement (recognition).

Although often overlooked, the desire to establish in the mind of the learner knowledge that will be retrievable at a later time is another factor of influence. To accomplish this task, the learner must become directly involved with the many intricate associations that establish the unique meaning of the concept. Activities that cause the learner to become directly involved will help him to retrieve the information at a later time. The transfer of knowledge from the initial learning experience to a future need happens in part because lessons have been designed to further this outcome.

The following list contains the five factors that influence the nature and length of activities in which the learner may become involved:

I. Teaching and Learning System

II. Level of Difficulty

III. Medium Selected

IV. Terminal Behavior Expectation

V. Type of Learning

As indicated by the preceding table, several factors determine the extent of the learner's involvement with the lesson. Activities, like other aspects of the learning experience, can be influenced by the teacher. Every facet of the learning experience should not be controlled in a rigid fashion; however, the teacher can be instrumental in bringing about desired outcomes. Activities, like other components of the learning experience, will vary in accord with the expectation of the learner. It is, therefore, reasonable to give some attention to the nature of both the student and the learning task when planning the extent of student involvement.

Learner-Based Instruction: A Format

The design of learning experiences is useless if the management of these events remains a mystery. Perhaps it would be

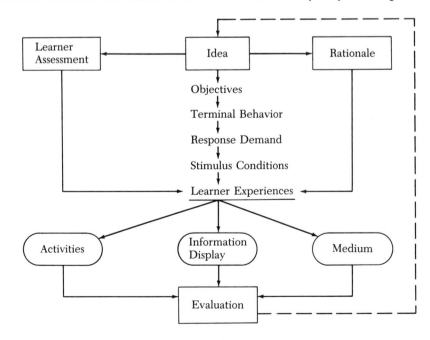

FIGURE 11–3

helpful if we considered the total process with a special emphasis on the transactions that occur which involve both learner and teacher. Figure 11–3 presents an outline of the steps involved and how they are interrelated.

The *idea* represents the meaning which the teacher attempts to communicate. In the broadest sense, the idea may be associated with all areas of human behavior (i.e., attitude, cognition, and psychomotor).

At the outset of preparing a lesson, it is important and desirable for the instructor to consider why the experience will be worthwhile to the learner. The teacher can better accomplish this task by assuming the role of the student. Explanations which serve as forerunners of the lesson should be attuned to the background of the target audience. The question to be answered is one which the student might ask and, therefore, the answer must be in terms that the student will understand. It is this answer that serves as the *rationale* for presenting the lesson at this time to this particular audience. In other words, the rationale simply addresses itself to the questions, Why bother presenting the lesson? and What value will it be to you, the intended learner?

When confronted with the task of communicating what you want the learner to do with the lesson, it is necessary to reduce ambiguity to a minimum. At this point, the linkage between what the student knows and how the student learns is established. After the terminal behaviors expected are linked to the levels of learning difficulty, how these behaviors are to be exhibited by the pupil becomes the teacher's next major concern.

It is here that the teacher demonstrates by his choice of words an awareness of the difference between behavior and response. I may want a student to identify the parts of a particular object or the elements of a particular set. Therefore, the test question must provoke the actual selection. Several demands can be made. For example, I might ask the student to draw a diagram of an object and label its parts, to label a diagram, or to select from a list of possibilities those elements which are correct. The learner may exhibit his knowledge by completing any one of these options, although one may be more suitable than the others. The latter response demand includes correct and incorrect labels; therefore, the student is required to select and reject information, thus showing his ability to discriminate. The goal is to make the responses correspond to the learning behaviors desired. Although they are different, objectives and test questions are closely related, and for the former to serve its function, the latter must be equivalent.

A host of stimulus options exist. Certain stimuli are more appropriate than others. Knowing which stimuli to choose for the elicitation of a particular response necessitates more than just casual involvement.

The design of learning experiences rests securely on attending to each of these milestones. The process, like a chain, is weakened by a neglect of any one particular link. The whole array of instructional technology is descriptive of methods and means for displaying different stimuli and response conditions. Therefore, prefacing a concern for these vehicles with an understanding of the stimulus and response options will assure that the appropriate medium is selected.

Many possibilities emerge when one considers the display format of a particular lesson. If the display is to be visual, many questions need to be answered. Is the visual to be graphic? Is it to be pictorial? If it is pictorial, will it be static or motion? Although the selection of a display format is often a matter of appeal, it can be the result of a logical transition from learning and communication considerations.

In the previous chapter, we discussed those factors which determine the *activities* you wish to provide for the learner, so we will not repeat them here. These transactions provide positive returns only after several trial runs. Achieving the skills which are essential to the design and management of learning experiences is a long range goal that may never be entirely achieved. However, such competence will not be forthcoming if we are not aware of the interactions involved.

All three components of the learning experience (i.e., activities, information displays, and media) are designed to fulfill two purposes. The more obvious of these is the satisfaction of the objectives for the lesson in terms of the terminal behaviors, the responses desired, and the stimuli selected. The experience includes a treatment of each objective—activities, display formats, and media are selected on the basis of what is considered appropriate.

Not so obvious is the fact that these components treat any discernible learner differences. For instance, if some students have indicated an ability to learn faster when they are given visual materials and others have shown an ability to learn better when directly involved with instruction, the teacher should provide both types of stimuli.

If attention is given to individual learning styles, each learning experience will be slightly different. In Figure 11–4, we imagine the lesson to consist of five objectives. Because we have separated the class into three groups of learning styles (i.e., A = visual, B = instructional involvement, C

Objectives	Individual Learning Styles	Learning Experiences
1–5	A	A_{1-5}
1–5	B	B_{1-5}
1–5	C	C_{1-5}

FIGURE 11–4 When the individual learning styles are considered, alternative learning experiences result.

= remainder of the class), three different learning experiences may convey the same lesson. Learning experiences A_{1-5} consist of treating all of the objectives with a special emphasis on accommodating a visual processing learning style. Learning experiences B_{1-5} consist of a treatment of all of the objectives with a special effort directed toward involving the learner. Learning experiences C_{1-5} include a treatment of the objectives in concert with the specified requirements.

At either end of the transactions that we have been discussing, an assessment is made of the learner's needs, and in the case of the posttest, an assessment is also made of the instructional approach (see Figure 11–3). Both pre- and postlesson procedures allow one to infer from the student's behavior the viability of the instructional strategies. The design and modification of instruction depend heavily on the effort expended to prepare this function.

If these transactions are to contribute to a fulfilling learning experience, all areas of the educational organization must work together. Administrator, librarian, and teacher can no longer go their separate ways. The teacher needs to obtain information and instructional materials from the librarian. The teacher needs to obtain sanction, support, and a logistical system from the administrator.

Library Support

The treatment of learning experiences can be described as a composition of activities, display formats, and mediating devices. The first component is related to the use of the student's time. How frequently and how long does the student interact with certain stimuli? The last two components refer to tangible materials or devices with which the student becomes involved.

Where are the necessary materials found? Are they something that the instructor created? Are they selections made from materials? Because of certain constraints, the teacher might compose the learning experience by using predesigned materials rather than by creating unique designs. The availability of these materials will determine to a large degree the extent to which the learning experience can be developed.

Our question concerns the source of these materials. The answer may reside with the traditional source of information, the library. Previously concerned only with printed materials, many libraries are slowly but definitely changing their images. To provide learner-based instruction effectively, you must have access to a library system that emphasizes retrieval. Materials must be available to both teacher and student.

When preparing learning experiences, two factors are critical to the decision-making process. The first is a need for information that will be helpful to the design of instructional strategies. It would appear that such information will only be forthcoming from a library that places a high priority on satisfying the needs of its consumers. This means that the library may have to accommodate requests that are often not made (e.g., the transport of a reference source or the transport of a medium normally used in the library center to the classroom).

The type of information needed depends on the priorities you attempt to satisfy when developing the instructional treatment. If you are able to gather from looking at a teacher's guide that accompanies a filmstrip the specific objectives that were covered, the levels of learning that were involved, the prerequisite concerns, and other common information, it will be much easier to make the decision to include or reject a particular medium.

There is much evaluative information available to teachers. However, some question exists regarding the value of this information. Certain organizations such as EPIE (Educational Product Information Exchange) are starting a most encouraging trend by investigating such evaluative information. This organization that has political sanction has managed to exert sufficient political pressure causing states to require producers to show some evidence of field testing exposure for the marketed product. If it is true that the major problems associated with instructional technology is software, then the solution lies in part with a concentrated effort focused on product evaluation.

Nothing is more convincing than an experience with success or failure. Minimizing error through field testing will enhance the persuasiveness of communications. It seems unreasonable to risk the efforts of the producer and the attitude of the user by avoiding this important step. Why do we find the majority of commercial manufacturers of programs apparently ignoring this factor?

Possibly, a large part of the problem is created by the existence of different priorities on the part of the commercial enterprise and the educational organization. Commercial enterprises seek to make a profit whereas educators seek to find an effective means for learning. The way to one goal may interfere with the accomplishment of the other. The producer views expediency, large consumer groups, and low investments as the road to success. If this is the case, one can see that producing materials quickly before your competition beats you to it might be an objective, or expanding the product over a large age group may be attempted with little thought given to learning difficulty; the delay and expense caused by field testing would be undesirable. From the standpoint of business, these practices are not unreasonable.

Perhaps, a member of the educational organization can do something constructive toward reaching a desirable end product that is in concert with instructional priorities. The librarian in the role of the manager of a storage and retrieval information system can do more than any other member of the educational organization to influence the availability of instructional materials.

You might disagree with the choice and suggest that the teacher can be more of an influence on instructional materials. It is true that the teacher and the student are the recipients of such products; however, the responsibility of competency with the subject area and the demands of learner-based instruction leave the teacher little room for other tasks. Since the librarian is

already expending effort in this direction, he is the likely candidate.

Let us assume that the EPIE influence causes a desired change in the effectiveness of certain products which facilitate the learning styles of a particular group of students. We might look with some interest at this product as a possible choice for a particular lesson. Yet, the design and development of learning experiences require more information than the results of field testing. If you will recall, we are concerned with the design and development of activities and display formats and the appropriate use of mediating devices. Therefore, we need information that will enable us to accomplish these tasks.

In Figure 11–5, the information needed about instructional materials is composed into categories. A completed product description enables the teacher to decide its appropriateness for a particular lesson. Each of the seven categories includes information that will assist the teacher; some of this information is general while certain categories include information more pertinent to learning.

Let us briefly explore the identity of each category in Figure 11–5. Incidentally, the arrangement of the chart is arbitrary. *Entry level* refers to information that will influence the student's performance with a particular lesson. The teacher and the student need to know if the product in question has any particular prerequisite requirements. It might be something as obvious as being able to operate the device which conveys the content. Perhaps the content of the product is based on the assumption that the learner possesses a certain amount of knowledge which is relevant to the lesson. Also, it is possible that certain learning styles are being accommodated inadvertently or deliberately. It is important to know whether the producer has allowed for the possibility that some students may have a command of the lesson.

Identification refers to any information that attempts to communicate the nature of the instructional materials content. You may be surprised by the inclusion of objectives in this category. If you will recall, our emphasis was to suggest their function to be one of communication. Because this can best be done with behavioral expressions, the learner is associated with content in terms of expected behavior change. Nevertheless, until objectives are linked to the levels of learning, they do nothing more than alert the learner to the intent of the lesson.

Design refers to the format in which the lesson is presented. In contrast to stimulus conditions, the concern here is with the particular display. The stimulus, for example, may be visual, but its format is a transparency with overlays; and the mediating device which conveys this format is an overhead projector.

Logistics is the term we have selected to label those items that have some association with the production or the use of the product. Thus, file code concerns the procedure of locating the item and is relevant to the utilization of this product to the lesson being designed.

Characteristics refer to the physical dimensions of the product. A filmstrip, for example, is a certain size; it has a certain number of frames; it may be in color or black and white; and it has subtitles or an accompanying sound tape.

Learning information alludes to information that is pertinent to the learning process. If the product requires no display of learning beyond recognition from the student and yet the producer specified

that the learner would be able to apply the information, there would be sufficient discrepancy to justify rejecting the product as a possible choice. What the learner is expected to do and the extent to which he will do this is information that is recorded under this category.

Evaluation is the category that reports any evidence of field testing or information that suggests some attempt was made to assess the value of the product. Also, the presence or absence of a posttest experience will be expressed in this category. Any information pertaining to the product that will be meaningful to the design and development of the evaluation section of the learning experience is placed in this category.

If a product lacks certain information, you should work to generate the missing data. If objectives are not specified, it is possible to generate objectives by working in reverse from the test questions that are usually available.

If a producer fails to supply information, his product may be in a questionable position as far as effective use is concerned. Perhaps this new posture will stimulate producers to provide information. The consequence of associating an instructional product with the design of learning experiences will bring more roles into the area. Librarians will require certain skills that they presently do not need, and producers will need to be more conscious of the educator's priorities. It would seem that broadening this sphere of involvement is in concert with the professed goal of greater cooperation between departments within the educational organization.

We can imagine the library providing teachers and students with the information listed under the categories in Figure

INSTRUCTIONAL MATERIALS
DESCRIPTIVE INFORMATION CHECKLIST

Date Produced _____

Title_____
Medium_____

ENTRY LEVEL ASSESSMENT	IDENTIFICATION	LOGISTICS	CHARACTERISTICS	DESIGN	LEARNING	EVALUATION
1. Prerequisite Requirements ( )	Clearly Stated Objectives ( )	Location ( )	Physical Dimensions ( )	Display Formats ( )	Levels ( )	Field Testing ( )
2. Pretest ( )	Title ( )	File Code ( )	Mode ( )	Mediating Devices ( )	Response Type ( )	Posttest ( )
3. Learning Styles ( )	Subject ( )	Producer ( )	Medium ( )		Stimulus Conditions ( )	Developmental Testing ( )
4. Grade Level ( )		Date of Production ( ) Distributor ( )			Learner Interaction ( )	

If an item is checked, that information is available for the instructional material.

FIGURE 11–5 **This checklist will indicate the availability of information that is important to the development of learning experiences.**

11–5. The librarian will peruse instructional materials for this information. The information which is not available will be sought from the producer. If data cannot be secured from either of these methods, the librarian will attempt to generate information.

Teachers who have this information will be better equipped to design and develop experiences for learners. Given this information, the notion of accommodating learning differences among students becomes feasible.

The librarian in this new role becomes an integral part of the design process sharing a partnership with the instructor. In this capacity, one would expect to find the librarian directly involved. The usual role of managing the storage and retrieval process must be extended to include the assimilation of relevant data if the involvement role is to be most effective.

Solutions to problems sometimes carry an ample supply of their own problems; and if one is not careful when recommending change, the suggested resolution may be a greater problem than the weakness it attempts to cure. The recommendation we have just made is no exception

for when we talk about information, we are referring to products. This information needs to be housed if it is to be made available.

A major constraint of most libraries is a limited storage capacity. A few years ago this constraint was without an alternative. However, with the advent of computer technology, this is no longer the case. We now have the means for storing and retrieving large amounts of information. Although the means exist, most schools do not have the technology; and if the technology is available, it is used primarily for clerical reasons.

It is not overly futuristic to imagine the use of computers for the purpose of extending the management capability of the librarian beyond his present limitations. The information so desperately needed by teachers for the purposes of designing learning experiences can be provided more quickly and with greater detail.

How can this be accomplished? The answer to this question requires that you clearly understand the integral parts of the computer operation. If you will look at Figure 11–6, you will notice that a terminal is associated with the input function of

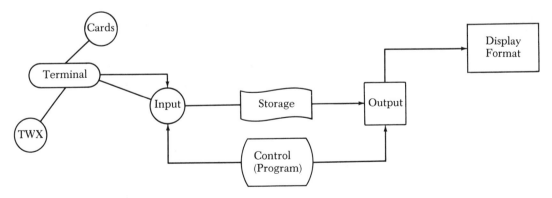

FIGURE 11–6 Information which enters the computer is stored, manipulated, and retrieved.

the total process. Information may be put into the computer with an IBM card format by using a teletypewriter (TWX). This data may be stored in the computer or in a portable storage format such as a disc or tape which is placed in the computer when you wish to retrieve the information. For our particular concern with the library function, we can file the evaluation information expressed in Figure 11–5 in the computer.

When one interacts with a computer which has been programmed to use the data in these files, the desired information can be retrieved in one of several display formats. The result may be a hard copy typewritten by a TWX machine, a video format through a television monitor, or a punch type produced by the TWX machine. Usually, the punch tape is an option that may or may not accompany the hard copy.

Imagine that you are one of several teachers in a public high school in a rather large district. In this district, there are thirteen schools (two high schools, two junior high schools, and nine elementary schools). You are presently involved with the preparation of a lesson—naturally, along the lines of learner-based instruction. Not having the inclination, time, or the necessary skills to design unique instructional materials, you go to the librarian for assistance.

In this situation, you are blessed with a retrieval-oriented library system and the technology to help you with your particular need. The response to your request for information directs you to a TWX terminal located in the library. Although the computer is several miles away, the terminal via telephone lines can activate it almost instantly. Located next to the terminal is a manual that includes a list of subject areas filed in the computer and a code for retrieving the information desired.

A library assistant feeds an array of numbers or words into the terminal which will direct the computer to render the information you want. The information is displayed on a hard copy that identifies the materials for the topic; the hard copy also lists which of the thirteen libraries has the material that you want (see Figure 11–7).

Whether by using a computer or by applying a manual means of providing descriptive and evaluative information, the librarian can provide a valuable service to teachers involved with designing lessons for learner-based instruction. Without such assistance, it is doubtful that many teachers will be able to or want to manage this approach.

We have emphasized the addition of information, but little discussion centers on the subtraction of information. And yet, if this function does not occur, it is impossible to accommodate the knowledge explosion. A criterion for removal is needed to prevent materials that should remain in the library from being removed. Two problems face the librarian. One is the tendency to keep obsolete materials which take up much needed space, and the other is the tendency to remove materials that should be retained.

Although we offer no immediate solution to this dilemma, evaluation information may help this decision-making process. Materials from which this information cannot be secured may be considered of questionable instructional value. These materials could be relegated to a lower priority status; and when the time arrives to make decisions about which materials to discard, these items would be the first to go. This strategy refers mainly to nonprint materials which create more of a space problem.

HHAALLFF
SITE 2- FOR ASSISTANCE PLEASE CALL 716-854-0242.
USER NUMBER- -N50944

PASSWORD-CESNOW

***ON AT 15:09.

SYSTEM- -FOR
EW OR OLD- -NEW OR OLD
OLD PROBLEM NAME- -SCHOOL

READY.

RUN

HOW MANY CONTENT CODES ARE YOU INPUTTING
EG: 300   ENTER 1
     310,613   ENTER 2
     310,613,973 ENTER 3
  ? 1
INPUT THE 1 CODES
- -

PORTRAIT FRESHMN CONGRSMN   ID- KT269   8 9

KITS-FILMSTRIP DISC   YEAR 69

LEVELS   CONTENT CODE
1 - JUNIOR HIGH SCHOOL   973-320- 0
2 - SENIOR HIGH SCHOOL
3 - ADULT EDUCATION

LOCATIONS
CICERO HIGH SCHOOL
- -

EMERGNCE U.S. WORLD POWER   ID- KT269   9 9

KITS-FILMSTRIP DISC   YEAR 69

LEVELS   CONTENT CODE
1 - JUNIOR HIGH SCHOOL   973- 0- 0
2 - SENIOR HIGH SCHOOL
3 - ADULT EDUCATION

LOCATIONS
CICERO HIGH SCHOOL

**FIGURE 11-7 A computer printout results from typing an
array of no more than nine digits.**

Objectives for course programs will help to resolve the problem of storing print and nonprint instructional materials. Those items which do not contribute to the achievement of objectives can be dis-carded or omitted from the collection. For example, there is presently a research battle over the value of pictures to reading comprehension. If empirical assessment should reject pictures that cause distractions due to a visual emphasis on irrelevant information, materials which contain such visuals can be classified with a low priority label.

This problem of storage limitations is a serious one and requires the attention of both librarians and teachers. Perhaps, the capability of computer technology holds the answer. Microfiche, of course, lends itself to the storage of information, and this along with other formats may offer some answers (see chapter 7).

Administrative Support

What kind of support can you, a teacher, expect from an administrator? You should be able to expect the administrator to give full support to any idea that may prove beneficial to students; however, as we noted previously, the bias of the administrator is often the determining factor. What you can expect from an administrator is a question of whether your need is perceived by him to be a high priority. Let us assume that the administrator is biased toward the learning and instructional needs. What can you expect from him in the way of support for affecting change in this direction?

First, regardless of his bias, the circumstances of his role demand that he give a fair amount of attention to other concerns. Therefore, the administrative time is divided in several directions to the extent that instruction may be compromised on occasion. For example, the physical plant requires considerable attention, and it is this tangible entity that parents and others with an invested interest see and understand.

The administrator, often the interpreter for the instructional process and the defender of instructional practices, may have learned the value of caution, conservatism, and compromise. Although these restraining factors may impede the wheels of progress, the initial learner bias, if present, will win out.

One very sensitive area that is worthy of your attention is the schedule. As a part of the administrative domain, the schedule can be as flexible as an administrator wishes it to be. The traditional lock step schedule in which students enter and leave class each day at the same time may force you to compromise much that is desired. Modular scheduling is one logistical strategy that attempts to accommodate new instructional configurations. This system of programming divides the school day into twenty-minute time modules. Each student is scheduled for group involvement in large, medium, or small configurations for 50 percent of his day, and he indulges in independent work for the other 50 percent of the day.

This scheduling system has worked in conjunction with other facets of learner-based instruction. Unfortunately, modular scheduling is often tried alone as a preparatory step to the end of achieving learner-based instruction; when the system is not combined with learner-based instruction, it seldom works. Not being trained to provide this type of instructional treatment has the student and teacher in a quandary as to how to manage the time.

If it is included as part of a total effort to provide learner-based instruction, modular scheduling can be helpful. Students can experience a wide range of instructional offerings, and teachers can pursue diagnostic and prescriptive ends without being interrupted by a ringing bell.

You should also be alert to how the power of technology may work against your best efforts. The preparation of information for the computer is a tedious process; and once the administrator has finally arrived at the point of routine for processing the original schedule, there may be some reluctance to risk involvement with a new one—especially if the new one is complex (e.g., CAI).

Few will argue with the notion that administrators strive to make their particular school the best. The consequence of this attitude provokes change and sometimes an exaggerated offering. An example of this condition is manifested when efforts are made to transplant success experiences from one school district to another. Often, no more than a few, brief orientation sessions precede the adoption of an innovation; such actions result in untrained personnel managing what they do not understand.

The success of the new practice in its previous setting may be and often is a combination of factors, some of which cannot be transplanted with the idea. If you should find yourself faced with this dilemma, be most critical of the conditions that prevail in the context from which the idea was borrowed. It may be that the idea is doomed from the start in your school because it lacks an important element peculiar to its previous setting. It may be that considerable training is necessary because the innovative technique demands a respecification of the present role. Your awareness of these possibilities will help you to manage your particular assignment better.

Summary

The message in this chapter attempts to acknowledge the value of extending our realm of interest and influence to other areas of the school organization besides the classroom. The teacher, librarian, and administrator each play key roles in the scheme of providing learner-based instruction. The climate in an educational institution is by nature transactional. For example, the outcome of the interactions that occur between teacher and administrator dictate the extent to which the learning needs of students are satisfied. Therefore, as a teacher, you will find that an understanding of the interpersonal dynamics that prevail in your school setting will help you reap the best for you and your students. The climate is no less political in schools than it is in other organizations, and the network of communications is no less important. If you realize that there exists a system of inputs and outputs from which many alternatives emerge, your professional situation will be much more tolerable.

REFERENCES

Banathy, B. H. *Instructional Systems.* Palo Alto, Calif.: Fearon Publishers, 1968.

Bidwell, C. M. *Coding Standards for Computerized Cataloging and Scheduling of Educational Media.* Syracuse, N.Y.: Center for Instructional Communications, 1967.

EPIE (Educational Products Information Exchange). "Educational Product Report." 463 West Street, New York, New York 10014.

Knirk, F. G. and Childs, J. W. *Instructional Technology, A Book of Readings.* New York: Holt, Rinehart & Winston, 1968.

Ofiesh, G. "University without Doors." Lecture presented March 1972 at University of North Carolina.

Chapter 12

Instructional Communicator

Introduction

Although it may be defensible and desirable to design unique materials for learning, it may not be possible in your school. The situation you are working in may not have the support areas that we have cited as being essential. Yet, our responsibility to provide learner-based instruction is inescapable if we are to prepare students to cope with the complexities of adult life. The trauma of Toffler's *Future Shock* may be partially avoided by our efforts to accommodate learning differences. However, the notion that a teacher can be all things to her students does boggle the mind a bit.

Altering our perceptions of media to include its function as a management tool will help. When we can be comfortable with the notion that materials and devices teach, we will be released from the constraints that are evident with teacher-group transactions. Such liberation will al-low us to assume a management role that will focus on the requirements of learning from which will emerge the blueprints for instruction.

In many schools where attempts are made to implement some form of learner-based instruction, it has become necessary to create a new faculty role. The role does not have a universal title. Because efforts to change incur resistance, it may take some time before the position is stabilized. In this text, we will call the person in this role the director of instructional communications or an instructional communicator.

The history of this new role is well documented by most textbooks that deal with the audiovisual concept. Since this concept is becoming more entrenched in the technical aspects of media, it is gradually experiencing a noticeable change. Since Edgar Dale's "Cone of Experience," there has been an assortment of interpretations on the role of the instructional communicator. What has evolved over this period of time are two distinct points of view. In one camp, the audiovisual specialist aligns himself closely with technology and approaches instructional concerns from a media bias. In contrast, the instructional communicator sees instruction as a communication process with a special emphasis on the selection of the appropriate medium for doing the job. It is the latter role that we will consider in this chapter. How the director of instructional communications functions to provide teachers with the assistance they need to accommodate learning needs will be the focus of our attention.

The goal of this chapter is to reveal the contributions that a director of instructional communications can make to the design and composition of learning experiences. When you finish this chapter, you should be able to accomplish the following objectives:

I. Identify the role of the director of communications.

II. Compare the director of communications role with the administrative and teaching roles.

III. Reveal possible constraints to the effectiveness of this role.

The Third Person

Each of the roles that composes the hierarchy of an educational institution has a major contribution to make toward the student's education. The administrator by necessity must concentrate on the operational functions of the institution; therefore, he is often forced to discount the teaching and learning process. The logistics of keeping everyone in the organization satisfied is a monumental task which is rapidly growing to gargantuan proportions.

More and more, teachers have been pulled into administrative duties beyond the classroom. Because the teacher is expected to survey the ever-changing body of knowledge, he has little time to translate theory into practical concerns.

Unless drastic changes occur which will provide teachers with a climate that is conducive to change, schools will adopt only that position which it can manage. For some, this will be modular scheduling and little more; for others, it may be mini-courses and nothing more.

Unless someone like a director of communications champions the cause of effective communications, instruction will remain virtually unchanged. The school needs someone that perceives teaching and learning as a communication process, that looks at learning in terms of its unique requirements, and who sees the relationship with others in the institution as reciprocal.

Equipped with competencies in instructional design, systematic decision-making tools, a command of learning theory, and the ability to communicate, the instructional communicator is an expert in process and a generalist in content. Unlike others on the educational team, the director of instructional communications has an opportunity to consider the issue of educational change without diluting effectiveness in other areas. For example, as a member of a committee of educators concerned with the issue of curriculum change, the instructional communicator can view the situation more objectively than the administrator or teacher.

The administrator, for instance, will be

concerned with the constraints imposed by the institution and others as well as logistical considerations. The teacher will most likely express concern for the content or knowledge factor or the proposed curriculum change. Both of these roles will consider the process to some extent; however, the instructional communicator is in an advantageous position to offer a more in-depth point of view.

The role of the librarian, as we mentioned in a previous chapter, has been altered to include the management of the storage and retrieval of nonprint materials. Already faced with the consequences of a knowledge explosion, the librarian has more to accomplish than time permits. Faced with a facility that often cannot house both print and nonprint materials, the librarian has a next to impossible charge.

The director of instructional communications can provide the school with an important service in this area. In some schools, the job of storing nonprint materials is shared by the librarian and the instructional communicator. In other schools, the instructional communicator assumes full responsibility for the storage and retrieval of nonprint materials. The nature of the school and of the persons involved will dictate the course to be followed.

Probably the most important role that the instructional communicator can provide teachers is with respect to classroom teaching and learning. The design of unique learning experiences can be managed through a team approach which results from the alliance of content specialist (teacher) and generalist (instructional communicator). Certainly, the expectations of desired results are higher with such a division of responsibility, and

it is reasonable to expect better results when several competencies operate as one. In Figure 12–1, we see a conceptualization of how a support service might interact with other areas of the school organization.

Candidates for a degree in this field may earn a master's degree or, depending on the university, a doctoral degree. Although most candidates in this field have a background in some phase of education, it is not essential; and we find people with diverse backgrounds in the field.

A typical program offering a master's degree provides experiences in the following areas: eighteen hours in education, six hours in radio, television and motion picture production, and six hours of electives. The eighteen hours in education may include instructional design, systems management, learning and communication theory, and curriculum development. Some programs also include courses in library science—this is regulated to a large extent by the bias expressed within a particular state.

Many states are now certifying this position; and in some cases, the certification is at the administrative level. Consequently, the number of hours required to be certified at the administrative level is greater than those listed in the preceding example. The program is usually operated on a cooperative basis between the state education department and the university.

It is apparent that the role of the instructional communicator is viewed as an administrative position. This attitude is reinforced by the step many community colleges have taken to provide a two year program of study that will provide a media technician. These two roles can be distinguished in the following way. The instructional communicator provides the institu-

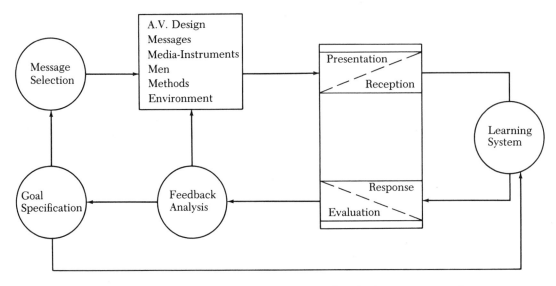

FIGURE 12-1   Relationship between the design system and other components of the educational process (Ely, p. 25).

tion with the competencies which are necessary for planning learner-based instruction. The rendering of the design is accomplished by the media technician. If the school does not have a media technician, students working with the instructional communicator can do the job or the instructional communicator can perform both the planning and rendering function. Obviously, there is considerable advantage to the first option because the planning phase is the most crucial and frequently the more time consuming.

From the standpoint of affecting curriculum change, an instructional communicator at the administrative level can wield much influence. Insofar as change is the result of political transactions, this is an important consideration. Having an instructional communicator in an administrative role whose bias is to reduce ambiguity will provide some assurance that issues are clearly communicated.

For those of you who aspire to become an instructional communicator, knowing the constraints that you may face has some measure of value. Because you will perceive education as a communication process, your perceptions of teaching and learning may differ measurably from those practiced at the school where you are employed. One of the biggest mistakes made by people in this position is to impose their convictions on others. It is imperative that you keep the channel of communications open between other faculty members and yourself; therefore, at times, it will be necessary for you to compromise what appears to be an effective technique.

If we accept Skinnerian psychology, we will meet people where they are. Providing them with satisfaction will do much to preserve the communication linkage. Gradually, through reciprocal transactions, a reasonable compromise will emerge from which the change desired is nurtured. Responding quickly with a solution to a repair problem or with materials when needed may pave the way for future collaboration on more substantiative issues.

You are not the expert in any particular classroom subject area; therefore, your receptivity to the input from teachers is essential to success. The giving is equal on both sides of the team effort; however, the teacher and his students must live with the consequences of the decisions. Therefore, the compromise should always be in the direction of the teacher's perceptions.

Facility and Service

One of the major expectations of the educational media department is service; therefore, the facility housing media, materials, and production activities should be easily accessible to teachers and students. Locating the department at a point where teachers pass during the day may stimulate usage that was not otherwise intended.

Many of the schools which have been built in the last ten years have combined the educational media facility with the library under the label of learning center. This association has proven to be desirable from several points of view. Both of these areas serve teachers and students; therefore, the alliance is a natural one. Each area is frequented by both teachers and students who seek some form of help. Some sharing of responsibilities which may maximize the output beyond which each area can individually provide is possible with this configuration.

As long as print and nonprint materials are placed in libraries, the traditional facilities will not suffice. More storage and storage of a different nature is required. One cannot sign out a film with the same procedures that one uses to sign out a book. Previewing a film requires considerably more than the presence of the film. Thus, unless the addition of this new responsibility is to have a debilitating effect on the storage and retrieval functions of the library, a major change in administrating this area is necessary. The collaboration of the educational media center with the library is one solution to this problem.

One of the major functions of this area is to provide teachers and students with easy access to all types of instructional materials. In some schools, the classification procedures used for films, tapes, and records are those systems used for book materials. Films, tapes, records, and materials that require the use of a device are often found in an area of the facility provided for this purpose.

In some schools there are study carrels in the library. Wet carrels will accommodate electrical equipment as well as learning materials, thereby affording the opportunity for independent learning experiences. Equipment such as small cassette tape recorders and 8 mm cartridge projectors physically lend themselves to carrel use. Some of the more sophisticated carrels have a video screen for television programming which is equipped with a dial access system so that students can request programs they need.

Although such centers house a large assortment of instructional materials and mediating devices, there is a paucity of good learning programs. We have to catch up with technology; but because of the mystic of technology, a considerable amount of money is allocated in this direction each year, and much of it remains idle. It is partially for this reason that an emphasis on how to use media is gradually shifting to the selection of appropriate media. Placing the stress on appropriateness will automatically focus attention on the worth of the instruction designed for such media.

One remedy for this problem is to produce unique instructional materials for teachers in a particular school. The production may result from team effort between the teacher and the instructional communicator, or it may result from a request to the instructional communicator who subsequently reacts to achieve the objective submitted. Production may also involve students directly with the design of instruction. In certain schools, it is a media technician who renders the instructional design.

Many learning experiences result from using materials produced by others. Often, a material by itself is not effective, but it may be effective when used in combination with another material. The teacher and the instructional communicator can work together to integrate diverse materials into one effective learning experience.

In addition to producing materials and planning learning experiences, the instructional communicator also provides training experiences. Many of the formats require a device to convey the information. Each device has its own idiosyncrasies which the user must be aware of. Therefore, a training program ranging from group to individual instruction is conducted for both teachers and students. Procedures for operating equipment as well as certain basic information is presented. The extent to which this type of program is carried out depends, among other factors, on the commitment of the school to the use of technology.

In some facilities, the distribution of in-structional materials and equipment composes the largest portion of their activity. In many schools, an instructional materials center handles the distribution. Functioning like a library, its primary goal is to provide teachers and students with learning materials which may be print (e.g., programmed instruction) or nonprint (e.g., simulation game).

Often, a teacher will want to preview a portion of the instructional items before deciding on their use. An area where such materials can be perused is helpful. Providing evaluation information to accompany materials has become, with the heavy emphasis on instructional technology, increasingly important.

Team Approach

Perhaps the best way to view the functions of the team effort between teacher and instructional communicator will be to consider an example. To accomplish this, we will imagine a situation where we consider you as the instructional communicator. Using one of the learning packages located in the appendix (i.e., "How Many?" by Jackie Radford), we will look at the interactions that might occur between teacher and designer.

The lesson is concerned with the concept of how many, and you are working with Miss Jackie Radford, a special education teacher. The class consists of educable mentally retarded students that range in age from seven to twelve years. The students have proven in a previous lesson their ability to count with whole numbers from zero to ten.

You might ask why Miss Radford felt that it was necessary to solicit your assistance for this lesson. The reasons for such action are varied and less important than the realization that such a request will not occur until the teacher has respect for your ability. This respect does not emanate as a natural condition from the position you hold but rather from the way you manage this position.

Undoubtedly, Miss Radford has experienced some difficulty on previous occasions with presenting the concept, and perhaps a casual reference to a need for some materials in this area initiated her discussion. On the other hand, you may have provided another teacher with some satisfying consultation regarding another lesson, and this was communicated to Miss Radford. Whatever the reason, your first target will be to understand clearly the instructional problem: what is meant by the expression "how many." You are told that the phrase refers to quantity which involves sequencing numbers in a particular order and abstracting a number when given a group of items. You are also told that it is a difficult concept for the students to grasp and that it is fundamental to the use of numbers. In the course of further discussion, you also discover that an understanding of equal, more, and less are included in this lesson. You are told, in an effort to reinforce the importance of this lesson, that a young girl who is learning how to make a cake needs to understand her mother's instruction that the recipe requires two eggs and that a boy needs to understand his father who tells him that the number of fish he caught was three more than the number of fish his buddy caught. Without an understanding of the concept "how many," these students would have a difficult time understanding everyday dialogue.

From just this basic exchange, you have acquired some very relevant information that is important to the design of the lesson. You have learned at least three things. You know what Miss Radford means by the phrase "how many." You know why she feels that it is important for her students to understand this concept. Also, you know that the reasons for understanding this lesson can be communicated to her students by citing incidents which are consonant with their backgrounds. This latter point is not always possible; yet, if we cannot show students how they will be able to use the knowledge, they may consider it unimportant.

At this point, you could verbalize the goal of this lesson to be that these students not only understand the lesson but also that they be able to apply its principles. However, at this point, you do not know how to accomplish this goal. That is, how Miss Radford intends to achieve this goal is still unknown.

The most obvious solution to this problem is to ask Miss Radford what her objectives are, but this solution may be impractical. At this juncture, you need to consider the nature of the person with whom you are collaborating because for some the request for specific learner objectives may be intimidating. To skip this step, however, hoping that it will somehow mysteriously appear in the course of further interaction, would be a mistake.

Assume that the preceding situation occurs with Miss Radford. What can you do to resolve the problem? If you said to ask her for an old test of this lesson, we agree. Although the test may be in need of considerable revision, it does delineate exactly what is expected of the students. From the specific responses requested on the test, you can work backwards to the objectives intended. The importance of this information to the design of this lesson is crucial if guessing is to be minimized.

If you look at the completed learning package, you will see how it is possible to infer the following objectives from the test questions:

I.   Be able to demonstrate an understanding of the numbered sequence 0–10.

II. Be able to indicate the number that represents any number of items up to ten.

III. Be able to form the correct group of items when given a particular number from 0–10.

IV. Be able to identify equal and unequal relationships between groups of elements.

After you have agreed on the objectives and decide that the behaviors expressed are specific enough, you have identified the targets for the intended design. However, you have not considered the level of difficulty for each target. One approach to this problem is to apply Bloom's taxonomy of cognitive behavior. It is not necessary for you to refer specifically to the tool, unless of course the particular circumstance dictates otherwise. You can simply assign a level value to each of the five objectives; these levels can serve as a reference for design considerations. This information may or may not be shared with the teacher. An appropriate assignment of these difficulties is indicated below:

I.   Objective One—Level Two (Comprehension)

II. Objective Two—Level Three (Application)

III. Objective Three—Level Three (Application)

IV. Objective Four—Level Three (Application)

To perform objective one, the student must be able to express his understanding of the concept. This suggests that the student must be able to show some form of comprehension.

To perform objectives three and four, students must be able to apply their understanding of objective one as a necessary prerequisite. A knowledge of the levels of learning difficulty will alert you to the different requirements demanded by each level.

At this point, you may wish to analyze the test questions from which you formulated the objectives. You should attempt to determine whether the test questions require the student to exhibit the appropriate responses for the learning behavior. Often, test questions fall down in this area by requiring that students give verbal responses only. This type of response would be unsatisfactory for objectives two and three which stipulate that items be used. A verbal representation of an item and the actual item are different stimuli, and you cannot assume that the learning performance will be the same for each. Also, because objectives three and four are at the application level, the student should be expected to perform the response at some time during the evaluation experience. A look at this learning package will reveal the need for students to evoke both kinds of responses.

The major input that you will contribute to the preparation of this lesson will be to keep the requirements that emerge from the interactions between you and the teacher to the forefront. The test instrument does not need to be a written experience—it reflects in its design whatever the objectives and their levels of difficulty dictate. Establishing the proper balance between these two events is important to the subsequent design process and, therefore, cannot be delayed.

You may recommend that the teacher give the finished test to students before the learning experience as well as after it. However, a pretest experience may be considered unwise with a group of mentally retarded children. This decision does not negate the effectiveness of a particular design; it simply prevents the teacher from inferring that all of the learning occurred as a result of the lesson. In any case, it will be up to the teacher to decide if he is going to give a pretest.

You are now ready to consider the design and composition of the learning experiences that are appropriate for this lesson. The difficulty that the students previously had with the lesson might have been the result of how it was communicated. A failure to acknowledge the different ways in which students learn may cause the use of inappropriate information displays and media selections.

With educable mentally retarded children, how they learn may be more important than what they learn. After considerable discussion about the past performances of her class, you decide that three different learning styles are evident in the group. Certain students seem to do better when given visual stimuli whereas others do better when assisted by an auditory means; others do better when given a tactile experience.

If you will look at the learning package to which we are referring, you will note that a variety of experiences have been provided to accommodate the specifications of the objectives as well as alternative experiences to accommodate the three learning styles. From previous discussions, you may recall that all of the objectives are treated in each alternative; therefore, a student may be exposed to only one alternative and succeed with the lesson. The advantage that Miss Radford has now that she did not have before is that a learning experience has been systematically planned for those students who might have experienced some difficulty. If the alternative learning experience fits the learning style of the student, the chances are better that success with the lesson will be experienced.

The value of approaching an instructional problem as a team is that while one member is focusing on what information is to be communicated, the other concentrates on how it can best be communicated. Armed with an in-depth knowledge of the subject, an understanding of the learning process, a model for effective communications, and a knowledge of the limitation of information displays and media options, the team applies the most appropriate strategy.

An appraisal of the learning package reveals the materials and media used to be rather simple. The experiences, however, are carefully matched to the requirement. Nothing is used that would appear beyond the management ability of an educable mentally retarded student. A high percentage of the information displayed is visual and heavily cued with mnemonics. There is even a simple programming effort designed for objective four which serves to select the attention of the student to the information.

You will notice that the treatment consists of both unique displays and materials that have been designed by others. Remember that the instructional treatment may consist of unique materials, materials designed by others, or a combination of these. Also, you will notice that unique experiences are not designed for each alternative (see objectives four and five). It is only necessary to design new experiences for a learning style when the efforts to accommodate an objective use an approach which is not in concert with a particular style of learning.

This particular package was selected as an exemplar for our discussion because it exhibits careful attention to the association of appropriate means for the ends specified. It is this matching rather than the use of sophisticated devices that makes a learning experience successful.

You will find a greater amount of sophistication among some of the other examples located in the appendix. It is not with a knowledge of media that the instructional communicator makes his greatest contribution but rather with a knowledge of systematic design. If the latter predominates, the former concern will fall into the appropriate place.

You may find it helpful to peruse the learning packages that are located in the appendix. They were selected because of the cross section of teaching areas covered as well as for their particular treatments. You will see many of the priorities which have been discussed in this book exhibited in them. They are unique for a particular instructional topic and learner characteristics—beyond this, generalizations should not be made.

Instructional design as a concept is less understood than the phrase, audiovisual instruction. It should not surprise you to find that the expectations of your services will be more along audiovisual lines. Accepting the challenge that accompanies this position means knowing when to compromise and when to affect change.

Summary

The director of communications assumes a role which functions in both an administrative and consultative capacity. As a manager of the educational media center, the instructional communicator in concert with the librarian can provide information and resource materials. The instructional communicator can provide training experiences to faculty and students in both production techniques and media operation. In the capacity of consultant, the instructional communicator can provide assistance to teachers for the design and composition of learning experiences. As a team, the instructional communicator and teacher can approach instructional design with a system worthy of the complexities confronted.

REFERENCES

Dale, E. *Audiovisual Methods in Teaching.* New York: Holt, Rinehart & Winston, 1969.

Ely, D., et al. "The Changing Role of the Audiovisual Process in Education: A Definition and a Glossary of Related Terms." *AV Communication Review* 11: 3–148.

Toffler, A. *Future Shock.* New York: Bantam Books, 1970.

Appendix

Student Papers

How Many?

Jackie Radford

Primary Idea

To teach the concept of how many.

RATIONALE

Introduction—The number as quantity (i.e., the "how many") concept involves the sequencing of numbers. It involves matching the number series of 0, 1, 2, 3. . . to corresponding groups of items. It involves abstracting the "threeness" from three apples, three blocks, three pennies, or any group of three items. It also involves an understanding of quantities in terms of being equal, not equal, more, and less. This learning activity package is concerned with the acquisition of these aspects of the concept of quantity or "how many," a basic arithmetic skill that is the foundation for other arithmetic skills and later mathematical skills.

Audience—The package is designed to aid the student in the primary grades (i.e., the primary educable mentally retarded student who is usually seven to twelve years old or the kindergarten to second grade student) who has previously proven his mastery of counting orally and writing the whole numbers from 0 to 10.

So What?—Has your mother ever remarked that she needed two eggs to make a cake? Maybe you have even heard an older brother or sister say to the clerk that he would like five pieces of a particular kind of candy. Has your father ever told you that he caught only three fish and that his friend caught less than he did? Sometimes a person will remark that there are only two more days until the weekend. A friend sharing his cookies with you could say that he has the same number of cookies as you do. Did you know how many things these people were talking about?

You have already learned to count from 0 to 10 orally, and you have also learned to write these numbers. Now, you are going to learn how many items each of these numbers mean. And you are going to learn what the terms equal, not equal, more, and less mean.

"How many," as you may presently realize, is an essential arithmetic skill concerning numbers which you must learn before you can learn other arithmetic skills. And we have already discussed the importance of numbers in our daily lives. We said that numbers are used in many everyday experiences—they are used to tell time, to determine the date, to indicate a page in a book, to tell how old you are, to call someone on the telephone, to travel on highways, to pay a clerk, to tell the "how many" of something, and for various other uses.

Secondary Ideas

BEHAVIORAL GOAL

Information will be provided through learning experiences and/or activities so that the learner will understand the concept of how many.

OBJECTIVES

I. The student will be able to demonstrate his understanding of the number sequence by arranging numbered cards which have been shuffled in the proper order. (Level I)

II. Given a group of items, the student will be able to indicate the number that represents how many items are in the group. (Level III)

III. Given a number, the student will be able to identify and correctly form a group with the number of items that the given number means. (Level III)

IV. Given two groups of items or two numbers or a number and a group of items, the student will be able to tell if they are equal or not equal. (Level III)

V. Given two groups of items or two numbers or a number and a group of items, the student will be able to tell which is more or less. (Level III)

PRETEST

The pretest is designed to discover to what extent the student understands the concept of how many. The evaluation procedure consists of observations and written tests. Objective 1 has only one exercise to be performed. Objectives 2, 3, 4, and 5 each have two exercises to be performed. The first exercise (a) is an oral exercise and the other one (b) is a written exercise. Depending on the student or students and the situation, the teacher may choose to do both or one of the exercises. While the written exercises must be done on an individual basis, the oral exercises can be done either on an individual or group basis; the group exercises develop a more relaxed testlike situation than do the written exercises.

Objective 1—I want you to arrange the following shuffled cards which are numbered from 0 to 10 in their proper sequence.

Objective 2—(Given a group or a picture of a group containing from 0 to 10 items, the student or students orally respond by stating the number of items in the group.) (a) I am going to show you a group of items, and I want you to tell me the number of items that are in this group. (b) See illustration on p. 248.

Objective 3—(Given a number between 0 and 10, the student or students use blocks or some other group of items to form a group with the number of items that the given number means.) (a) I am going to say a number, and I want you to form a group with the number of items that the number means, from the blocks that you have. (b) See illustration on p. 249.

Objective 4—(While being shown two pictures of two groups of items, two numbers, or a group of items and a number, the student or students will indicate whether they are equal or not equal by holding up the appropriately marked card.) (a) I am going to show you two pictures, and I want you to hold up the card marked equal if the pictures represent two equal groups or the card marked not equal if the pictures represent two groups that are not equal. (b) See illustration on p. 250.

Objective 5—(While being shown two pictures of two groups of items, two numbers, or a group of items and a number, the student or students will indicate whether the group pointed out is more or less than

In the blank, write the number of items in each group. Look at the example.

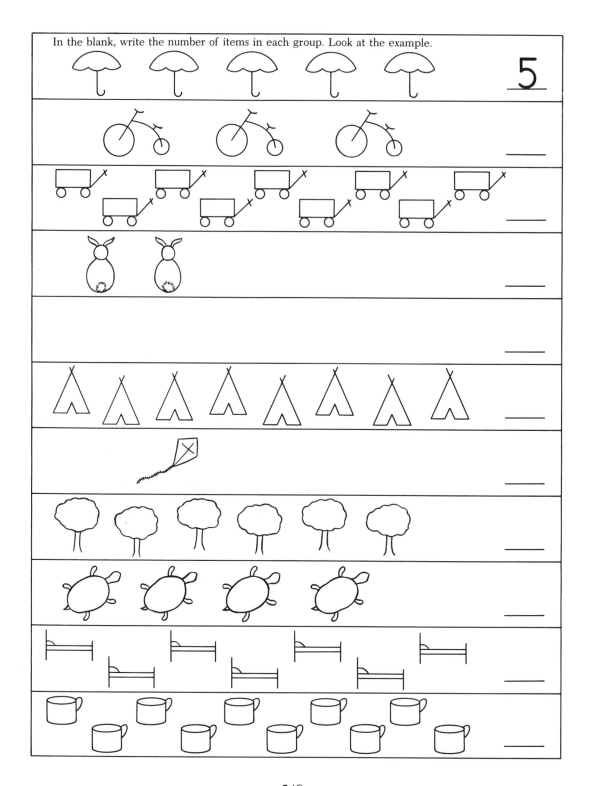

5
___

___

___

___

___

___

___

___

___

___

___

248

Complete the following by drawing the number of items that the number in the blank means.
Look at the example.

○ ○ ○ ○ ○ ○ ○ 7

△ 10

⌣ 5

□ 2

○ 4

○ 8

0

人 3

○ 6

X 9

1

Place a check (✓) in the box if the 2 groups are equal and place a cross (X) in the box if the 2 groups are not equal. Look at the examples.

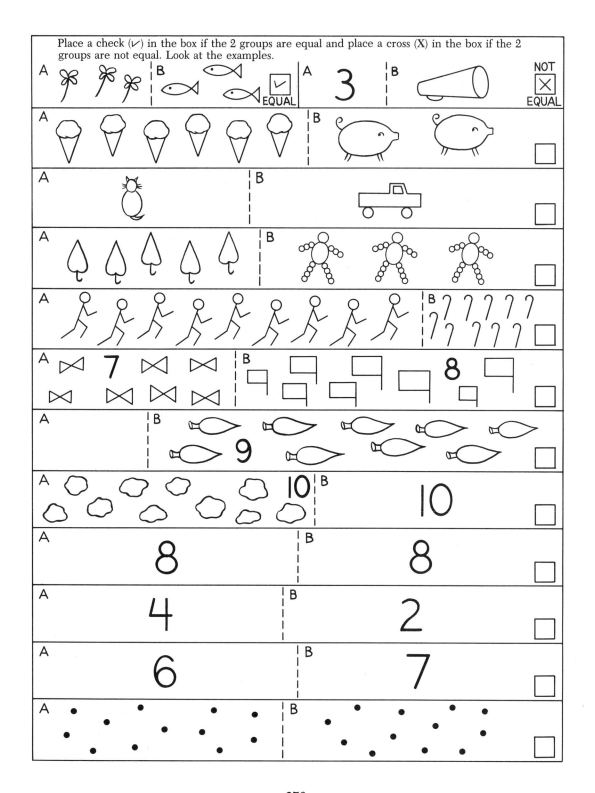

250

the other group by holding up the appropriately marked card.) (a) I am going to show you two pictures. After I point out one of the pictures, I want you to hold up the card marked more or less depending on whether the picture represents a group of more or less items than the other picture.

(b) See illustration on p. 252.

Activities and/or Learning Experiences

(Alternative 1 is mainly concerned with the visual learner; alternative 2, the auditory learner; and alternative 3, the tactile learner.)

OBJECTIVE

Method—Begin by letting the student or students count orally, and then let them write the numbers from 0 to 10.

Alternative 1—Using laminated cards numbered from 0 to 10, the student observes the teacher arrange them in the proper sequence on a chart such as the one in Figure 1.

As the teacher arranges the cards, he should point out several visual cues that the student can attend to. There is a hole in the top of each of the laminated cards

which is matched to the dot in the appropriate box on the chart. Also, there are red arrows between each box indicating the sequence of the numbers from 0 to 10. After the teacher has arranged the cards and pointed out the visual cues, he picks the cards up, shuffles them, and lets a student arrange them. When the student has completed the activity, there is a chart to which he may refer that shows the numbers from 0 to 10 in proper sequence.

Considerations—Such an activity should appeal to the visually oriented learner because of the visual cues to which he must attend. It further provides him with materials that he can hold, examine, and maneuver, as well as demonstrate himself.

Alternative 2—To establish the sequence of the numbers from 0 to 10, you can use games, counting rhymes, number stories, finger plays, number songs, and other related activities. Some of these activities include the following:

(a) "What Number Am I?" is a game in which the numbers from 0 to 10 are verbally described. By using different parts of his body, the listener moves in the position of the numbers as the speaker describes them. After practice, the listener will be able to do the appropriate movements as they are described by the speaker for the numbers from 0 to 10 in a continuous sequence.

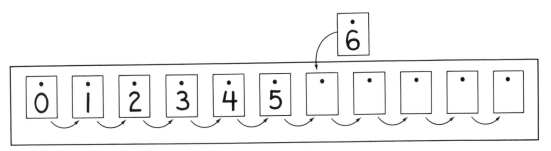

FIGURE 1

Underline the correct answer. Look at the examples.

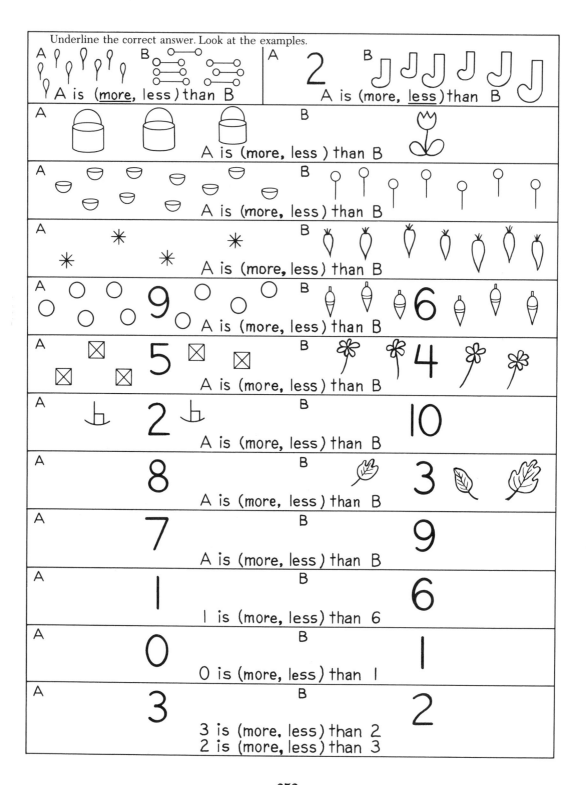

A is (<u>more</u>, less) than B

A is (more, <u>less</u>) than B

A is (more, less) than B

A is (more, less) than B

A is (more, less) than B

A is (more, less) than B

A is (more, less) than B

A is (more, less) than B

A is (more, less) than B

A is (more, less) than B

1 is (more, less) than 6

0 is (more, less) than 1

3 is (more, less) than 2
2 is (more, less) than 3

(b) A finger play is:

1, 2, 3, 4, 5,
I caught a bird alive;
6, 7, 8, 9, 10,
I let him go again.

(c) There are the number songs: "Ten Little Indians," "This Old Man, He Played One," and "1, 2, 3, The Devil's after Me." (d) An example of a counting rhyme which could be used is:

1, 2, touch your shoe;
3, 4, touch the floor;
5, 6, pick up sticks;
7, 8, stand up straight;
9, 10, sit down again.

Another counting rhyme is "One, Two—Buckle My Shoe."
These activities and others can be recorded on tape and played by the student or students. The teacher should tell the students to feel free to participate with the movements described in the activities and to talk and to sing along when possible.

Considerations—While this design is aimed at the aurally oriented learner, it also permits the learner to respond through movement and vocalization.

Alternative 3—This alternative is based on the same procedures as alternative 1 of this objective. The only difference is that the materials are developed for the tactile learner. The cards have the numbers from 0 to 10 done in felt, and there is still a hole in the top of each one of them. However, in this experience, instead of matching the hole to the dot in the appropriate box on the chart, the student will put the card on a hook in the appropriate box on the chart. The arrows between each of the boxes indicating the sequence are made of sandpa-

per. As in alternative 1, the teacher first arranges the numbered cards in the proper sequence from 0 to 10. Then, he points out the tactile cues to which the student should attend by moving his hand across the felt number and the sandpaper arrows. After the teacher has picked up the cards and shuffled them, he should let the student arrange them. A chart with the numbers in felt should be available for the student to check his work.

Considerations—The tactile oriented student will profit most from this learning experience. Moreover, this experience also provides visual cues.

OBJECTIVES 2 and 3

Method—You should introduce students to this session by emphasizing that the term "how many" is concerned with the group of items that each number means.

Alternative 1—To help the student understand the relationship between the numbers from 0 to 10 and their corresponding group of items, he will do work with puzzles. There are eleven separate puzzles which are divided so that one half of the puzzle has the number on it and the other half has the corresponding group of items on it. There is a visual cue, a straight line running across the top and bottom of the puzzle, to aid the student in correctly placing the two parts of the puzzle together. To make sure that the student puts the appropriate two parts together, the two lines are the same color on the two matching puzzle parts. Plus, on the back of the two matching puzzle parts, there are the same numbers. This is shown in Figure 2. A frame is also provided to help the student put the two puzzle parts together. After pointing out all the different

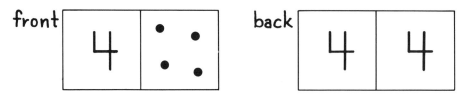

FIGURE 2

visual cues to aid the student in matching the numbers from 0 to 10 with their corresponding group of items, the teacher should give the student the number of pieces of puzzle that he can successfully work until he can eventually work with all twenty-two pieces. In the beginning, the student should be given groups of items with which he is to match the appropriate number, and later he should be given the number with which he is to match the appropriate group of items.

Considerations—This puzzle design should appeal to the learner who is visually oriented since he must respond to many visual cues. It also enables him to be actively involved in the learning experience since he will be in charge of manipulating the various puzzle parts.

Alternative 2—Matho is a game which is very similar to the game of bingo, except

this game is concerned with the numbers from 0 to 10 and their corresponding group of items. The student has a card which has MATHO printed across the top in large capital letters. These are five columns—one under each letter of MATHO —and each of these five columns is subdivided into five blocks. Consequently, there are a total of twenty-five blocks. Twenty-four of these blocks contain a number or a group of dots, from 0 to 10 printed within them. The twenty-fifth or center block is a free space with "how many" printed in it. Figure 3 gives a pictorial representation of a Matho card. There are large chips with a letter of MATHO and a number or group of dots from 0 to 10 printed on them. For every block on any of the Matho cards, there is a chip. A caller draws a chip from a pile and he then orally calls the letter of

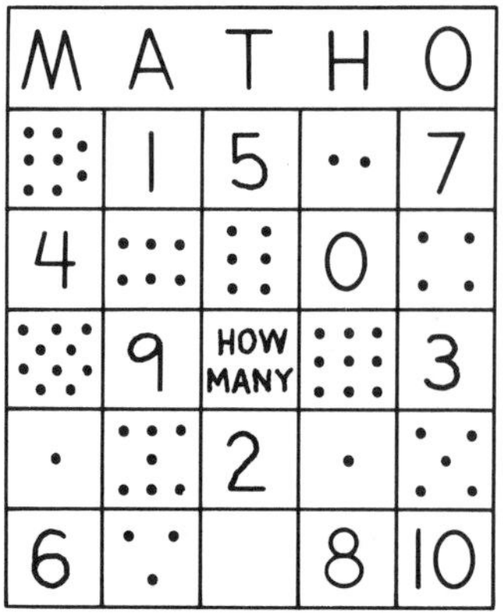

FIGURE 3

MATHO and the number or he orally calls the letter of MATHO and claps (makes some type of noise) the number of dots which are on the chip that he drew. If the person with a card has the called block on his card, he covers it with a small piece of paper. At first and any other time that he is requested to do so, the caller will show what he has called by holding up the chip. The game continues as bingo with a person having MATHO when he covers five blocks in a row (five blocks vertically, horizontally, or diagonally) or all four corner blocks. Then, he becomes the caller.

Considerations—Matho is a game which basically depends on the student's ability to listen and respond to what he hears. This game also relies on visual stimuli. Matho enables the student to become an active learner.

Alternative 3—The student who learns best by tactile experiences can learn how many items each number means by working with a pegboard. The pegboard has the numbers from 0 to 10 carved out on the left-hand side and the corresponding peg holes beside that number, as represented in Figure 4. The student is instructed to put the pegs, as he counts them, in the holes beside the numbers which he should trace over with his finger. After the student has put the pegs in the

holes, he is to cover the numbers with pieces of cardboard. Now, he can count the pegs, say the number of pegs to himself, and then look to make sure he is correct.

Considerations—The pegboard learning experience is especially appropriate for the tactile learner; in addition, it presents visual stimuli to the student and permits him to be an active participant in the learning experience.

OBJECTIVE 4

Method—These alternatives are concerned with teaching the terms *equal* and *not equal*.

Alternative 1—Language Master cards, having two groups of items, two numbers, or a group of items and a number, are used by the student to help him learn the terms *equal* and *not equal*. These cards are concerned with the numbers 0 to 10. Along with the pictorial stimuli, there is a corresponding message taped on the card by the instructor. Figure 5 represents the format used on these Language Master cards. The cards begin with many cues, but these fade out as the student proceeds through them. On the first cards, there are two groups of items; later, there are two groups of items and their corresponding

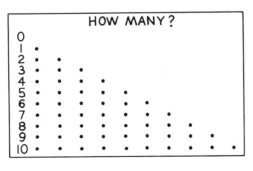

FIGURE 4

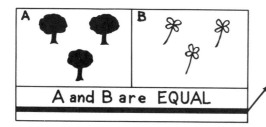

Tape says, "Group A has three trees and group B has three flowers. So groups A and B are equal."

FIGURE 5

numbers; and finally, there are only two numbers given. The student should be instructed to go through the Language Master cards, which are numbered in order, listening to what the instructor has to say and responding when indicated.

Considerations—Such an activity should hold the attention of the visually oriented learner, as well as the auditory oriented learner. At the same time, this activity relies on a motor and vocal response.

Alternative 2—I feel that the preceding learning experience is sufficient in accommodating the student who learns best by auditory experiences.

Alternative 3—Using the numbers from 0 to 10, a sequence of cards such as the ones in Figure 6 are used to teach the terms *equal* and *not equal*. These cards have on them two groups of dots or two numbers or both or a group of dots and a number, all of which are made from felt. At the bottom of each of the cards is the phrase "A and B are EQUAL" or the phrase "A and B are NOT EQUAL" which is also done in felt. The word "EQUAL" or the words "NOT EQUAL" are covered by an opaque overlay on each of the cards. The student looks at the picture and decides if the two groups are equal or not equal and then lifts up the overlay to receive an immediate feedback on his answer. Beginning with many cues, these numbered cards have the cues faded out

as the student progresses through them. The first cards have two groups of items on them; later cards have two groups of items and their corresponding numbers on them; and the last few cards have only two numbers on them. The student should be instructed to proceed through the cards in the proper sequence and to move his hand over the felt.

Considerations—The tactile learner should benefit most from this learning experience. It also holds appeal for the visually oriented learner.

OBJECTIVE 5

Method—The learning experiences used in alternatives 1, 2, and 3 of objective 4 are also suitable for objective 5. The only difference being that objective 4 is concerned with teaching the terms *equal* and *not equal* whereas objective 5 is concerned with teaching the terms *more* and *less*.

POSTTEST

Same as the pretest.

CONCLUSION

After completing one or all three of these alternatives or additional ones for these objectives, depending on what is

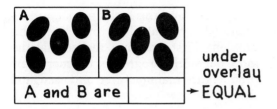 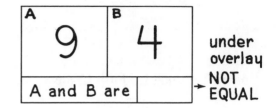

FIGURE 6

necessary for the individual student to be able to respond correctly to each of the objectives of this learning activity package, the learner will have an understanding of the concept "how many." From this point, he may continue to acquire more sophisticated arithmetic skills.

Unit on Pollution for Fifth Grade Students

Alice Card

Primary Idea

To teach fifth grade students the meaning of the word "pollution" and how the problem of pollution affects the United States and each citizen as an individual.

Rationale

Pollution is a problem which, of course, cannot be neglected by our society. We cannot take for granted that fifth grade students have a thorough understanding of this problem. Therefore, it is necessary that each child has a knowledge of the problem and knows how he might help protect his environment and himself.

Audience

Fifth grade students who are oriented in the visual, auditory, and manipulative senses.

SO WHAT QUESTION   (Addressed to fifth graders)

We want to learn about pollution because it is a big problem which must be solved.

The people, and this includes *you,* are responsible for controlling or solving this problem. First, we must realize that the more our world progresses, the more new products are manufactured and used, and thus more new pollutants are produced. Everything is affected by these waste products. That includes all living plants and animals and *you.* If pollution is not kept under control, you may suffer very much in the future. It is harmful for us to breathe polluted air. Playing outside may have to be limited or stopped all together if air pollution continues. We cannot swim or fish in polluted water, nor can we drink it. We would not be happy to sit by and watch America become ugly, would we? Therefore, each of us must learn to do our part in fighting pollution so that we can continue to have a happy life and bright future.

Goal

It is hoped that at the end of this unit the students will have a positive attitude towards cleaning up their environment. It is also hoped that the students will have gained more knowledge about the pollution problem.

COGNITIVE OBJECTIVES

1. The student will be able to recall the definition of the word "pollution" and name the four major types of pollution that were given in class.

LEARNING LEVEL   RESPONSE
Recall   Selective

2. The student will be able to recall the

various causes of pollution that were discussed in class.

Recall   Selective

3. The student will be able to give examples of things other than those given in class that pollution affects.

Comprehension   Selective, Constructed

4. The student will be able to demonstrate the knowledge that he gains from a class presentation on methods and ways that the consumer can help protect his environment through his daily living.

Application   Selective, Motor

5. The student will be able to analyze a unique situation and tell (in writing) whether or not pollution is a major factor. And if it is, why? And if it is not, how could pollution possibly affect the situation?

Analysis   Selective, Constructed

AFFECTIVE OBJECTIVES

First Objective of the Unit

1. The student will develop a positive attitude towards the cleaning up of his environment. His change in attitude will be indicated by his:

   I.   increased responding
   II. doing unassigned outside work
   III. offering examples
   IV. volunteering

Last Objective of the Unit

2. Using the "criteria for criticism" given in class, the student will be willing to criticize a recent method or idea of pollution control and will be able to express his opinion or reasons for his position.

PRETEST

To evaluate the entry level behavior of each student, I have designed a pretest which is disguised as the making of a bulletin board. I have already tried my pretest on some fifth grade students. I had the children answer five questions which dealt directly with the cognitive objectives. The children answered the questions using felt-tipped pens on construction paper (with the purpose in mind of making a bulletin board). Each child's response is followed by a question mark. This means that the child's answer may or may not be true. It is hoped that by the end of the unit on pollution, the children will want to change or add to their bulletin board.

In a classroom situation, I would give the pretest at the end of the day or just before a break, so that I would have a chance to evaluate the children's responses before making the bulletin board.

In the class situation, I will provide about three pictures (dry mounted) for the children to choose from for Objective 5. If they like, the children may gather in groups around the picture, but they may not discuss it with each other. All three pictures will be put on the bulletin board along with the students' responses.

PRETEST QUESTIONS

1. What is pollution? You may make up your own definition.

2. What causes pollution?

3. What does pollution affect? Name as many things as you can.

4. What can you do to help stop pollution?

5. Look at this picture. Do you think that there is evidence of pollution in the picture? Why? Why not? Could pollution enter the scene in the future? How?

POSSIBLE ANSWERS TO PRETEST QUESTIONS

1. Pollution is the process whereby man, primarily through his continuous advancement in technology, contaminates his environment.

2. fossil-fuel burning (factories, mines, electricity)
automobiles (auto service stations dump oil)
nuclear power plants (radioactive pollution)
ships and boats
machines
people

3. human health—eyes, ears, lungs, accidents
property
vegetation
weather
fish
animals
the beauty of our land

4. Do not litter.
Use litter bag in your car.
Do not use electricity that you do not need.
Do not use dyed toilet and tissue paper.
Keep your car in good condition.
Use low phosphate detergents.
Use returnable bottles.
Write to congressmen and factories about the problem.

5. The pollution in the picture involves air, water, noise, and land.

Activities

ALTERNATIVE 1   for the visually oriented individual

Activity 1

In order to elicit a selective response from the students for cognitive objectives 1 and 2, I have designed a flannel board arrangement. Through the use of the flannel board and class discussion, the students should be able to learn a definition of pollution, the four major types of pollution, and the things that cause pollution.

How to Use the Flannel Board

On the chalkboard, I will write:

buildings	water	restaurant
factories	signs	fishing pole
sidewalk	lights	dirt
ship	people	paper
store	telephone poles	trash can
		service
cars	wires	station
streets	hills	bottles
flowers	shore	airplane
trees	clouds	
smoke	fish	

I have made felt pieces for all of the above items. Students may add to these.

Explanation

We are going to build a city and also a landscape. First let's start building the city. Look at the words on the board and tell me what to put on the flannel board in order to start making our city.

Example: If a student says "smoke," I would ask, "Why? Does it really belong in a city? What things cause smoke? (factories, cars) What may smoke be called? (a pollutant) What kind of pollution is smoke pollution? (air pollution)"

Activity 2

I have made a transparency to provide activity for the third objective. Through the use of the transparency and class discussion, the student should be able to understand and comprehend the effects of pollution.

First, the transparency will contain only the question, What does pollution affect? As the students respond, the windows of the transparency will be opened. For example, if a student says "vegetation," I will open the window on the transparency and show the picture of some trees. If a student says, "human health," I would open the window and show a picture of a doctor.

Outline of what the transparency involves:

WHAT DOES POLLUTION AFFECT?

Air Pollution	Water Pollution	Noise Pollution	Litter Pollution
human health	drinking water	property	beauty of our country
vegetation	fish	hearing	accidents
property	under-water vegeta-tion	small animals	
vision			
weather			

Activity 3

I have made slides so that the child may select from them those things that he

thinks he can do about pollution; hopefully, he will then do it. This activity should get at objective 4. After the slides, it would be good to follow up the idea with a clean-up campaign for our school and home. It is hoped that students will volunteer to pick up trash and write to congressmen, etc.

The slides are relevant to fifth grade students. Children of this age are on some of the slides. While showing the slides, I will ask the class "What can you do?" and will comment on their responses. Example: One slide shows a lot of trash on the ground. I would ask "What can you do?" Then I would show the next slide which shows fifth graders putting the trash into a trash can.

In my slide series, the first slide always presents a problem. The second slide offers a solution or a means of coping with the pollution problem.

Activity 4

In order to help the student be able to analyze a situation and tell about the pollution, I will let them again carefully observe the three pictures of the pretest and write about them. This assignment will not be graded. This activity deals with objective 5.

ALTERNATIVE 2 for the individual who is oriented towards auditory stimuli

Activity 1

In order to provide for objectives 1 and 2, I would use the tape recorder. I would record various sounds to stimulate the students' minds about the following questions, What is pollution? What are some types of pollution? and What causes pollution? These sounds will be representative of the felt pieces used for the flannel board in alternative 1. The recorded sounds will include sounds of horns, water running, wind blowing through the trees, ships, airplanes, paper being torn, and people, etc. The individual who is oriented towards auditory stimuli may discover noise pollution more readily than the other individuals. Noise pollution may be of more interest to this child and, therefore, should be thoroughly covered.

Activity 2

In order to select and construct their ideas on "What Pollution Affects," the students will go on a listening walk. It is hoped that they will return and be ready to talk about what they've heard. (cars, birds, people, trees, wind, etc.)

Activity 3

We will bring a television and radios into the classroom. The students will listen for advertisements. I will ask them if they think that the product is or is not safe for our environment.

Activity 4

The students will look at a picture and play a cassette recording which tells about the situation in the picture. However, the recording will not tell anything about pollution. The students will write whether or not they think that pollution is a factor and state the reason for their answers. Later on, they will not use the cassette.

ALTERNATIVE 3 for the individual oriented towards manipulative stimuli

Activity 1

I would use the same activity described for alternative 1, which is the flannel board. However, I would make sure that the students participate in the making of the felt pieces and in putting the pieces on the flannel board.

Activity 2

I would have the students draw pictures or construct some sort of model of those things which they think pollution affects. Those who are interested could make transparencies.

Activity 3

Given some magazines, the students will find and cut out some pictures about which they can write. If possible, they may dry mount their pictures. They will tell whether or not pollution is a factor.

Affective Objectives—How Will They Be Met?

1. The student will develop a positive attitude towards the cleaning up of his environment.

In order to provide an atmosphere for this change, I will use a transparency, pictures, and discussion. By using the transparency, I can show how the child is affected personally. The transparency first shows a young boy enjoying nature. Through the use of overlays, pollutants are added to the scene and the boy becomes sad. The pictures show some bad results of pollution. Through class discussion and allowing the children to talk and participate at any time, I feel that my indicator objectives will be accomplished.

EVALUATION

Unit-Pollution

Name	Pretest Question					Posttest					Evaluation
	#1	#2	#3	#4	#5	#1	#2	#3	#4	#5	
Daintly	✓	✓ 2	− 3	− 1							
Jim	+	✓ 3	+ 6	✓ 3							
Fredric	−	✓ 2	− 3	✓ 3							

Key

+ good answer
✓ fair
− poor
○ needs extra help

The numbers represent how many examples the child gave.

It is hoped that on the posttest that the quality of response (+, ✓,−,0) will improve and that the number of responses will increase.

2. Using the "criteria for criticism" which will be given, the student will be willing to criticize a recent method or idea concerning pollution control. He will be able to express his opinion or reasons for his position. The criteria will simply be to look at both sides of the solution, argue with reason and logic, find factual information to support your views if necessary, etc.

I will provide for this affective objective by using a small packet of note cards. The cards will present an idea on pollution control and ask questions about it. Any student who is interested may use the packet. It is hoped that students who have reached this level will write to their congressmen and get others interested. Example on note card:

> The President has proposed a tax on factories that pollute. Congress objected on the grounds that this would simply give factories a license to pollute.
> Do you agree with the President or Congress? Why?

My goal for the unit has definitely been accomplished for each student who reaches this affective level. The student must have developed a positive attitude towards protecting his environment if he is interested in expressing his opinion about various methods of pollution control.

POSTTEST

The posttest will be almost the same as the pretest. The only change will be in the fifth question. I will give a different set of three pictures about which the student is to write.

I will tell the students that we are going to improve and correct our bulletin board. The posttest will be more like a test situation because I will express to the students my desire that they do their best. I will let them know that I am going to evaluate their responses.

Organization of the Unit Plan for Visually Oriented Individuals

Pretest—build bulletin board

Answer the So What Question

Affective Objective 1   The student will develop a positive attitude towards the cleaning up of our environment.

    I. transparency—How Pollution Affects <u>You</u>

   II. pictures—Pass around pictures showing some bad effects of pollution.

Cognitive Objectives 1 and 2   Use the flannel board and discussion to seek some basic definitions and causes.

Cognitive Objective 3   Use a transparency and discuss those things that pollution affects.

Cognitive Objective 4   Show slides (e.g., What Can You Do about Pollution) on pollution and discuss them.

Cognitive Objective 5   Show mounted pictures, and ask the students to write about them.

Affective Objective 2   Show note cards with ideas about pollution control written on them.

Posttest   Basically same as pretest.

Development of Oral Language Skills

Paula Harrington

Idea

This learning activity package is designed to be used by a kindergarten or first grade teacher in the development of oral language skills. This package includes listening and speaking activities that attempt to involve all of the children in the class. It gives the student the opportunity to listen to the teacher and other students. It also gives him the opportunity to speak himself and in this way improve his oral language skills.

Rationale

Introduction—Many young children begin school with no previous experience in communicating with people other than their parents and close relatives. They may have never had to express themselves before a large group or in front of a group of strangers. They also may have never been taught to listen in the correct way (i.e., they may not know how to listen for and follow directions). The first duty of the teacher is to start the development of receptive (listening) and expressive (speaking) skills in the students.

So What Question—(as explained to the learner)

There will be many fun and interesting things that we will be doing in school this year. But to be a part of these activities, you must be able to listen carefully and follow the directions that the teacher or your friends give to you. Let's see how well you can follow these directions now. An important part of our days in class this year will be the time we have for just talking among ourselves. I want you to feel free to tell the class and your friends things that you feel will interest them. Would somebody like to tell me and the other people about a favorite pet that they have at home?

(from teacher's standpoint)

I feel that the ability to express one's feelings orally is very important for the young child. Many children are shy and need aid in overcoming this trait. On the other hand, many children tend to over express themselves and need help in knowing when and where to talk. They need to be taught how to be good listeners because for every talker, there needs to be at least one listener. When children enter school, most often they do not know how to listen. Today, children are experts at tuning out auditory stimuli. Some children tune out everything that is uttered in a normal voice because they are used to responding only to shouting and harsh tones. The teacher must teach the child selective listening by helping him know which sounds to tune out and which to tune in. Children need to be taught that there are different ways to listen to different activities. Listening to directions given by the teacher requires a different listening technique than listening to a record while playing the game, musical chairs. As a child develops other learning skills, his listening and speaking skills should be given some attention.

Goal

The main goal of this package is to improve the child's oral communication skills. This goal will be accomplished by engaging the entire class, small groups, and individual students in various activities that should improve listening skills and increase speaking skills.

Objectives

1. To describe the four types of listening by telling how one would listen differently during different activities. (Level 2—Comprehension)

2. To demonstrate the ability to listen differently for different purposes by successfully completing at least four of the following activities.

    I.   The child will identify sounds that he hears on a tape. (Level 3—Application) (Attentive)

    II.   The child will raise his hand every time he hears a specified word in a class discussion. (Attentive)

    III.   The child will choose to finger paint while listening to a record. (Appreciative)

    IV.   The child will tell which of two pictures on a flannel board matches the description given by the teacher. (Analytical)

    V.   The students will play the game, musical chairs. (Marginal)

    VI.   The child will follow directions given on an activity record. (Analytical)

3. The child will verbally communicate ideas to classmates (individually and to groups) given the following situations. (Level 3—Application)

    I.   The child will tell a story given a picture to use as his main idea.

    II.   Using the flannel board, the child will retell a story that was told by the teacher.

    III.   The child will tell a story using puppets.

    IV.   The child will demonstrate his ability to ask appropriate questions by playing the game, treasure hunt.

Pretest and Posttest

The most useful pretest for oral language skills is careful observation of the student by the teacher. But for the purpose of organization, these observations need to be recorded in some systematic fashion. In this learning activity package, the grid system will be used as a checklist for individual student accomplishments. In this system, each objective or desired behavior is listed across the top of the page and each child's name is listed down the side of the page. As a pretest, the teacher will check each behavior that the child exhibits. From this evaluation, it will be easy to determine where each child needs help and to plan the lesson accordingly.

After the lesson has been presented, a checklist like the first one will be used to check off the behaviors that the child now exhibits. Then a comparison of the two checklists can be made to determine the progress made by each child.

To help in accurately assessing each

child's behavior and needs, a tape will be made (without the knowledge of the students) of a class discussion or activity. At a later time, the teacher will use this tape in assessing individual student needs. Tapes may be made at various times during the lesson to determine the progress of the students. A tape can also be used to aid in the final evaluation. An ideal situation would include a one-way mirror so that the teacher could observe her students unnoticed.

Individual Differences

Individual differences specifically treated in this learning activity package are:

I. Quiet, shy child

II. Extremely verbal child—almost to the point of being uncontrollable

III. Extremely physically active child

INDIVIDUAL DIFFERENCES

OBJECTIVE	QUIET, SHY CHILD	EXTREMELY VERBAL CHILD	EXTREMELY PHYSICALLY ACTIVE CHILD
1. To describe the four types of listening by telling how one would listen differently during different activities.	Divide class into small groups for this discussion. Have shy student discuss something with another student. Student draws pictures illustrating how to listen differently for different listening situations. He then describes his picture to the class or a small group.	Let this child help the quiet, shy child. Ask direct questions to help the child express himself. Act out (without talking) different listening situations.	Have several short discussions so this child does not become bored. Have groups of four or five children act out different listening situations (can talk).
2. To demonstrate the ability to listen differently for different purposes by successfully completing at least four of the following activities:			No activity should last too long because the child becomes tired easily.

a. The child will identify sounds that he hears on tape. (Attentive)			
b. The child will raise his hand every time he hears a specified word in a class discussion. (Attentive)			Instead of raising his hand, he will stand up.
c. The child will fingerpaint while listening to a record. (Appreciative)	State before starting that no one has to see the picture but the child unless he wants them to see it.		Play records with different tempos.
d. The child will tell which of two pictures on a flannel board matches the description given the teacher. (Analytical)			
e. The students will play the game, musical chairs. (Marginal)		Play record softly so the child will have to be quiet in order to hear.	Play slow record.
f. The child will follow directions given on an activity record. (Analytical)		Same as above	
3. The child will verbally communicate ideas to classmates (individually and to groups) given the following situations:	Start with small groups and slowly build up to large groups.	Must learn to control his verbal output.	
a. The child will tell a story given a picture to use as his main idea.	At first, help the child to get started talking by asking him questions. Eventually, will not have to do this.	Limit this child to one sentence or phrase to describe the picture. This will make him think before he speaks.	Limit the discussion to a short story or description so the child will not become bored.

b. Using the flannel
board, the child
will retell a story
that was told by
the teacher.

c. The child will tell
a story using
puppets.

d. The child will dem-
onstrate his ability
to ask appropriate
questions by playing
the game, treasure
hunt.

Let this child write clues
down as other children
figure them out.

Film Splicing

Bob Gibson

Dave Hale

Introduction

The ultimate aim of the educational experience as described in this paper is the teaching of a skill. The process of teaching any manipulative physical skill ultimately falls into one of two categories. The first, and simplest, level of instruction is that which we shall call the trade school approach. This approach involves instruction in the skill without an understanding of the process and is by nature tool specific (i.e., the emphasis being on proficiency, maximum instructional time is expended on the physical working of materials through the application of the special tool available to the student). The second approach is more philosophical but far less practical than the first approach and involves the teaching of pure theory, with minimal lab time in the manipulative art.

The disadvantages of each of these approaches are immediately apparent. The trade school approach leaves the student well-versed in the sequence of actions involved in a specific task. However, rote learning can be physical as well as mental. Faced with some new tool outside his learned physical repertoire, the learner must reorient himself completely and learn his task again—without an understanding of the process, he cannot expand his application of it. On the other hand, the student who knows the theory of the process, but who has never become familiar with any sort of physical application of that theory, is probably worse off than his trade school counterpart—he will probably not be able to function in any application situation.

The specific task with which this project is concerned is the use of a film editing machine called a hot splicer. Mostly, the approach followed is the trade school one, for the simple reason that it is more advantageous to the student to possess an ability (in the sense of a function-skill) than it is for him to have stored in his brain any sort of ultimately idle understanding. In recognition of the long term disadvantages of such an approach, certain elements of theoretical knowledge are introduced, with the hope that these will aid in providing a sufficient level of adaptability in the learner so that he can confront new tools and new situations with minimal additional instruction and minimal initial fear.

Audience

The class consists of college level students, having their introduction to the film medium. The learner must be familiar with film and film formats; it would be good if he has also been introduced to editing theory. The learner is expected to be completely unfamiliar with splicing. The learning biases treated are visual, auditory, and verbal orientations. The students must be able to operate an overhead projector, a cassette recorder, and a videotape recorder.

Primary Idea

To teach the use of the hot splicer.

Rationale

The physical disassembly and subsequent reassembly of sections of film is a process that is basic to the production of any film beyond the home movie level. Lacking the ability to splice, the learner is practically prevented from exploiting the medium for any purpose—personal, aesthetic, or commercial.

The film industry characteristically adopts tools that are best suited for a given purpose. For the splicing process, the hot splicer has come into universal use, as it provides the quickest made, strongest, and most durable splice possible. More specifically, the hot splicer made by Maier-Hancock is most commonly used; this particular brand has the reputation of being the highest quality machine on the market. It is the Maier-Hancock hot splicer that the student will most probably encounter in a real-life situation. Hot splicers that are made by other manufacturers such as Bell and Howell, S-O-S, and Hollywood Film, are almost exact imitations of the Maier-Hancock model.

Goal

The student will be given practical experience in the use of the hot splicer and introduced to the principle on which the machine works. By this means, the student will overcome his initial fear of a compli-cated looking tool and process, thereby lowering the risk factor involved in his continued exploration of the process through the use of new tools and materials.

OBJECTIVES

I. The learner will identify the parts of the hot splicer: the clamps, the platen, the scraper.

II. The learner will identify the base, binder, and emulsion layers on a diagram of a section of film.

III. Given a piece of film, the student will distinguish between the emulsion and base sides.

IV. The learner will make a satisfactory splice on a Maier-Hancock hot splicer.

V. The learner will list two advantages of the hot splicer over other types of splicers and defend his answer.

VI. The learner will explain at least one disadvantage of the hot splicer as compared to another type of splicer.

VII. When exposed to another type of splicer, such as the guillotine splicer, the student will manifest an interest in the machine and will ask to be allowed to attempt a splice on it.

Pretest

Aside from the testing of the learner's knowledge of the splicing process, the pretest is intended to allow the instructor to gauge the degree of reluctance on the part of the learner to attempt the splicing process. In this approach, it must be noted that a student's ability to make a splice on the Maier-Hancock machine is not entirely adequate to satisfy the lesson's goal; it is important that he be willing to approach an unfamiliar, related activity without excessive fear. The pretest represents an attempt to distill this basically subjective test to a more manageable yes or no proposition. Obviously, this must be supplemented to a certain degree by the instructor's personal analysis of the student's mental frame.

Activities

1. Videotape on splicing on the hot splicer.

Method: The videotape is played in a classroom situation. A question-and-answer period might follow. The tape is then made available to the students for reviewing, either within or outside the classroom.

Considerations: This activity is primarily aimed at the visually oriented student. However, the tape is designed with built-in accommodations for other learning abilities. The narration is independently complete, aiming for the aurally oriented student, and all diagrams are labelled as well as described, an accommodation for the verbally oriented student.

2. Handout describing the splicing process.

Method: The handout is distributed to the class.

Considerations: The handout should appeal to the verbally oriented student; it should also provide an immediately accessible means of review.

3. Audio cassette.

Method: The cassette recorder is placed beside the splicer(s) to which the students have access.

Considerations: The cassette gives a step-by-step description of the splicing procedure; this process allows for hands-on instruction in the absence of the instructor. Also, the cassette would accommodate those audio-oriented learners who were unable to follow the splicing procedure on the videotape.

4. Transparencies.

Method: The transparencies duplicate the graphics used in the videotape and are intended to be used primarily by the individual student in review of the tape graphics.

Considerations: The transparencies allow the verbally or visually oriented student to remove the graphic portions of the tape from the sequential time restraint inherent in the medium. The transparencies are also used in the pretest and posttest situations.

5. Hands-on instruction on the splicer.

Method: After all informational materials have been made available to the students, the instructor demonstrates the splicing technique in the classroom. Then, under the instructor's supervision, each student makes a splice.

Considerations: The live demonstration of splicing is the final step in the process of providing the learner with maximum mental rehearsal time before the actual making of the splice. Producing a splice under supervision provides a formalized instructional approach for the student's first manipulative contact with the tool.

6. Individual practice in the making of splices.

Method: Practice time must be provided within or outside the classroom situation. Alternative types of splicers should be present in the area provided for individual practice. Materials for activities 3 and 4 should also be available.

Considerations: Practice allows the student to gain confidence in the physical activity. As this confidence increases, it is hoped that the student might examine and attempt to operate one of the other types of splicers.

Posttest

It is essentially the same as the pretest; however, it is administered in a stress situation. When the student has completed objectives one through six, testing for objective seven should proceed in a non-stress situation.

Conclusion

The fear in undertaking an attempt at an unfamiliar activity derives largely from an incomplete knowledge of the specific procedure required. This project is designed with the aim of providing an "over-kill" situation in the presentation of preliminary information, following up with hands-on instruction and practice time to allow the student to become thoroughly comfortable with the splicing procedure. Hopefully, this familiarity will be achieved

with a minimum of difficulty and trepidation. This familiarity, along with a fundamental knowledge of the theory behind the practice, will reduce the feelings of risk in the learner toward the use of a new machine and process.

The Pretest

The pretest is conducted in two parts.

The first part consists of the identification of those students who have previously acquired the skills for operating a hot splicer. This portion of the pretest should be conducted well in advance of the presentation of the lesson in an effort to minimize the learner risk involved in the situation. The instructor simply asks if there is anyone in the class who knows how to operate a hot splicer. In the event of an affirmative response, the instructor should set up an appointment with the student(s) under the guise of a request by the instructor to splice some film for the class. When the student comes to make the splices, the instructor should prominently display some type of splicer other than the hot splicer. If the student successfully makes a splice and comments on the other splicer as well, objectives 3, 4, and 7 can be considered to be fulfilled; this student can be assigned to help his fellow students learn to use the hot splicer. Should the student fail to notice or comment on the other splicer, a certain amount of tension about the task may be assumed; the instructor's task is to determine whether the situation or the student's rigid inadaptability is to blame. If the latter is the case, the most advisable course of action might be to put the student through the entire lesson.

The second part of the pretest is conducted as a written test. In order to minimize risk, students should be assured that the test will have no bearing on their grade and will not be returned to them. While it would be ideal to instruct the class not to put their names on the tests, the resultant crippling of the pretest as an evaluative tool makes this practice inadvisable.

After they have completed section III of the pretest, the students should be asked to examine the hot splicer displayed in the class. You should place a cold cement splicer and a guillotine splicer alongside the hot splicer. The instructor should closely observe the members of the class during this procedure in order to gauge the degree of interest manifested by the class in other machines.

The Posttest

The written posttest is identical to the written pretest. The students make a hot splice. They should be asked if they would like to try another type of splice on a guillotine or cold cement machine. Results are gauged as follows:

Refusal = failure to achieve objective 7.
One attempt = some success in achieving objective 7.
Repeated attempts = greater success in achieving objective 7.
Self-activated attempt = complete achieving of objective 7.

ANSWER AS MANY OF THE QUESTIONS BELOW AS POSSIBLE.

   I. Refer to the projected transparency (T-1)

   A. The transparency represents a magnified cross section of a piece of motion picture film. If layer 1 is the base, identify layers 2 and 3.

   B. In cement splicing, which of these two layers are joined?

  II. Refer to the projected transparency (T-2)

   A. Identify the parts of the hot splicer labeled 1, 2, 3, and 4.

 III. Refer to the piece of film being passed around the class. Until the film reaches you, proceed with the test.

   A. The sides of the film are labeled (1) and (2). Identify the two sides of the film.

   B. Which side would be placed up when loading it into a hot splicer?

   C. List two advantages of the hot splicer over other types of splicers; defend your answer.

   D. Identify at least one disadvantage of the hot splicer as compared to other types of splicers.

Sample Handout

One of the essential facts of the film medium is that the film must be physically arranged into the desired sequence after it is shot. The process used in this reassembly is called splicing.

The splicer most commonly used in the motion picture industry is called the *hot splicer.* In order to understand the workings of the hot splicer, it is important that one have some idea of the physical construction of the film.

A strip of movie film consists of three separate layers, each with a distinct function. These are as follows:

I. The *BASE LAYER* is a plastic material which is clear and flexible; it provides a secure mounting surface for the emulsion layer.

II. The *BINDER LAYER* consists of an adhesive substance which is used to secure the emulsion to the base.

III. The *EMULSION LAYER* consists of a chemical substance which is sensitive to light and records and preserves the photographic image.

In cement splicing, the base layers of two pieces of film are bonded together—the splice becomes an integral part of the film. Other methods of splicing, such as tape splicing, rely on an external bond; this process is much like using adhesive tape between two sheets of paper. Understandably enough, cement splicing is far stronger than tape splicing.

In hot splicing, the cemented bond is subjected to heat, which not only produces the splice more quickly but actually welds the base layers together. Hot splices are extremely strong. They can withstand such treatment as ultrasonic cleaning, a process which dissolves a tape splice. For this reason, hot splices are used for almost all applications such as laboratory printing or repeated projection, where the splice will be subjected to strain.

There are four major parts of the hot splicer:

I. Left Clamp. This instrument is used to hold the film firmly in alignment during the splicing procedure.

II. Right Clamp. The right clamp not only holds the film in place but also secures the large platen lever which is below the right clamp lever; therefore, the entire right side of the platen can be swung up. This allows the film in the right side of the splicer to be laid down on top of the film in the left side.

III. Scraper. The large curved lever in the center of the splicer controls the scraper. The scraper has a knife blade which, when lowered onto the film and pushed, peels away the emulsion and binder layers of the film, leaving the base exposed.

IV. Platen. The flat stainless plate under the clamps is electrically heated to weld the film.

The hot splicing procedure is as follows:

I. Open both clamps by lifting the small, round levers on the far left and far right. You will notice four guidepins or *posts* protruding from the platen.

II. Place the *tail* of the film (the end of the piece to which you intend to attach another section of film) in the right side of the splicer. The film must have the *emulsion side up.* The emulsion side can be determined by flexing the film under a light. The base side will shine; the emulsion side will be dull. Place the film so that the post passes through a sprocket hole and that the last frame that can be cut off protrudes past the line of the joint of the platen.

III. Close the right clamp and lock the lever by pressing down firmly. Next, lift the large round lever below the right clamp lever and lock it in place. This joins the right platen to the clamp. Unlock the clamp lever and raise it. *The clamp and the platen* on the right should swing up and out of the way.

IV. Place the head (beginning) of the piece of film to be attached in the left clamp, *emulsion side up*, in the same way as you did with the right side.

V. Close and lock the left clamp.

VI. Holding the thumb lever in the center of the splicer with your thumb and forefinger, pull the scraper up and toward you. Then carefully lower the scraper *as far as it will go* and with *gentle* pressure downward, push it away from you and across the film. Repeat this process until there is an even, clear stripe across the film. Take care not to scrape too deeply and *do not* attempt to drag the scraper toward you across the film. Push it away from you on the cutting stroke. Brush the scrape clean with your finger.

VII. Remove the cap from the film cement. With the application brush

sparingly apply cement to the scraped surface. Close the right clamp and platen immediately, lowering it and locking the right clamp lever. Do not slam the clamp down; lower it quickly and firmly. The excess film in either clamp will be automatically trimmed. Brush any loose pieces of film away from the splicer.

VIII. STOP. Allow ten seconds for the splice to set.

IX. Release all three levers on the clamps and raise the clamps up to an open position. With your finger, gently rub away any excess cement or editing marks from the film.

X. Lift the film from the platen. Test the splice by twisting the film about a quarter turn and then by gently tugging the film. If the splice is good, it will not break. Should it break, the splicing procedure must be repeated. *Do not* attempt to use the same scraped frame; use the next frame from the headpiece.

Some rules for splicing:

I. ALWAYS WEAR LINT-FREE GLOVES to prevent marking the film.

II. ALWAYS CAP THE FILM CEMENT TIGHTLY AFTER EACH USE.

III. *ALWAYS LEAVE THE SPLICER WITH THE CLAMPS CLOSED* when you are finished.

Preoperative Teaching of Pediatric Open Heart Patients

Rebecca S. Wilson

This learning package is designed for children with congenital heart defects who have been admitted to the hospital for surgical repair of their defect.

Primary Idea

To provide the child who is scheduled for open heart surgery with knowledge and understanding about his surgery and postoperative care.

Rationale

The value of preoperative teaching as a means of improving postoperative recovery has been widely discussed. Certain studies have indicated that patients are more cooperative and generally have a shorter period of convalescence when they are prepared in advance for surgical procedures and postoperative care. The preparation of children scheduled for open heart surgery is especially important. Because of the seriousness of the surgery, close monitoring and care of these children during the postoperative period is essential. For this reason, they are transferred directly from the operating room to the intensive care unit (hereafter termed ICU). They remain in ICU for several days before returning to the general pediatric floor. ICU can be very frightening to these children. They awaken in a strange environment filled with unfamiliar equipment and unfamiliar faces. When children are prepared for this experience, they usually accept these conditions and are able to return to their room on the pediatric floor within four or five days. Children who are unprepared become extremely frightened and uncooperative, making postoperative care very difficult.

Nurses have assumed a major responsibility in providing selected activities for teaching these children; however, most of the teaching has been based on the individual nurse's intuition and past experience with little consideration given to the principles of teaching and learning. At North Carolina Memorial Hospital, preoperative teaching is done the night before surgery by one of the nurses from ICU. The lesson consists of a verbal description of what the child will experience while he is a patient in ICU. The value of such teaching is questionable. The nurse usually spends from twenty to thirty minutes with the child. Sometimes, the child is encouraged to ask questions, but usually the child is frightened and will not ask questions. No consideration is given to individual differences, and there is no alternative for the child who is unable to verbally communicate his feelings, fears, and misconceptions. In other hospitals where a organized teaching plan has been established, the preoperative teaching is done in two or three sessions and begins the day of the child's admission to the hospital.

The importance of preoperative teaching of pediatric open heart patients should be obvious. One of my concerns is the haphazard way in which it is being done in this hospital. The staff nurse on the general pediatric floor would seem to be the most logical person to do preoperative teaching to these children. She sees the child when he is first admitted and cares for him until the day of surgery. It is this nurse who has the opportunity to establish a relationship with the child and who is available to provide preoperative teaching over a span of two to three days. Therefore, the purpose for developing this learning package is twofold:

1. to provide information which will hopefully reduce the fear and anxiety of the child who is scheduled for open heart surgery
2. to provide a learning package which will be used by general pediatric nurses to prepare these children for surgery

LEARNER CHARACTERISTICS

I. Age: approximately four to six years of age
   Although children of all ages undergo open heart surgery, this age group was selected because they are able to communicate verbally, they are curious and interested in their environment, and they are able to postpone need gratification.

II. Educational Level: no formal education
   Some children have attended nursery school, kindergarten, or Head Start. Others have not had these opportunities.

III. Medical History: congenital heart defect requiring surgical repair
   All of these children have been hospitalized at least once, and some have been hospitalized several times for diagnostic tests and/or surgical procedures.

LEARNER INTRODUCTION TO PACKAGE

There are many children like you who have come to the hospital to have their hearts fixed. Today I am going to read you a story about one of these children. The story tells about the experiences the little boy had while he was in the hospital. There are pictures which show how the nurses and doctors took care of the boy and how they helped him to get well. After we read the story, I will show you pictures of some special equipment that the doctors and nurses used to help the little boy get well. It is like the equipment you will have when you get your heart fixed.

Before we read the story, tell me about some of the other times you were in the hospital. (pretest follows)

OBJECTIVES

I. Show the location of the heart on the body. (level I)

II. Show the location of the operating room and tell what it will look like. (level I)

III. Identify the following equipment and tell what it is used for by showing which part of the body uses it. (levels I and II)
   A. chest tube

B. urine catheter (wee wee tube)

C. N. G. tube (stomach tube)

D. I. V. set up (fluid or feeding tube)

E. EKG monitor (heartbeat machine)

F. respirator (breathing machine)

ATTITUDINAL OBJECTIVE (not given to the learner): The learner will cooperate during the postoperative period by following the instructions given by the ICU nurse.

PRETEST: (to be given orally)

After the child relates his previous hospital experiences, he will be asked the following questions:

I. Have you ever had any operations before?

II. You came to the hospital to get your heart fixed. Can you show me where your heart is?

III. This is a picture of a little boy who is going to have a heart operation. Point to where you think the doctor will operate.

IV. Try to draw lines on the picture to show what the operation site will look like.

V. Here are drawings of some equipment. You may have never seen some of these things. Do you know what any of them are?

VI. If so, can you tell me what the different pieces are used for?

Activities

1. "Johnny Gets His Heart Fixed" is a story about the experiences of a little boy who goes to the hospital for a heart operation.

The story is read to the child after the pretest is given. It introduces him to some of the experiences he will have before and after surgery. There are pictures of a doctor listening to Johnny's heart (Objective 1), Johnny in ICU with some of the equipment used for his care (Objective 3), and Johnny at his operation site (Objective 2). Although this activity is directed toward all of the objectives, its main purpose is to make the hospitalization less frightening to the child and to hasten his recovery (Attitudinal Objective).

2. Flannel board with the figure of a little boy is used to show the location of the heart, the operation site, and the equipment used in the ICU. (Objectives 1, 2, and 3)

The following explanation is given to the learner:

Now that we have read the story about Johnny, let's take a close look at him.

This is where his heart would be if we could see it. (Place a red heart on the figure.) Here is your heart. (Show location of the heart on the child's body.) Of course, we can't really see Johnny's heart because it is inside his chest, just like your heart is inside your chest.

Johnny has a bandage on his chest. Let's see what is under the bandage. (Remove white bandage to reveal operation scar.) This is where Johnny had his operation. Your operation scar will look something like Johnny's.

Now I am going to show you some of the equipment the nurses and doctors used to take care of Johnny while he was in the intensive care unit. This is the same equipment they will use to take care of you while you are in the intensive care unit. (As each piece of equipment is placed on the board, it is identified, then connected to the figure as its use is explained.)

This is an EKG monitor. It shows a continuous picture of your heartbeat. These are pads which are placed on your chest and connected to the monitor. The monitor won't show your heartbeat unless it is connected to these pads.

This is a urine catheter. It is a tube which is placed into your penis (wee wee). It catches all your urine so you won't have to worry about going to the bathroom.

This bottle is called a chest bottle. It is connected to a tube in your chest. The chest tube drains fluid out of your chest. This makes it easier for your heart to beat. It also makes it easier to breathe.

This is another tube. It is called an N.G. or a stomach tube. It goes down your nose and all the way to your stomach. It keeps your stomach empty so you won't vomit (throw up).

This bottle and tubing is called an I.V. It is used to give you fluid and medicine. You will not be able to eat or drink anything right after surgery. The I.V. is put into a vein. This is the way we feed you until you are able to eat.

3. Show the child cards with pictures of equipment showing their use.

As each card is shown, ask the child to tell the name of the equipment and its function. Each card has a visual cue to help the child answer. For example, the I.V. card has a drawing of an I.V. set up and some food. If the child is unable to answer, he receives the same explanation that was given with the flannel board ac-

tivity. The following explanation is given to the learner:

That was a lot of equipment. Let's talk some more about how it is used. I am going to show you some cards with pictures of the equipment. Beside each piece of equipment is a picture to help you remember what it is used for. As I show you the card, tell me the name of the equipment and what it is used for. If you don't know, I will help you by telling you about the equipment and its function, like I did with the flannel board.

Individual Differences

This package was designed for the child who is frightened by the total hospital experience. He is extremely anxious and is threatened by equipment. The activities allow him to become acquainted with hospital routines and familiar with some equipment before he is actually confronted with them.

For the learner who needs to be actively involved, the package would consist of the following activities:

I. A model of the intensive care unit with two dolls, a nurse, and a patient. The patient would have a bandage which could be removed to reveal the operation scar. The unit would include models of the equipment which could be attached to the doll patient. As the equipment was explained, the child could be involved in connecting it to the patient.

II. A tour of the intensive care units which would provide an opportunity for the child to touch and see some of the equipment.

III. The child is given a stethoscope and shown how to listen to his heartbeat.

For the visually oriented learner, the activities would be as follows:

I. A videotape about a child who is admitted to the hospital for open heart surgery. The tape would include a physical exam of the child which shows the doctor listening to his heart. The child would receive preoperative teaching which would include a demonstration of equipment. He would be seen going from surgery to ICU. In ICU, all the equipment would be seen and its use would be demonstrated by the nurse as she provided care for the postoperative child. While the child was in ICU, his bandages would be removed and the operation scar could be seen.

II. Slides of the equipment. Even though the equipment would be identified and explained on the videotape, I would include slides in this learning package. This would reinforce information given on the videotape as well as allow the learner time to ask questions which he would have been unable to answer during the videotape.

Posttest: (to be given orally)

Introduction to learner: We have spent a lot of time talking about what will happen after you have your heart operation. Let's see if you can tell me what the doctors and nurses will do to help you get well after your operation.

I. As each piece of equipment is placed on the flannel board, tell its name.

II. Tell what the equipment is used for.

III. Show me where your heart is on your body.

IV. This is a picture of a little boy who is going to have a heart operation. Point to where the doctor will operate.

VI. Draw lines on the picture to show what the operation scar will look like.

Summary

This learning package was designed for the anxious child who has been admitted to the hospital for open heart surgery. My experience has been that most children admitted to the hospital for open heart surgery fall into this category. It is my belief that if this learning package is used by the staff nurses on the pediatric floor, the majority of these children will be less frightened and more cooperative during their postoperative experience in ICU.

The Introduction of the Concept of Sets to Young Children

Helen E. Atwood

Primary Idea

The introduction of the concept of sets and subsets to young children who are in kindergarten and first grade, only some of whom will have attended preschool programs.

Rationale

FOR THE TEACHER

This concept is fundamental to the child's later mathematical development. Sets are basic to the understanding of cardinal numbers—concepts of quantity as a form of group identity as opposed to counting on or ordinal number concepts involving ranking. Thus, as an illustration, when you ask a child, "How many animals?" and he responds "Five—two dogs and three cats," he is dealing with a number set and its constituent subsets.

FOR THE LEARNER

Have you noticed how we are always putting people or things together and giving them a name? Sometimes, we take large groups of things and sort them into smaller groups. If you think about some of the things you do, you'll see what I mean.

For example:

I.   grownups = mothers + fathers
II. people = children + grownups
III. toys = yours + mine

At other times, we take small groups of things, put them all together, and give them a new name. For example:

I.   cats + dogs = animals
II. shirts + sweaters + socks = clothes

We are going to be talking about groups like this a great deal in the next few weeks. We will be taking them apart and putting them together.

I have deliberately avoided using the term "set" at this point since a strange term used in an abstract introduction such as this may simply confuse the pupil. A rationale such as the preceding one may be usefully restated in a variety of ways during the course of the learning experience. Given the nature of young children, however, the very excitement of the learning process and mastery of a new skill are often sufficient justification in themselves. Therefore, while an adult rationale may be helpful in providing the child with a different perspective, it should not be overstressed.

General Comments

Most children will have previously had some very informal experience with sets since from a very early age, they tend to order and group toys and other objects about them. It is therefore assumed that children entering school for the first time will not be at any disadvantage in this respect as compared with those entering from other programs. The concept of sets is not normally covered in preschool programs in any formal manner, partly because the young age of the children does not make this a very relevant activity. However, children entering kindergarten and first grade with previous preschool experience will probably be at an advantage in regard to interim objectives, that is, concepts of color, shape, and size. For this reason, an alternative lesson has been designed for those children who are identified in the pretest as having a mastery of interim objectives.

Finally, it should be noted that the understanding of set theory involves cognitive ability which is developmental in nature—specifically, in Piagetian terms, decentration and nesting of classes. Therefore, while it is highly desirable that all children be exposed to basic set theory, not all of them will be in a position at this time to benefit equally. For this reason, all activities need to be as open ended as possible, and it is of the utmost importance that each child progress according to his own needs. Since it is anticipated that this learning package will take several weeks, depending on the individual student, activities suggested in the following pages are provided as examples.

It should perhaps be added that the learning activities package has been purposefully designed so that the development of basic reading skills is neither a prerequisite nor a stated objective, although some incidental learning may take place.

Objectives

See page 284.

Pretest

This test is to be administered orally and informally, with small groups (approximately four) of children.

A. QUESTIONS COVERING INTERIM OBJECTIVES

1. Present a display of colored (i.e., blue, red, orange, brown, green, black, yellow, and white) objects. Children are to identify the colors that they recognize. This may be done singly with the others watching. A record should be taken discreetly, the emphasis being on informality. Repeat the process with different objects. This time specify the color you wish to be identified.

2. Present a display of different shaped objects (i.e., square, triangle, rectangle, circle, cube, cuboid, sphere, cylinder). Repeat the process that was followed for objective 1.

3. Present a display of different sized (i.e., tall/short, wide/narrow, and large/small) objects. Again, repeat the process that was followed for objective 1.

B. QUESTIONS COVERING OBJECTIVES AND SUBOBJECTIVES

1. (Objective Ia)
Place an assortment of plastic cows and horses in one group. (They should be of assorted sizes and colors) How are these things alike?
—all are animals
—all have four legs
—all eat grass, etc.
—any or all of these answers

COGNITIVE TAXONOMY	In a new situation, that is, when presented with unfamiliar sets, the learner must be able

1. to identify a set as a collection of objects having a common property by

    (a) starting with the set and identifying the common property

II
Comprehension

    (b) starting with a specified property and selecting those objects from a mixed group which constitute a set according to the specified criteria

II
Comprehension

2. to identify members of a set in terms of three specific properties—color, shape, and size

II
Comprehension

3. when given a universal set containing one subset, to identify that subset and name the property which differentiates the members of the subset from the universal set

SUBOBJECTIVES

I
Knowledge

1. Presented with a new set and the common characteristic specified, the learner must be able to name the collection "a set of _____ "

I
Knowledge

2. Given a new set containing one subset and the differentiating characteristic specified, the learner must be able to label the subset "a subset of _____ " specifying the universal set

INTERIM OBJECTIVES

COLOR

I
Knowledge
I
Knowledge

When presented with familiar and unfamiliar objects, the student must be able
1. to identify objects according to a specified color
2. to name the color of given objects
These objectives apply to the following hues:

blue	red	green	yellow
orange	brown	black	white

SHAPE

I
Knowledge
I
Knowledge

The student should be able
3. to select (identify) objects according to a specified shape
4. to name the shape of given objects
This objective applies to both familiar and unfamiliar objects and the following specific shapes:

triangle	square	rectangle	circle
cube	cylinder	cuboid	sphere

SIZE

I
Knowledge
I
Knowledge

The student must be able
5. to select (identify) objects (familiar and unfamiliar) according to a specified size
6. to name the size of given objects
This objective refers to the following characteristics:

tall/short	wide/narrow	large/small

2. (Subobjective 1)
Does anyone know a special name for things that are put together like this when they are the same? (a set)

3. (Objective 1b)
How are these animals different? After they have offered some suggestions, ask each child to select a group of animals according to some criteria you specify.

4. (Objective 3)
See how many different ways you can sort them. One might devise "fields" and ask the children to put different animals in different fields, thus avoiding any vocabulary problems with the concept of sorting.

5. (Subobjective 2) A query to elicit the response "a subset" should only be introduced if the answer to B(2) was positive.

6. Repeat B(1), B(3), and B(4) using other objects such as toy cars and trucks. Children who responded last in the previous questions should be encouraged to respond first this time so you can check for any limitation.

C. QUESTIONS COVERING
   OBJECTIVE 2 (only to be tested if section A was positive)

Use two collections of objects.
1. Ask the children to sort triangles, squares, circles, and rectangles of different colors and sizes (large or small) as they wish and then to sort the objects according to (a) shape, (b) color, and (c) size.

2. Repeat this process using solid shapes (i.e., cubes, cuboids, cylinders, and spheres).

Learning Experiences

ALTERNATIVE I

(For those students who learn best through manipulative activities.)

COLOR

1. Using sorting boxes and a collection of colored buttons, colored beads, and colored farm animals, let the children (1) sort them as they wish and (2) sort by specific color sets.

2. Organize several "color tables" in the classroom; put everyday objects of a particular color on the tables. Encourage the children to collect the objects. Label the table or area. e.g. "We have made a set of red objects."

3. Make an autumn tree with paper collage. Have each child select a specific color of paper from magazines to make a single colored leaf; different children will select and make different colored leaves.

On a large painted tree, arrange clusters of leaves of the same color together; add "hoops" around these leaves either in paint or by glueing on rope, and then label the display as shown in Figure 1.

a set of
black leaves   a set of
                      red leaves

FIGURE 1

4. Devise paper and crayon activity as shown in Figure 2. It would also be helpful to have a large color chart in a semipermanent position in the room to which all children might refer when they are confronted with the written word, which they do not recognize, for a color.

4. Use straws and pipe cleaners to make triangles, squares, rectangles, and cubes. These can be put on display in a form of a mobile and labelled.

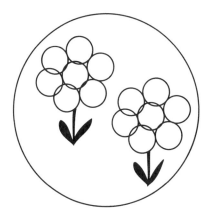

color these flowers red

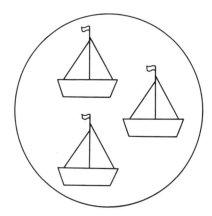

color these boats black

FIGURE 2

SHAPE

1. Set up shape tables in the same way that you set up color tables.

2. Provide a box of assorted shapes, and have the children sort them in the same way as they did for the color activity, using a sorting tray or hoops, (1) as they wish and (2) according to specified characteristics (e.g., "Can you make a set of triangles?")

3. Devise a paper and crayon activity. The students are to draw a set of shapes, preferably from everyday objects (e.g., for a set of circles, use jar tops, coffee tins, cottage cheese lids, etc.).

SIZE

1. Draw around the outline of the two tallest and the three shortest children in the room or in this particular group. Cut out the outlines and put them on display, labelled as two different sets. With some guidance, the children can do much of this themselves.

2. Use sorting trays or hoops and a box of objects of assorted sizes in the same way as was done for the color and shape activities.

3. With guidance, the children can make two giants out of painted cardboard boxes, and these can be displayed as a set of tall

people. Children can then make a set of short people out of plasticene and wooden lollipop sticks. Again, these can be displayed and labelled.

SUBSETS

The crucial questions for you to ask the student and for them to ask themselves are:

How are these objects alike?
How are they different?

For the following activities, provide objects that are related by function, but which differ in color, shape, or size.
1. Devise a sorting tray activity, using for example, small and large plastic toy cars, different colored cubes, different sized triangles, or assorted triangles, circles, and squares of the same color. Allow the children to sort one of the above groups as they wish and then discuss the way in which they sorted the objects using the two questions above. Demonstrate to the students how to place objects in a universal set and then sort them into subsets with a rod, a rope, or a small hoop.

2. Have the children to draw around each others' feet and also those of any adults to be found in the vicinity. Have them cut these drawings out and paste them on a brightly colored board. Display the cutouts as a universal set of feet with a subset of particular sized feet.

3. Devise a crayon and paper activity such as the completed one in Figure 3.

ALTERNATIVE II

(For those students who have already achieved the interim objectives involving concepts of color, shape, and size.)

1. Use assorted objects and a sorting tray or hoops as was done for alternative I. However, properties of sets may be selected other than on the basis of color, shape, and size, although naturally these need not be excluded. For example, these following groups may be used separately or mixed together:
knives, forks, and spoons
cups and saucers
toy animals
toy vehicles

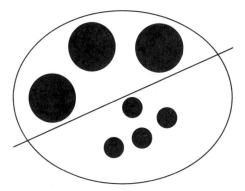 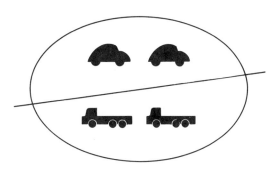

Partition into subsets

FIGURE 3

 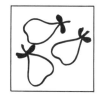 

FIGURE 4

It may actually be better to mix them at first so that the differences are *very* clear (e.g., forks, cars, and cows).

2. Plan crayon and paper activities. For additional practice, one might introduce color, shape, and size in some secondary capacity. For example, you might use the following exercises.

a. Draw a set of boats 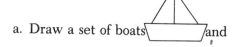 and

color them **blue**, or draw a set of bananas

and color them **yellow**.

b. Draw a square, triangle, rectangle, etc. around each set (see Figure 4).

Again, at first one would do well to ask students to distinguish between sets whose different characteristics are very obvious. Do not have them distinguish between subtle differences until they are more confident and almost ready to move on to subsets. The preceding example would provide something of a transition stage.

c. See Figure 5.

(Since children using this alternative are not having to master the concepts involved in the interim objectives, more demand has been placed on them in other

FIGURE 5

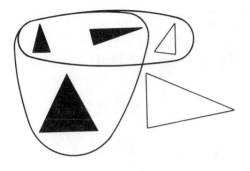

FIGURE 6

areas, e.g., reading. This does not mean that reading is essential; however, it is still incidental.)

SUBSETS

1. Sort concrete objects into a universal set and divide them into subsets by means of a rope, rod, or hoop. Since color, shape, and size are already familiar concepts to the children, one might introduce two variables, either in concrete terms, as above, or symbolically in crayon and paper activities, or both when subsets are

fully understood. For example, you could ask the children to construct two subsets using color and size. Draw a line around the *blue* triangles, and then draw a line around the *small* triangles (see Figure 6).
2. Construct subsets within the class. Have each child to write his name on a piece of paper and stick it on the wall chart illustrated in Figure 7.
3. Give each child an identical piece of paper on which to draw his pet. Each child then places his pet on the block graph, which will have been discussed as an alternative way of representing sets and subsets (see Figure 8).

ALTERNATIVE III

(For those children who learn best through visual activities.)

Some of the activities mentioned in this alternative are similar to those used in alternative I; however, the underlying purpose for using the activity is different. The emphasis, in this case, is on the *visual*

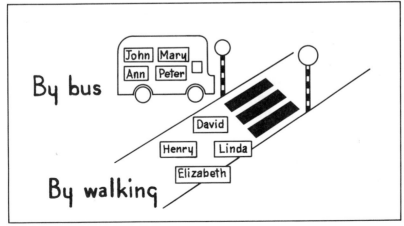

FIGURE 7

These are our pets.

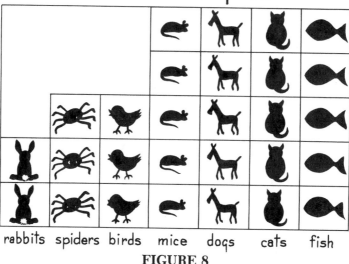

rabbits spiders birds mice dogs cats fish

FIGURE 8

product rather than the *manipulative process.*

COLOR

1. Set up color tables using environmental objects and a color chart for reference as you did for alternative I.

2. Ask the children to identify different objects around the room by color and label them. Group some of these items into sets, put a hoop around them, and label them as a color set.

3. On several different occasions, sort the children into color sets using skipping ropes or chalk marks, and help them to make visual representations of this process (see examples in Figure 9).

4. Plan a group game. For example, say to the class, "I spy a set whose members are all green," etc. The room needs to be set up strategically for this purpose beforehand.

5. Use a Language Master with individual children or small groups, working independently. For example, display color sets on Language Master cards using everyday objects cut out of magazines or familiar scrap materials. On the audio strip, record a statement that describes the property of the set.

SHAPE

1. Set up shape tables and a shape chart for reference.

2. Identify everyday objects around the room and label them according to their shapes.

3. Devise a group game. For example, you might use the "I Spy" game in this context also (See No. 4 above). Alternatively, you might ask the students to guess the property of a set of itemized objects. Again, this activity needs to be visual, either by using concrete objects or pictorial representations.

4. Use a Language Master as you did for the color activity. This would be most suitable for presenting sets of two-dimensional shapes to young children; however,

a set of red sweaters

a set of blue sweaters

a set of brown eyes

a set of blue eyes

FIGURE 9

it is probably too abstract for presenting three-dimensional shapes to young children.

SIZE

1. Label objects around the room and also group them as sets.

2. Construct representational set diagrams and block graphs, as previously described, with an emphasis on visual clarity.

3. Devise group games such as those described above. Once again, this activity needs to be visual.

SUBSETS

1. Make visual representations of concrete objects and put them on display. For example, have the children make a collection of stamps and place them into subsets on the basis of some specific criteria (e.g., shape, size, etc.). You could also divide the children into subsets by means of a rope according to some criteria such as size. For example, after making a circle, sit the smallest children in the middle with a rope around them.

2. You can use templates to provide a useful transition from the concrete to the symbolic in the same way that you used drawings around objects to produce two-dimensional diagrams of shapes. The children can sort the templates into a universal set and a subset, and then draw around them and display their results.

3. Devise paper and crayon activities similar to those used in alternative I.

4. Use a Language Master.

Posttest

This test is to be administered orally on an individual basis. Section A is designed for students who undertook alternatives I or III only. Sections B and C are designed for all students.

QUESTIONS COVERING INTERIM OBJECTIVES

The test for colors described below should be repeated, using shapes and then sizes.

Color test—As for the pretest, present the student with an assortment of colored objects and ask him to identify the colors that he recognizes. Then, using different objects, ask him to identify an object of the color specified by the tester.

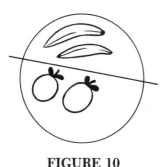

FIGURE 10

QUESTIONS COVERING SUBOBJECTIVES

Using a collection of apples and bananas, pose the question, "What name do we use for these items when we put them together like this?" The student's response must contain the word *set* and a reasonable description of the property of the set. Pose a similar question about subsets. "If we put all the bananas together like this, do you know what special word we use?" (See Figure 10.) The student's response

should contain the word *subset*. This process should be repeated a second time using other objects (e.g., large and small fish).

QUESTIONS COVERING MAIN OBJECTIVES

Use two groups of shapes. Each shape is to be represented in different sizes and four different colors (see Figures 11 and 12). This situation can be used to test for all three objectives.

Questions Covering Objective 1(a)

1. Arrange a set containing a single color, and ask the student to identify the common characteristic.
2. Do the same thing by shape and size. (Not all colors, shapes, and sizes need be covered. The actual knowledge of all these is covered in the interim objectives. It is the process of identifying a common characteristic which is being tested here.)

Questions Covering Objective 1(b) and Objective 2

1. How many different color sets can you make?

GROUP I

X 4

RED, BLUE, YELLOW, BROWN
LARGE/SMALL

FIGURE 11

GROUP II

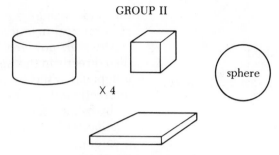

X 4

sphere

GREEN, BLACK, WHITE, ORANGE
TALL/SHORT
WIDE/NARROW

FIGURE 12

2. How many different sets of shapes can you make?

3. How many sets of different sizes can you make?

Questions Covering
Objective 3

1. Take a color set and ask the student to sort it into subsets (the word subset does not necessarily have to be used) and name the differentiating property that he identified in order to perform this task (shape/size).

2. Take a shape set and repeat the preceding process.

Teaching Musical Notation

Karen M. Wiley

Audience

My husband and I teach a junior choir of fifteen eight to twelve year olds who present an anthem about once a month. A few of the children have had piano lessons and can read some music, but the majority of them cannot. One child cannot match pitch. Two of the children are boys whose voices have changed enough that they are doubling the girls' pitch an octave lower.

Rationale (addressed to the Junior Choir)

Why should you learn how to read music? So you can pick up the hymnbook, select a hymn, and know how it goes without having somebody play it for you. So you can watch the notes in the introduction as Mr. Wiley plays them and be ready to sing when the time comes. So you don't have to memorize every song. You can read the music as well as the words. So you can learn more music in a shorter time. You won't have to drill over and over the same piece. The more music you can learn, the better you can sing, and, hopefully, the more you will enjoy singing.

Primary Idea

The purpose of this instructional design is to provide the child with a second tool for understanding music, the ability to read musical notation.

Although no affective purpose is handled directly in this instructional design, it is hoped that success in reading music will indirectly foster good attitudes about music by facilitating a successful musical production which will ultimately result in a greater enjoyment of and appreciation for music. One reason for not attacking attitudes about music in this design is the nature of the audience. The choir members are volunteers. They frequently ask to do solos; they moan when rehearsals are canceled. There has been no evidence that any of them are being forced by their parents to sing in the choir. However, there is a great deal of evidence that each choir member enjoys and appreciates music. We only hope to enhance these attitudes by providing tools that make music production easier.

Secondary Ideas

I. Note values

    A. Goal

        The child will demonstrate a knowledge and understanding of note values.

    B. Objectives

        1. The child will label the symbol.

        2. The child will produce the symbol when he is given the label.

        3. The child will indicate the duration of the notes by

            a. counting the number of beats.

            b. clapping the notes in rhythm.

Objective	Response Demanded	Learning Level
1. The child will label the symbol.	Constructed*	Knowledge
2. The child will produce the symbol when he is given the label.	Constructed	Knowledge
3. The child will indicate the duration of the notes by		
a. counting the number of beats.	Constructed	Comprehension
b. clapping the notes in rhythm.	Motoric	Application
4. The child will write the note values he hears.	Constructed	Application
5. The child will follow a line of music he hears.	Covert*	Application

*but tested by selection

4. The child will write the note values he hears.

5. The child will follow a line of music he hears.

II. Meter and rhythm

III. Pitch notation

Alternative Designs

Reading music necessarily involves two sensory modalities: vision and audition. The visible symbol represents an auditory signal. Therefore, any alternative to teaching and learning music notation must involve both modalities.

Alternative I is designed for children with little or no background in rhythmic notation who can respond easily to a visual-aural presentation. They are good listeners and readers. They have no difficulty keeping up with the speed of the tape as it follows the printed handout.

It is hoped that the students will read the notes and words in time to the music, establishing a relationship between the visual and auditory symbols they receive. As words are taken away, the child must depend on note value alone; and finally, the child will clap or sing the rhythms he sees and take rhythmic dictation.

Alternative II is designed for those children who need to work at a slower tempo or who prefer to work alone. A sequential set of Language Master cards could be used (see Figures 1 and 2).

"This is a whole note."

FIGURE 1

the rhythm clapped for the student

FIGURE 2

Alternative III is designed for those children who need kinesthetic input in addition to the other modes. A tape presentation based on eurythmics could meet this need. The child makes motoric responses to instructions and music on the tape. Later, transparencies of notation are projected. Motoric responses are elicited from the child by both the visual and auditory inputs. Example:

"Listen to the metronome. Every time it clicks take a step. Ready . . . walk. Click . . . click . . . click . . . click, etc. Now walk twice as fast. Take two steps for every click. Ready . . . walk."

Note: This experience should be an especially helpful remediation for students who began Alternative I but were unable to apply the principles of notation by clapping or singing the rhythms.

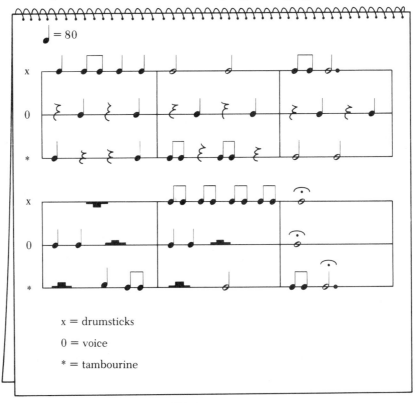

x = drumsticks

0 = voice

* = tambourine

FIGURE 3

Alternative IV is designed for advanced students who, upon entry, can meet all of the objectives. For them, you can use a flip chart and metronome. On each sheet is a score for several instruments. Each member of the group will follow his instrument's line of music and play the rhythms indicated (see Figure 3).

The rhythms will be more complicated than those used in Alternatives I through III. The simultaneous playing of several instruments further complicates matters and is more like the rhythms that really occur in music. Objectives dealing with higher levels of the taxonomy may be added. For example, students may compose their own scores for group performance (synthesis). Group members may select the compositions they feel are most interesting rhythmically and defend their choices (evaluation).

PRETEST

(See Figure 4.)

ACROSS

2. the name of this note:
4. the name of this note:
7. the name of this note:
9. If ♩ gets 1 beat, ♩ gets _____ beat(s).
10. If the whole note gets 2 beats, the half note gets _____ beat(s).

DOWN

1. The whole note is _____ as long as the half note.
3. the name of this note:
5. The quarter note is _____ as long as a half note.
6. If ♩ gets two beats, then ♩. gets _____ beat(s).
8. ⌢ This means to hold the note _____.

FIGURE 4

1. These	are	whole	notes.
2. They	are	long	notes.
3. Add a	stem and	make a	half note
4. half as	long as	whole	notes.
5. Fol - low	the notes	as the	play - er
6. plays	them	for	you.
7.			
8.			
9.		half	Whole

298

1.	Quarter notes go	faster than the	other notes we've	looked at so far.
2.	Whole	notes	half notes	quarter quarter
3.	Now we can	sing songs that	are more fun to	sing.
4.	Counting sometimes	helps us.	Listen while I	count.
5.	1 2 3 4	1 2 3 4	1 2 3 4	1 2 3 4
6.	1 & 2 &	1 & 2 &	1 & 2 &	1 & 2 &
7.	It makes no	difference how you	count	just as long as
8.	whole	notes	are	twice as
9.	long as	half notes	and quarter notes	are shorter yet!
10.		quarter	half	whole

1. Quarter notes go	twice as fast as	half notes.	Now watch eighth notes.
2. 1 2 3 4 5 6 7 8	1 & 2 & 3 & 4 &	1 2 3 4	1 2 3 & 4 &
3. Clap eighth Ready? the notes. Go!	(clap)		
4. STOP!!	Sometimes eighth notes	go much slower,	then the quarters
5. sound like this	and this	and half	notes go
6. slow,	oh	so	slow!
7.			
8.			
9.	eighth	eighth	

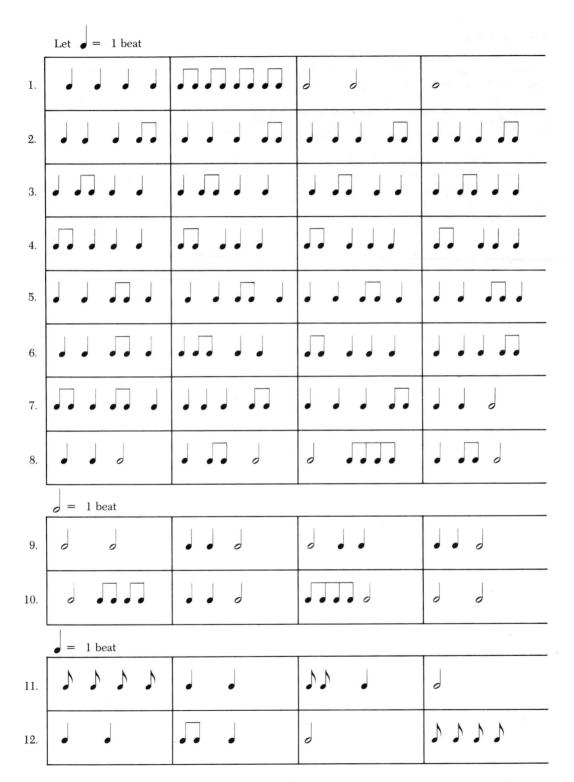

Now, let a ♩ equal 1 beat. If the composer wants a note to last *one* beat, he writes ♩ . If he wants it to last *two* beats, he writes ♩ . If he wants it to last *four* beats, he writes 𝅝 . But what if the composer wants to write a note that lasts *three* beats?

He could write ♩+♩+♩

He could write 𝅗𝅥+♩

But instead he writes: 𝅗𝅥.

𝅗𝅥 = 2 beats and the dot means add ½ of ♩ or 1 beat.

$$𝅗𝅥 + . = 𝅗𝅥.$$

2 beats + 1 beat = 3 beats

A dot after the note means that you should add ½ of the value of the note before the dot.

Listen as the instrumentalist plays line 1, then line 2. Play.

Listen again as I count with the music (see Figure 5).

If a quarter note gets one beat, how many beats does ♩. get?

$$♩ + . = ♩.$$

1 + ½ of 1 = ?

Listen as the instrumentalist plays this line (see Figure 6).

Listen again as I count with the music.

Sometimes a composer wants to make a note last longer so he puts a fermata sign above the note. It means to s t r e t c h the note out until the conductor tells you to stop. Look at the fermata in the box.

(Some people call it a bird's eye because it looks like one, but its real name is fermata.)

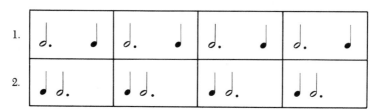

FIGURE 5

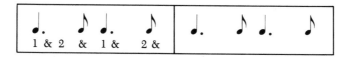

FIGURE 6

Listen to the players play the first line of music (see Figure 7).
Now write in a fermata over the very last

note in line 1 and listen to the difference. Listen and write a fermata over each note that needs one (see Figure 8).

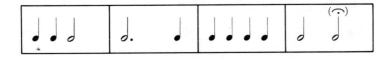

FIGURE 7

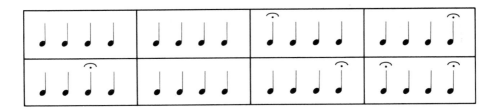

FIGURE 8

POSTTEST

I.

II. 1. 𝅗𝅥 = 1 beat   2. 𝅗𝅥 = 1 beat   3. ♩ = 1 beat

   o = 2 beat(s)   ♩. = ½ beat(s)   𝅗𝅥 = 2 beat(s)

4. ♩ = 1 beat   5. ♩ = 1 beat   6. ♪ = 1 beat

   ♪ = ½ beat(s)   o = 4 beat(s)   ♩ = 2 beat(s)

7. o = 1 beat

   𝅗𝅥 = ½ beat(s)

III.

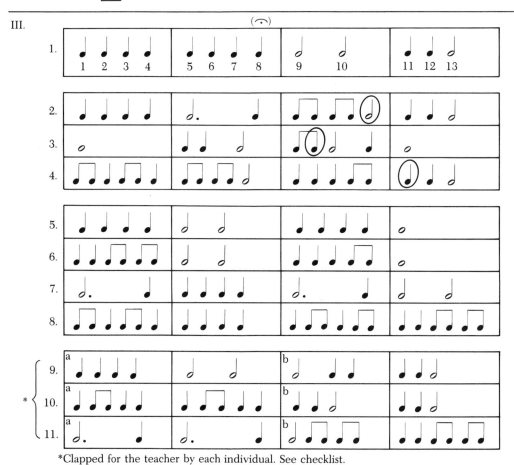

*Clapped for the teacher by each individual. See checklist.

Checklist for III. 9–11

Rhythm clapped correctly = ✓

Name	9a	9b	10a	10b	11a	11b

Picturing Functions and Relations
Algebra II

Michael D. Priddy

I. Introduction

In our previous work, a function and a relation were defined in terms of their possible domains and ranges. The ordered pair with its domain and range is now used again with its parts serving as the coordinates of a point on a graph. By locating several of these points on a graph, one can determine what type of line represents a particular function or relation. The method used to picture or graph a function or relation will be the concern of this lesson.

This will not be your first encounter with graphs, but it will be your first opportunity to graph a function or relation in this course. In future math courses, you will be using the graphing method for representing more complicated functions and relations.

II. Primary Idea

To introduce and illustrate the technique of graphing on the plane Cartesian coordinate system by picturing various functions and relations on the graph.

III. Rationale

The students express a willingness to take Algebra II, an elective, thus some

basic interests are already present. Many of the students realize the course serves as a college preparatory math course, so it will be beneficial to them in their future studies. Whatever the case, most of the students are self-motivated before coming into the course, so motivation is not one of the areas of concern. The students indicate that they like to produce pictorial representations of their work (i.e., sets), so this topic should be quite interesting to them.

This beginning phase in the picturing of functions will lead into several other areas. Initially, the student will be placing both straight lines and curved lines on the graph, and a subsequent discussion will concentrate specifically on the linear function. Following that topic will be a problem-solving lesson where graphing will be employed to determine the common solution of simultaneous equations. After that lesson, the student will be able to use the graphing method at his discretion in solving simultaneous equations.

IV. Goal

Using a given statement and a given domain, the learner will be able to graph the function or relation on the plane Cartesian coordinate system and state whether the picture is a function or relation.

V. Objectives

I. Be able to name two methods for picturing a function or relation. (Knowledge)

II. Be able to name the parts of the plane Cartesian coordinate system. (Knowledge)

III. Be able to locate any point on the graph. (Comprehension)

IV. Be able to find the range of a function or relation. (Application)

V. Be able to picture a function or relation on the graph. (Application)

VI. Be able to state which of three graphs represents a function. (Analysis)

VII. Be able when given two statements to take a position on whether their graphic representations illustrate a function or relation. Defend your position. (Evaluation)

VI. Pretest

The students will be given a sheet with a choice of answers on it for each question.

If the first answer is correct, then he will hold up a red card; the second answer, a yellow card; and the third answer, both cards.

1. What are two ways of picturing a function or relation? (See Figure 1.)

2. Choose the picture that shows the function with a domain of { 1, 2, 3, } and a range of {4} in the two accepted ways. (See Figure 2.)

3. Choose the coordinate system which is labeled correctly. (See Figure 3.)

4. Choose the coordinate system which is labeled correctly. (See Figure 4.)

5. Is this the correct location of the point (-3, -5) on the graph? (See Figure 5.)

6. Which graph has the point (4,–2) located correctly? (See Figure 6.)

7. What is the range of the given function, f:x $\longrightarrow$ 3x–5, when the domain is {1,2,3,4}?

   a) {–2,1,4,7}

   b) {8,11,14,17}

a)

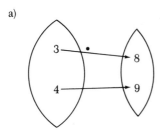

b)

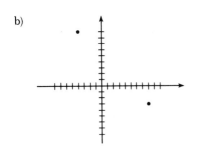

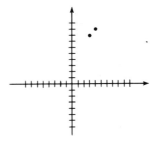

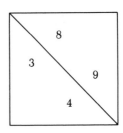

FIGURE 1

a)

 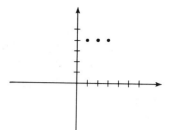

b)

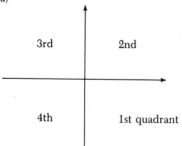 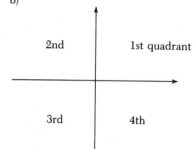

FIGURE 2

a)

b)

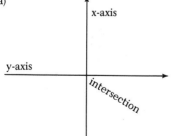 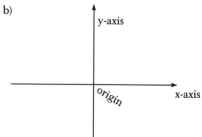

FIGURE 3

a)

b)

FIGURE 4

308

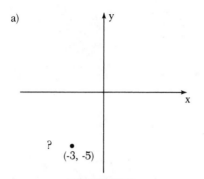

FIGURE 5

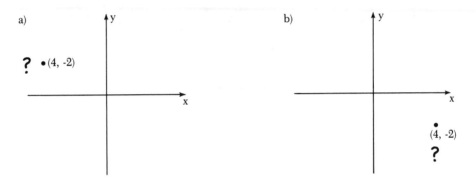

FIGURE 6

8. If the given statement is f:x $\longrightarrow$ 2x+1, what is the range when the domain is {0,1,–1}?

 a){1,3,–1}
 b){3,9,–1}

9. Which graph represents the function in #7? (See Figure 7.)

10. Which graph represents the statement in #8? (See Figure 8.)

11. Choose the graph that represents a function. (See Figure 9.)

12. Choose the graph that represents a relation. (See Figure 10.)

13. Given f:x $\longrightarrow$ 4 and g:y $\longrightarrow$ 2x–5, which pictures represent these statements, when the domain is {2,3,4,5}? (See Figure 11.)

14. Which of the graphs in #13 represent a function? Justify your answers.

1st	a) Yes	b) No	Why?
2nd	a) Yes	b) No	Why?
3rd	a) Yes	b) No	Why?
4th	a) Yes	b) No	Why?

15. Which of the graphs in #13 represent a relation? Justify your answers.

1st	a) Yes	b) No	Why?
2nd	a) Yes	b) No	Why?
3rd	a) Yes	b) No	Why?
4th	a) Yes	b) No	Why?

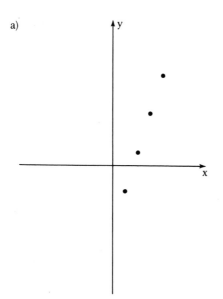

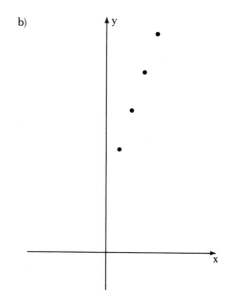

FIGURE 7

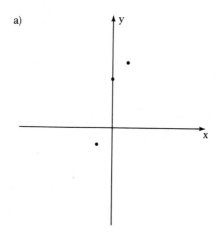

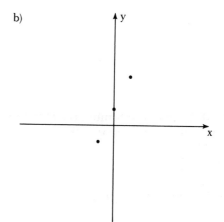

FIGURE 8

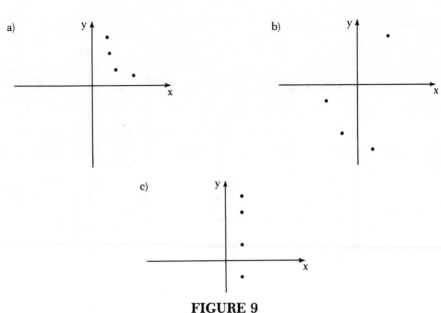

FIGURE 9

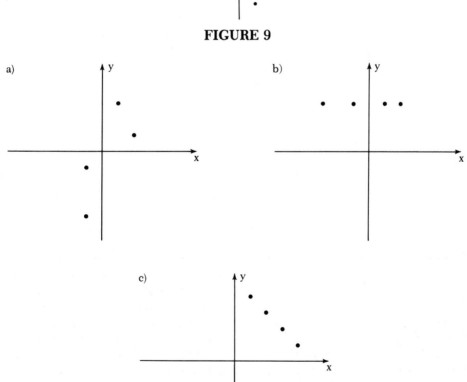

FIGURE 10

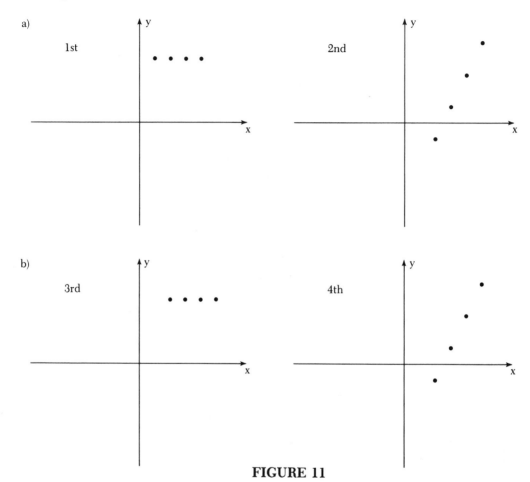

FIGURE 11

VII. Objectives with Alternatives

Each objective will be treated in three different ways; this procedure allows for at least three different learning styles. The three alternatives treated will be oriented toward the verbal student, the manipulative student, and the visual student. A verbal student is one whose learning is facilitated by listening to an explanation of the idea or method that is to be understood or employed by the student. A manipulative student's learning is facilitated by physically interacting with the materials that are involved in the learning exercise. The visual student learns most easily by seeing how operations are used to obtain a final product. This learning activity package will include a description of the verbal and manipulative alternatives; the visual alternative will be developed using the appropriate media.

OBJECTIVE 1

Be able to name two methods for picturing a function or relation. (Knowledge)

Alternative 1 (verbal)

The student will listen to a cassette recording that describes, in general terms, the two methods for picturing a function or relation. The recording will refer the student to several pictorial examples of mapping diagrams and of graphing, so that he will be able to successfully name the two methods after listening to the tape.

Alternative 2 (manipulative)

The student will be given an example of a mapping diagram in the form of a picture with a statement below the picture which states, "This function (or relation) is illustrated by the use of *a mapping diagram*." Next, the student will use a flannel board to reproduce the picture, including the sentence, that he has been given. This process will be repeated using an example of a graph to allow the student to associate the picture of a graph with a sentence that states, "This function (or relation) is illustrated by the use of *a graph.*"

Alternative 3 (visual)

Refer to the transparency for Objective 1, Alternative 3. In all cases, see end of project for media descriptions.

OBJECTIVE 2

Be able to name the parts of the plane Cartesian coordinate system. (Knowledge)

Alternative 1 (verbal)

Using another prerecorded cassette tape, listen to the description of a plane Cartesian coordinate, while you look at the picture of a graph. Be sure to note the location of the following: 1) origin, 2) y-axis, 3) x-axis, 4) first quadrant, 5) second quadrant, 6) third quadrant, and 7) fourth quadrant. Next, locate these parts on the Cartesian plane coordinate system without the use of the tape.

Alternative 2 (manipulative)

Using a large picture (20" x 20") of the plane coordinate system that is labeled with the seven items listed in Alternative 1 as a guide, locate and place an appropriate identification label on each of the corresponding parts of the magnetic plane Cartesian coordinate system.

Alternative 3

Refer to the dry mounts labeled Objective 2, Alternative 3.

OBJECTIVE 3

Be able to locate any point on the graph. (Comprehension)

Alternative 1 (verbal)

Attend the mini-lecture, "Locating Points on the Plane Coordinate System" during one of the three days it is offered in class. After listening to the lecture, turn to another student and explain how to locate a point. The lecturer may prompt you when necessary.

Alternative 2 (manipulative)

Using the "Learning-by-Doing" series of filmstrips and records and a chalkboard plane coordinate system graph, follow the directions for locating a point, as they are stated in the record/filmstrip set "Plotting a Point." As you follow the directions given by the voice on the record, you can check your work on the chalk graph by comparing it to the appropriate frame on the filmstrip.

Alternative 3

Refer to the dry mounts for Objective 3, Alternative 3.

OBJECTIVE 4

Be able to find the range of a function or relation. (Application)

Alternative 1 (verbal)

Using three examples with given statements and given domains, follow the steps that are displayed on the chart, as you listen to the explanation of the process involved in moving through each step. The first example has each step included; the second example requires you to fill in some answers as you listen to the tape; and the third example requires you to fill in the answers before checking them. All answers are on the back of each chart.

Alternative 2 (manipulative)

Using the three examples from Alternative 1, reproduce each problem on a transparency, and mentally work through the steps as you copy the example onto the transparency. Next, erase the steps in the solution and share the step-by-step solution to the problem with a friend. Repeat this operation with the next two examples from Alternative 1. The answers to all blanks can be found on the back of the chart with the example on it.

Alternative 3

Refer to the dry mount for Objective 4, Alternative 3.

OBJECTIVE 5

Be able to picture a function or relation on the graph. (Application) Note: Use the three examples from Objective 4 for these alternatives. (In this way, the student can practice having to refer to other materials.)

Alternative 1 (verbal)

First, you need to find two other classmates to work with you. Individually, each of you must state the ordered pairs that can be determined from the chart for Example 1, Objective 4. Work one problem at a time to avoid confusion. After you have determined each ordered pair, com-

pare your answers with your partners. If any of the answers are not alike, then explain to each other how you determined your answer. Next, working together, locate each point on the plane coordinate system. Repeat this procedure for each of the other two examples.

Alternative 2 (manipulative)

You must first obtain a blackboard/pegboard combination set. Using Example 1, Objective 4, write the ordered pairs on the blackboard that correspond to the related domains and ranges. Next, using the pegboard, locate each point. Place a peg in the holes that correspond to the ordered pairs. Check with the teacher to see if your work is correct. Do this again for the other two examples. (The teacher is asked to check the work because no other check points have been provided.)

Alternative 3

Refer to the dry mounts for Objective 5, Alternative 3 (visual).

OBJECTIVE 6

Be able to state which of three graphs represents a function. (Analysis)

Alternative 1 (verbal)

In a group of three students (including yourself), discuss the definition of function that was adopted in the previous lesson. You should bring out the importance of the characteristics of the domain. Compare your conclusions with the points made by another individual which are recorded on the reel-to-reel tape identified as "Functions, Objective 5, Alternative 1." Next, as a group, decide whether the graphic examples provided for this alternative are functions. If they are not functions, then they must be_____.* You can then check

_____

*relations

your answer, by listening to the remainder of the tape. If any answers were incorrect, try to decide why.

Alternative 2 (manipulative)

First you will need a plastic T-square which is available in the materials center. Using the graphic representations provided and your T-square, you will be able to determine if a problem is a function. To do this, follow these instructions very carefully.

    I.   Place the graph in front of you on a flat surface.

    II.   Lay the T-square on the graph so that the longer part is parallel to the y-axis and the "T" part is flush with x-axis.

Look at the example provided. (See Figure 12.)

Now you are ready to determine if a graph represents a function. Move the T-square along the x-axis. If any two points fall on the same edge of the T-square, then the points have the same domain; therefore, the graph does not represent a function. Use this method for the rest of the examples. The answer to each problem is on the back of the graph.

Alternative 3

Refer to the Language Master cards for Objective 6, Alternative 3 (visual).

OBJECTIVE 7

Given two statements, you will be able to take a position on whether their graphic representations illustrate a function or a relation. Defend your position. (Evaluation)

Alternative 1 (verbal)

Using the examples given—which are three different problems each with two separate statements—determine the range and the ordered pairs of each statement and graph each statement. Next, explain why the two statements are both functions, both relations, or one of each. Your explanation should be recorded on a cassette tape. Show your completed work to a friend. Ask him to look at the graphs and listen to the tape. Does he agree with your reasoning? Repeat this problem-solving method for the other two problems.

Alternative 2 (manipulative)

Using the blackboard/pegboard and the three problems in Alternative 1, find the range of each statement in problem 1 and the ordered pairs. Write your solutions on the blackboard. Graph each statement on the pegboard. Now write a statement on the blackboard telling why both statements are functions, relations, or one of each.

Alternative 3

Refer to the dry mounts for Objective 7, Alternative 3 (visual).

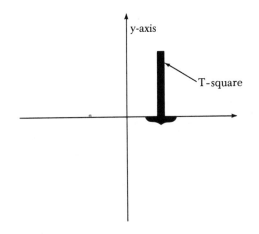

FIGURE 12

VIII. Posttest

The pretest in this package will also serve as the posttest. The students will be given an individual copy of the posttest and encouraged to show their work for each problem, although this is not a mandatory requirement.

The following is a description of the media which was used in the preceding project.

OBJ. 1, ALT. 3

The transparency illustrates two ways to represent a set, either with a mapping diagram or with a graph.

OBJ. 2, ALT. 3

The dry mount uses a programmed instruction technique to help the student become familiar with the seven basic parts of a graph. The parts are the origin, the y-axis, the x-axis, the 1st quadrant, the 2nd quadrant, the 3rd quadrant, and the 4th quadrant.

OBJ. 3, ALT. 3

Four dry mounts are used in teaching the student how to plot a point on the graph. The first dry mount illustrates each step in the process. The second, third, and fourth dry mounts provide the student with fewer and fewer helping steps. Answers are provided on the back of the second and third dry mounts. The examples are: (a) Plot (3,–5), (b) Plot (2,4), (c) Plot (–2,–1) (d) Plot (–1,3).

OBJ. 4, ALT. 3

The student is exposed to the concepts of the domain and the range of functions, and he is asked to determine the range for each of three examples. The examples provide the student with fewer and fewer helping steps, as the student progresses from #1 to #3. The answers are supplied

on the reverse side of the second and third dry mounts. The examples are:

I. Given that $S = \{-3,-2,-1,0,1,2,3\}$ and $f = \{(x,y): y = 1 - x, x \epsilon S\}$, find the range.

II. Given that $S: x \longrightarrow 3x - 5$, $x \epsilon \{1,2,3,4,\}$, determine the range.

III. Given that the domain of $x \epsilon \{-2,-1,0,1,2\}$, determine the range of $L = \{(x,y): y = 4\}$.

OBJ. 5, ALT. 3

In this objective, the student is required to synthesize what he has thus far done in distinct stages. Using the three examples in Objective 4, Alternative 3, he is asked to plot the coordinates of each problem on separate graphs. With each graph, fewer helping steps are provided. Answers are not given.

OBJ. 6, ALT. 3

Language Master cards are used in teaching the students to recognize a function and a relation, either from set notation or from a graph. Eight examples are supplied; for instance, is $\{(3,1),\ (-2,1),\ (3,2)\}$ a function or a relation? Which of the following is a function? $\{(-3,0),\ (0,-3),\ (1,0)\}$ or $\{(-1,1),\ (1,1),\ (1,3)\}$

OBJ. 7, ALT. 3

Three sets of problems are given for the student to graph. The activities in the previous objectives contribute to the successful completion of each problem. Questions are asked about each pair of completed graphs. The problems are:

1.

   a) Given $f : x \longrightarrow x - 1$,
      when $x \in \{-3,-1,0,1,3\}$

   b) Given $g : x \longrightarrow 3\,(x + 1)$,
      when $x \in \{-5,0,5\}$

2.

   a) Given $t : y \longrightarrow -5$
      when $y \in \{1,2,3,4\}$

   b) Given $y : x \longrightarrow x^2 - 1$
      when $x = \{-1,0,1\}$

3.

   a) Given $\{(x,y) : y = x^2 - 1\}$,
      when $x \in \{-3,-2,-1,0,1,2,3\}$

   b) Given $\{(x,y) : y = 1 - 2x^2\}$,
      when $x \in \{-3,-2,-1,0,1,2,3\}$

Index